VISUAL QUICKSTART GUIDE

THE GIMP

FOR LINUX AND UNIX

Phyllis Davis

 Peachpit Press

Visual QuickStart Guide
The GIMP for Linux and Unix
Phyllis Davis

Peachpit Press
1249 Eighth Street
Berkeley, CA 94710
510-524-2178
800-283-9444
510-524-2221 (fax)

Find us on the World Wide Web at: http://www.peachpit.com

Peachpit Press is a division of Addison Wesley Longman

Editor: Nancy Davis
Production Coordinator: Kate Reber
Interior design and production: Phyllis Davis
Cover design: The Visual Group

Photographs on pages 131–146, 168, 185, 226, 234, 235, 238, and 274 are © 2000 by Harold Davis.

ISBN 0-201-70253-3

9 8 7 6 5 4 3 2 1

Printed and bound in the United States of America

This book is dedicated to

JULIAN

the sweetest little boy in the world...

...and to the Knights that say "Ni!"

Heartfelt Thanks

to

Nancy Davis, the best editor in the world and a sweet friend. Hi Matty!

and

Kate Reber and Mimi Heft for your assistance and sage advice. I couldn't have done it without you.

and

Harold and Julian for putting up with me while I pounded away at the keyboard. You're my men!

and

Those of you in the GIMP community who offered invaluable suggestions, help, and contributions. I'd especially like to thank Seth Burgess, Ben Crowder, Alex Dekker, Tuomas Kuosmanen, Marco Lamberto, Hirotsuna Mizuno, Nate Oostendorp, Federico Mena Quintero, Jeremy Rumpf, and Jakub Steiner.

TABLE OF CONTENTS

TABLE OF CONTENTS

Chapter 8   **Painting Lines and Shapes**   **107**

Chapter 9   **Adjusting Color and Tone**   **129**

Chapter 16   **Plug-ins and Script-fus**   **247**

Chapter 17   **Creating Images for the Web**   **261**

TABLE OF CONTENTS

THE BASICS

Welcome to the amazing world of the GIMP! The GNU Image Manipulation Program (fondly called the GIMP) offers a professional set of tools for creating and manipulating images. This program has incredible power and loads of features, all incorporated in an interface that is *way cool*. You can run with the GIMP as far as you please. With the GIMP and your imagination, the sky's the limit!

So, just what is the GIMP? The GIMP is a *pixel*-based image manipulation program (also called a *bitmap* or *raster* program). In the GIMP (and other pixel-based programs such as Adobe Photoshop and Corel Photo-Paint), images are made up of tiny dots called pixels. These pixels are arranged in horizontal and vertical rows, and are colored to create a pattern. The shape and color of a pixel-based image appear smooth from a distance, but if you were to view a pixel-based image close up, you would see tiny individual squares. Pixel-based images depend on the resolution at which they are saved for printout quality.

My purpose in writing this book is to show you just how easy it is to create amazing imagery with the GIMP. In keeping with the *Visual QuickStart Guide* format, my aim is to present easy, step-by-step directions with illustrations to take the mystery out of even the most complicated feature.

If you are new to the GIMP, the program may seem a bit dense at first because it is so rich in features. But, if you take it one step at a time, you'll be creating beautiful images in no time. For those of you who are already acquainted with the GIMP, use this book as a guide to new features and techniques, and as a handy reference.

Have fun!

Is the GIMP Installed? (And What to Do if it Isn't)

Whether the GIMP was installed or not depends upon the selections you made during installation of your Linux/Unix distribution. A missing menu item does not necessarily indicate the absence of the GIMP; it just may not have been added to the menu. Below are some steps to take to find the GIMP. These steps assume you're using the RedHat Linux 6 distribution; if you're using another distribution, refer to the documentation that came with your distribution or check out the Web site that supports your flavor of Unix.

◆ Look on the menus on your desktop. If you find a GIMP item, select it to launch the GIMP.

◆ If a menu item isn't present, use File Manager to find if a file named gimp is present in the /usr/bin directory. If the gimp file is there, double-click on it to start the GIMP.

◆ If a menu item isn't present and you can't find the gimp file in /usr/bin, then the GIMP probably has not been installed. You can check this by running GnoRPM and seeing whether the GIMP package is present. It should be listed with the Multimedia packages in the Applications hierarchy.

◆ If the GIMP is not listed in GnoRPM, then you will have to install it from the RedHat Linux 6 CD-ROM.

◆ If all else fails, you can download the most recent stable version of the GIMP from http://www.gimp.org/ download.html. Instructions for installing the GIMP can be found at http://www.gimp.org/install_help.html

Working with Scanners, Digital and Video Cameras, and Drawing Tablets

Scanners, cameras, pens, and other pointing devices are great for creating digital images that you can use in the GIMP. Unfortunately, you can't just plug a peripheral in and have it automatically work with the GIMP. You need to install drivers and compile programs. Compilation is easiest for programmers to achieve, involves a number of tricky steps, and is different for each hardware platform and operating system. As such, compilation is beyond the scope of this book, but I'll give a brief description of what's needed for each peripheral and where you can get help with compilation if you need to do it.

Digital scanners come as either parallel or SCSI devices, though a scanner with a SCSI interface is the easiest to configure and use with the GIMP. SANE (Scanner Access Now Easy) is the universal scanner interface that is most frequently used with the GIMP. To find out which scanners are supported by SANE, and how to compile, and install SANE, go to http://www.mostang.com.

Digital and video cameras are a bit more straightforward. With a camera hooked up to a parallel port and the appropriate driver installed, the GIMP can be used to capture digital and video snapshots. To find out what's supported, go to http://metalab.unc.edu/ pub/Linux/apps/video/!INDEX.short.html.

Wacom pens and other drawing tablets need to be recognized by X Windows before the GIMP can use this device. In addition, you'll need to have a recent version of the GIMP Toolkit (GTK) installed on your computer so the GIMP supports Xinput. For the current Wacom driver, go to http://www.lepied.com/ xfree86/. Check out http://www.gtk.org/ for the latest version of the GTK.

GIMP Resources on the Web

There are many wonderful GIMP resources available for you on the Web. This is just a small list of sites. Try a search engine to find more.

The companion site for this book: http://www.peachpit.com/vqs/gimp/

The official GIMP site: http://www.gimp.org

GIMP news: http://www.xach.com/gimp/news

WilberWorks distributes and offers support for the GIMP: http://www.wilberworks.com

The GIMP 16 project, extending the GIMP for film production: http://www.film.gimp.org

Compiling the GIMP

If you want to install the development version of the GIMP (see the sidebar below), or use a peripheral device driver (see page 2), you will need to compile a new version of the GIMP. If you are a Linux/Unix programmer with experience in compiling programs, you won't find this difficult. If you don't have this kind of technical background, this can still be done (I did!), but you may find yourself using online resources and discussion groups to get past the sticky spots.

Generally, the process of compiling the GIMP starts with downloading the GIMP source code. You will need to have the Gnu C Compiler (gcc) loaded on your system. In addition, there are some code libraries that also need to be present on your computer.

Compiling the GIMP is beyond the scope of this book, but if you're interested in doing so, you can go to http://www.gimp.org/INSTALL for detailed instructions.

The Next New New Version of the GIMP

I wrote this book using RedHat Linux 6 and Version 1.0.4 of the GIMP. However, new versions of the GIMP are always being created. If you discover that you love the GIMP (as many folks do!) and want to be on the cutting edge of everything gimpish, you can download the latest Development Version of the GIMP at http://www.gimp.org/devel_ver.html. Be warned that the Development Version is uncompiled source code that needs to be compiled into a program. If you're an experienced programmer, this shouldn't be a problem. But, for mere mortal users, compilation of a new GIMP version will likely be difficult. And once the program is running, it's not guaranteed to be free of bugs.

The GIMP Screen (Figure 1)

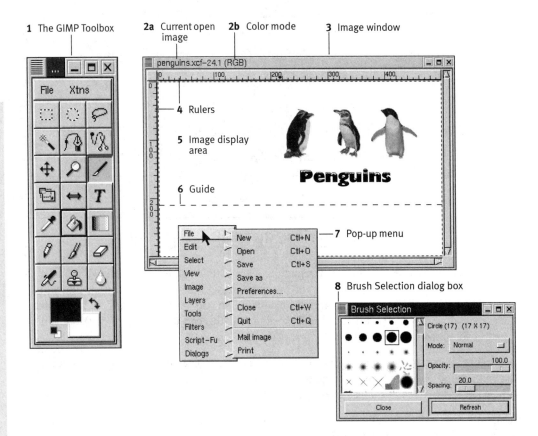

1 The GIMP Toolbox **2a** Current open image **2b** Color mode **3** Image window

4 Rulers

5 Image display area

6 Guide

7 Pop-up menu

8 Brush Selection dialog box

Key to the GIMP Screen

1 *The GIMP Toolbox*
The GIMP Toolbox is your gateway to creating amazing images. The Toolbox contains twenty-one tools that perform various functions from selecting and painting to erasing and blurring.

2A–B *Titlebar*
The Titlebar displays the currently open image name and the color mode in which the image is set.

3 *Image window*
The image window is the area on the screen where images are created. You can have as many image windows open at one time as you want.

4 *Rulers*
The mouse pointer's current position is indicated with marks on the vertical and horizontal rulers. The measurement unit they display is fixed at pixels.

5 *Image display area*
The image display area or canvas is the area of the image window where graphics appear. It is bounded by a dashed line.

6 *Guides*
Guides are non-printing lines that come in two flavors—vertical and horizontal. Guides are used for aligning selections or layers, or for exactly delineating an area to be selected.

7 *Pop-up menu*
The pop-up menu contains the myriad commands, filters, etc., used to manipulate an object. The pop-up menu is accessed by positioning the mouse pointer over the image window and clicking the right mouse button.

8 *Special GIMP dialog boxes*
There are seven dialog boxes that give access to essential items such as brushes, color palettes, layers, and tool options.

Changing Keystroke Combinations on the Fly

The GIMP comes preconfigured with many keystroke combinations (also called hotkeys), such as Ctrl+N to start a new graphic and Ctrl+S to save a graphic. If you are used to working with other image manipulation programs and want to use the keystroke combinations you are familiar with, you can change the preset GIMP combinations on the fly. Here's how:

1. Use the mouse pointer to highlight the menu item you want to change. For instance, you could right-click on the image window and highlight Image→Grayscale on the pop-up menu.

2. With the menu item highlighted, press the new keystroke combination on the keyboard you wish to use for that menu item, for example Ctrl+G. The keystroke combination will be reassigned to that menu item. The next time you want to access the menu item, just press your custom keystroke.

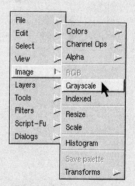

✔ Tips

■ Be aware that changing a keystroke combination for one item can affect another. For instance, in the example above, Ctrl+G is assigned to the Image→Grayscale command. By default, Ctrl+G opens the Gradient Editor. Changing this keystroke means that Ctrl+G will no longer open the Gradient Editor.

■ This book uses the standard preset GIMP keystroke combinations. If you create your own, they won't match the directions.

■ If you want to reset the keystroke combinations to the preset default, open a Terminal window and type `rm .gimp/menurc` at the command prompt. To find out how to open a Terminal window, take a look at step 1 on page 23.

The GIMP Toolbox (Figure 2)

The GIMP Toolbox is the first (and only) thing you'll see when you launch the GIMP. (To create or open an image, use the File menu in the GIMP Toolbox.) The 21 tools in the Toolbox are used to manipulate a graphic in various ways. If you've used other graphics programs, the Toolbox works just as you would expect: click the tool button to select the tool. To access the options for a tool, double-click on the tool button.

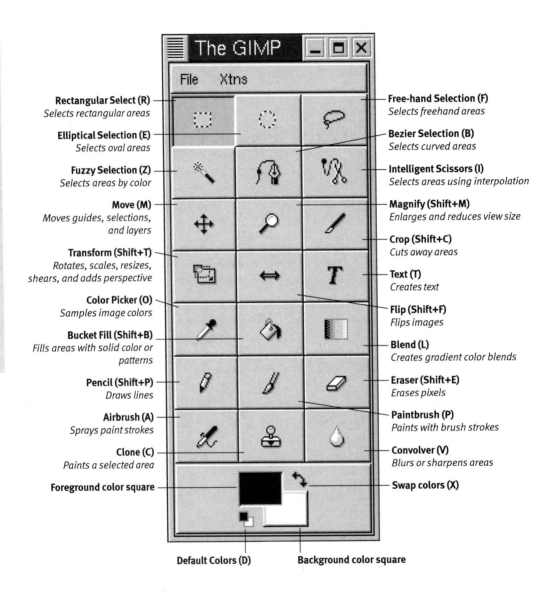

Rectangular Select (R)
Selects rectangular areas

Elliptical Selection (E)
Selects oval areas

Fuzzy Selection (Z)
Selects areas by color

Move (M)
Moves guides, selections, and layers

Transform (Shift+T)
Rotates, scales, resizes, shears, and adds perspective

Color Picker (O)
Samples image colors

Bucket Fill (Shift+B)
Fills areas with solid color or patterns

Pencil (Shift+P)
Draws lines

Airbrush (A)
Sprays paint strokes

Clone (C)
Paints a selected area

Foreground color square

Free-hand Selection (F)
Selects freehand areas

Bezier Selection (B)
Selects curved areas

Intelligent Scissors (I)
Selects areas using interpolation

Magnify (Shift+M)
Enlarges and reduces view size

Crop (Shift+C)
Cuts away areas

Text (T)
Creates text

Flip (Shift+F)
Flips images

Blend (L)
Creates gradient color blends

Eraser (Shift+E)
Erases pixels

Paintbrush (P)
Paints with brush strokes

Convolver (V)
Blurs or sharpens areas

Swap colors (X)

Default Colors (D)   **Background color square**

The GIMP Toolbox Menus

There are two menus available in the GIMP Toolbox (**Figures 3–4**). These menus give access to general commands, such as starting a new graphic, setting preferences, or creating new images using script-fus.

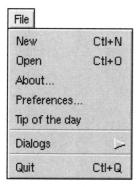

Figure 3. The File menu is used to create and open images, and exit the GIMP. It is also used to set user preferences, view the Tip of the day, learn about the creators of the GIMP, and access the special GIMP dialogs.

Figure 4. The Xtns menu is used to open the DB Browser, create screen shots, access script-fus, and view GIMP-related Web sites using a browser. Typically, the script-fus located on the Xtns menu create new images in a new image window.

Script-fus and Plug-ins

Script-fus and plug-ins are two very powerful programming features that add functionality to the GIMP.

Plug-ins are little programs that let the user add extra features to the GIMP. In fact, much of the GIMP, except for core features, are plug-ins that have been integrated into the GIMP program. Since the GIMP is a modular program, it's easy to enhance the GIMP directly through the use of plug-ins without having to recompile or reinstall the entire program. Typically, plug-ins are coded in C. If you have some experience with C and want to create your own plug-ins, visit `http://gimp-plug-ins.sourceforge.net/doc/Writing/html/plug-in.html` for directions.

Script-fus are essentially the macros of the GIMP. If you are familiar with macros (or scripting languages) from word processing programs, you know that a macro will replay various actions or repetitive tasks. Script-fus are usually written using a programming language called SCHEME. Go to `http://xcf.berkeley.edu/~gimp/script-fu/script-fu.html` to find out more about script-fus and how they are created.

To find out how to use the script-fus and plug-ins that come with the GIMP, turn to Chapter 16, *Plug-ins and Script-fus*, starting on page 247.

The GIMP Pop-up Menus

The GIMP works mainly through the use of pop-up menus. These menus give access to all possible commands that affect an image, such as copying, adding layers, or applying a filter. All of the GIMP menus are shown in **Figures 5–14** on the following three pages.

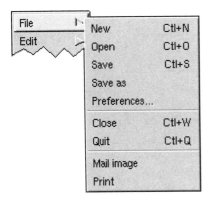

Figure 5. The File menu is used to create, open, save, close, and print images. It is also used to set user preferences, email an image, and exit the GIMP. (You can also create and open images, set user preferences, and exit the GIMP using the File menu in the GIMP Toolbox.)

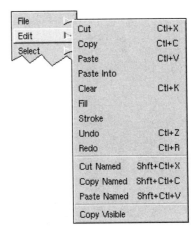

Figure 6. The Edit menu is used to cut, copy, and paste images, paste into selected areas, clear areas of color, fill areas with color, add an outline to a selection, and undo and redo actions. The Cut, Copy, and Paste Named commands let you cut, copy, and paste multiple items.

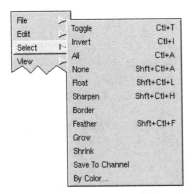

Figure 7. On the Select menu, the All command selects an entire layer. The None command removes all selections (not the areas inside the selections, just the selections, themselves). Other Select menu commands hide the selection boundary (toggle), and sharpen, float, grow, feather, or save selections to channels.

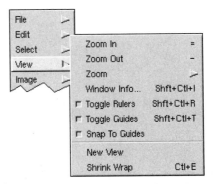

Figure 8. The View menu is used to zoom in or out (changing your view of an image) and toggle rulers, guides, and snap to guides on and off. The New View command displays the same image in a secondary image window. Shrink Wrap lets you see the entire image window regardless of the zoom.

GIMP POP-UP MENUS

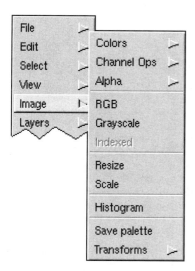

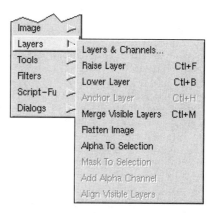

Figure 9. The Image menu is used to adjust the color of an image, add and manipulate alpha channels, set an image in one of three color modes, save image palettes, and rotate and crop an image. The Resize and Scale commands change image size to specified proportions.

Figure 10. The Layers menu is used to access the Layers & Channels dialog box where you can create, copy, and delete layers and channels. The menu also lets you raise, lower, anchor, and merge layers, flatten an image, add alpha channels, and align layers.

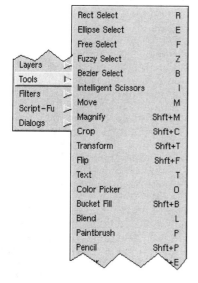

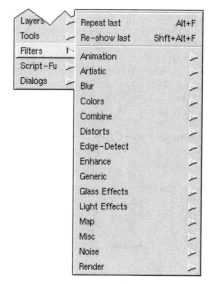

Figure 11. The Tools menu is used to access all the tools available in the GIMP Toolbox.

Figure 12. Filters are used to perform a wide range of image editing functions. On the Filter menu, they are divided into submenu categories that are available on fly-out menus.

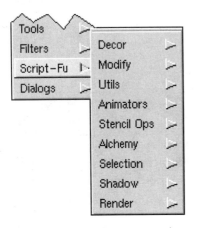

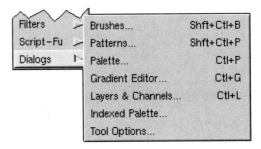

Figure 13. Script-fus are mini-programs used to automate special effects containing many steps. On the Script-Fu menu, they are divided into submenu categories that are available on fly-out menus.

Figure 14. The Dialogs menu is used to view the seven special GIMP dialog boxes. (All of these menu items, except Indexed Palette, are also available on the Dialogs fly-out on the GIMP Toolbox File menu.) These dialog boxes are described on pages 11–13.

Large Menus and Dialog Boxes

GIMP menus and dialog boxes contain many commands and items to select. Consequently, some of them are quite large. Many of the figures in this *Visual QuickStart Guide* are too big to display in their entirety or become very small when sized to fit the page. In order to fit these large items, some menus have been shortened using a jagged edge (**Figure 14**). The menu item being selected is shown, but upper, middle, or lower menu items are removed to conserve space. In a large dialog box, a circle is drawn around the area under discussion (**Figure 15**).

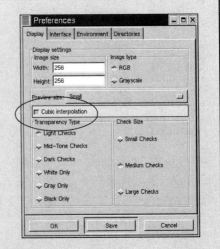

Figure 15. A circle appears around the area under discussion in a large dialog box.

GIMP POP-UP MENUS

Special GIMP Dialog Boxes

There are seven special GIMP dialog boxes that are used for image editing (**Figures 16–22**). To open one of these dialog boxes, choose File→Dialogs in the GIMP Toolbox or right-click on an image window and choose Dialogs from the pop-up menu. (The Indexed Palette dialog box is only available on the pop-up menu.) If you are working with several dialog boxes at once, you can maximize screen real estate by rolling up a dialog box that is not in use—just double-click on the dialog box's Title Bar.

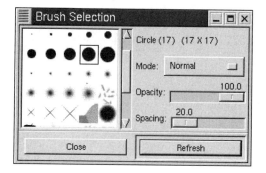

Brush Selection dialog box (Figure 16)

Use the Brush Selection dialog box to select preset or custom brushes for use with a painting or editing tool. You can also use the Brush Selection dialog box to set a *blending mode*, opacity, and stroke spacing. To find out more about the Brush Selection dialog box, turn to page 110.

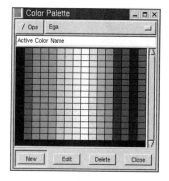

Color Palette dialog box (Figure 17)

The Color Palette dialog box lets you select colors from predefined palettes. These colors are applied using a painting or editing tool, or using a command such as Stroke or Fill. You can also use the Color Palette dialog box to edit existing palettes and colors, and create new color palettes. To learn more about the Color Palette dialog box and how to use it, turn to page 47.

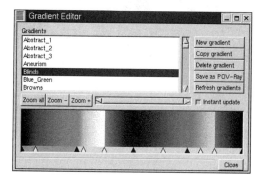

Gradient Editor dialog box (Figure 18)

The Gradient Editor dialog box works in conjunction with the Blend Tool. Using the Gradient Editor dialog box, you can select from the extensive list of gradients, edit an existing gradient, or create a new one. Turn to page 127 to find out more about the Gradient Editor dialog box.

SPECIAL DIALOG BOXES

Indexed Color Palette dialog box (Figure 19)

The Indexed Color Palette dialog box is similar to the Color Palette dialog box in that it does show a color palette and let you edit existing colors. But, that's where the similarity ends. This color palette is composed of the colors in an open image set in indexed color mode. It is a temporary palette that is only available while the image is open. To find out more about the Indexed Color Palette, turn to page 51.

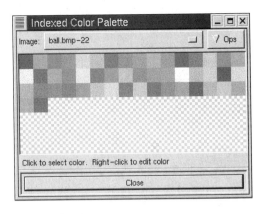

Layers & Channels dialog box (Figure 20)

The Layers & Channels dialog box is used to display the layers and channels that make up an image. Using this dialog box, you can create, duplicate, and delete layers and channels. In addition, you can move layers and channels up or down in the *stacking order* and anchor *floating* layers.

By default, when you create a new image, it will have one layer called the Background layer. The number of channels an image has depends upon the color mode the image is set in. (An RGB image has three channels and an indexed, grayscale, or bitmap image has one channel.)

You can edit each layer separately without changing the other layers and set a blending mode and opacity for each layer. The *active* layer is highlighted. The eye icon indicates a visible layer. Take a look at page 92 to learn more about this dialog box.

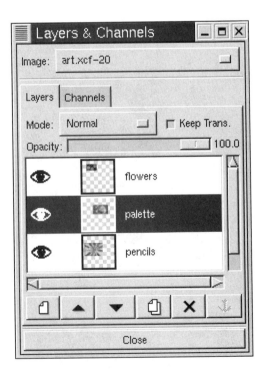

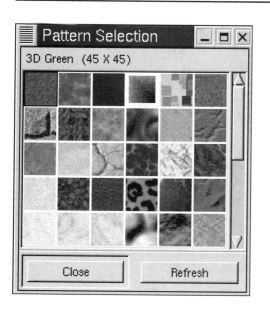

Pattern Selection dialog box (Figure 21)

The Pattern Selection dialog box contains many preloaded patterns. These patterns are used in conjunction with the Bucket Fill Tool to fill areas with the selected pattern. To find out how to use the Pattern Selection dialog box turn to pages 121–122.

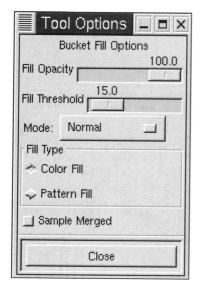

Tool Options dialog box (Figure 22)

The contents of this dialog box change depending upon which tool is selected in the GIMP Toolbox. Access this dialog box by double-clicking on a tool button in the Toolbox or by choosing the menu item on the File→Dialogs menu in the GIMP Toolbox or by right-clicking and choosing the Dialogs menu item from the pop-up menu. The Tool Options dialog box can be seen in its various permutations on pages 63, 68, 74, 75, 116, 118, 126, 152, 154, 188, and 189.

SPECIAL DIALOG BOXES

Setting Levels of Undo and Redo

By default, the GIMP lets you undo the last five actions you've performed. You can change this to any number you want, though this does take up extra space in RAM and may slow your computer down. The number of redo levels automatically corresponds to the number of undo levels.

To set the levels of undo:

1. Right-click on the image window and choose File→Preferences (**Figure 23**).

   or

   Choose File→Preferences in the GIMP Toolbox (**Figure 24**).

   The Preferences dialog box will open with the Display tab page in front (**Figure 25**).

2. Click the Interface tab page to bring it to the front (**Figure 26**).

3. In the Levels of undo text box, enter the number of levels you would like.

4. Click OK. The Preferences dialog box will close and the levels of undo will change to your setting.

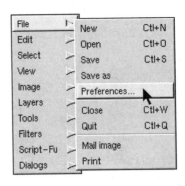

Figure 23. Right-click on the image and choose File→ Preferences from the pop-up menu.

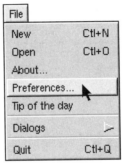

Figure 24. Choose File→ Preferences in the GIMP Toolbox.

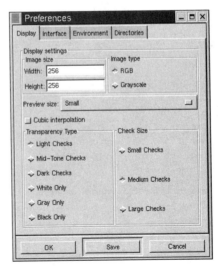

Figure 25. The Preferences dialog box opens with the Display tab page in front.

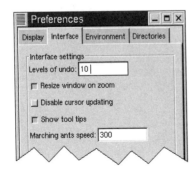

Figure 26. On the Interface tab page, enter a number in the Levels of undo text box.

The GIMP Controls

Figures 27a–f show the controls you will use when working with GIMP dialog boxes.

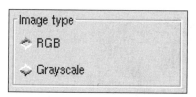

Figure 27a. *Radio buttons.* Radio buttons are usually contained in an area, and you can select only one item from two or more options. Click the diamond to select a radio button. Some folks call these option buttons.

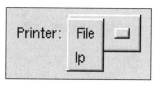

Figure 27d. *Drop-down lists.* Drop-down lists present a selection of items from which to choose. To open the list, click the list box button or the little rectangle to the right of the list box. You can only choose one item from a drop-down list.

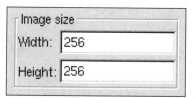

Figure 27b. *Text boxes.* Text or numbers are typed in text boxes to set the specification for an item.

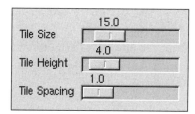

Figure 27e. *Sliders.* Sliders are used to set the value for a specific item. To use a slider, position the mouse pointer over the slider, press the left mouse button, and drag left or right.

Figure 27c. *Check buttons.* Click a check button (also called check boxes) to turn an option on or off. Depending upon your desktop settings, a check may or may not appear in the button when it's selected.

Figure 27f. *Preview areas.* Some dialog boxes include a preview area that lets you see how changes look before clicking OK and applying an effect to an image.

Some Terms You Should Know

On the next three pages is a quick list of just a few GIMP terms that you will see throughout this book. Take a look at them to get an idea of what the GIMP can do. For more about GIMP terms, turn to Appendix A, *Glossary*, starting on page 293.

Active layer and transparent layer (Figure 28)

The highlighted layer on the Layers tab page of the Layers & Channels dialog box is the active layer. When a layer is active, it is the only layer that can be edited. An image can have just one layer—usually named the Background layer—or more than one layer. Most typically, all layers in an image except the background layer are transparent. Layer transparency can be set using the Opacity slider. Layers can be moved and aligned, and their stacking order changed. A *layer mask* controls the way a layer is revealed. Turn to Chapter 7, *A Layer Primer*, and Chapter 11, *Layer Techniques*, to find out more about layers.

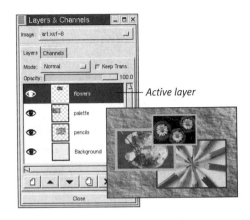

Active layer

Alpha channel (Figure 29)

A special grayscale channel that is used to save selections. These selections are used to protect areas of an image from editing. To find out more about alpha channels, take a look at page 194.

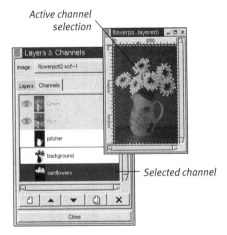

Active channel selection

Selected channel

Blending mode (Figure 30)

A blending mode changes the way a layer's pixels blend with the pixels in the layer directly below it. In the image to the right, a white semitransparent layer using an Addition blending mode has been placed on top of the point shoe. To learn more about blending modes, turn to pages 170–173.

Original image

Red channel

Green channel

Blue channel

Channel (Figure 31)

A component of an image that contains the pixel information for an individual color. An RGB image has three color channels while a grayscale image has one color channel. The rose image to the left has been broken down into its three channels. To learn more about channels and how to use them, turn Chapter 13, *Channels and Layer Masks*.

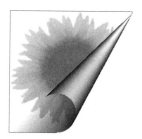

Filter (Figure 32)

Filters are used to apply special effects to an image or selected area. All of the filters are plug-ins. Many script-fus use several filters to create complex effects. The Pagecurl filter has been applied to the image at the left. Take a look at Chapter 15, *Using Filters*, to find out how they work and the effects they create.

Hue window

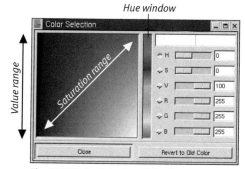

Value range

Saturation range

The GIMP Color Selection dialog box

Hue, Saturation, and Value (Figure 33)

Hue is the actual color itself, such as green or purple, regardless of the saturation or value. Saturation is a description of a color's purity. The less gray a color contains, the higher the saturation. Value is a description of the brightness of a color. To find out about the HSV color model, turn to page 35.

Pixels (Figure 34)

The dots used to display bitmap images in a pattern on the computer screen. The GIMP is a pixel-based image manipulation program. Viewed at 200% magnification, the bananas at left are showing their pixels. Take a look at page 25 to learn more about pixels.

Selected area

Selection (Figure 35)

An area of an image that has been isolated to restrict changes to that area. A dashed, moving *selection boundary* (also called *marching ants*) delineates the selected area. If a selection is moved, the space left behind is filled with the current background color if the selection is on the Background layer; if the selection is on another layer, the space becomes transparent. A *floating selection* is a selection that is not anchored to a layer. Take a look at Chapter 6, *Making Selections*, to learn about the ins and outs of selecting.

Semi-transparent layer

Transparency (Figure 36)

An area of an image where the pixels contain no color. A transparent area in an image is shown in the GIMP image window with a light and dark gray checkerboard pattern. To learn more about layer transparency, turn to page 174. To learn about creating transparent effects with layer masks, turn to page 200.

SOME TERMS YOU SHOULD KNOW

Summary

In this chapter you learned about:

- GIMP installation
- GIMP resources on the Web
- The GIMP screen
- Changing keystroke combinations
- The GIMP Toolbox
- The GIMP Toolbox menus

- The pop-up menus
- Large menus and dialog boxes
- Special GIMP dialog boxes
- Setting levels of undo and redo
- The GIMP controls
- Some GIMP terms you should know

STARTUP

When the GIMP is launched, a small Toolbox appears on the screen (**Figure 1**). Using this Toolbox, you can open an *image window*.

The image window is the area on the screen where images are created. The image window consists of the *image display area* or *canvas* edged with a dashed line. There are rulers across the top and at the left of the image window divided into *pixels*. If the image display area is too large to show all at once, you can use scrollbars at the bottom and to the right of the image window to move the image display area around. You can resize an image window by positioning the mouse pointer at any edge or corner, pressing the left mouse button, and dragging to a new size.

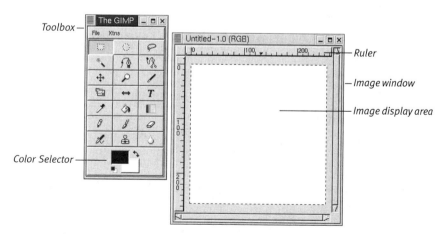

Figure 1. The GIMP Toolbox is your gateway to creating amazing images.

Menu Items and Desktop Shortcuts

Sometimes a shortcut for the GIMP isn't present after installation. (For the RedHat and KDE distributions of Linux it is usually available on the Graphics fly-out on the Main Menu.) Below are directions for the KDE and Gnome distributions.

To put a menu item on the K Main Menu:

1. Choose Utilities→Menu Editor from the K Main Menu (**Figure 2**). The Menu Editor window will appear (**Figure 3**).

2. Right-click on the Empty button and choose New from the pop-up menu (**Figure 4**). The kmenuedit dialog box will open (**Figure 5**).

3. Type GIMP in the Name text box.

4. Click the icon button to the right of the dialog box and select an icon from the Select Icon dialog box. This is the icon that will appear on the menu.

5. On the Execute tab page in the Execute text box, type the full pathname of the location where the GIMP is installed plus the command to launch the GIMP. In **Figure 5** /usr/bin/gimp has been typed.

6. Click OK to close the kmenuedit dialog box and return to the Menu Editor window.

7. Choose Save from the File menu.

8. Press Ctrl+Q on the keyboard to close the Menu Editor. The GIMP menu item will appear under the Personal fly-out on the K Main Menu (**Figure 6**).

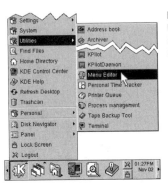

Figure 2. Choose Utilities→Menu Editor from the K Main Menu.

Figure 3. The K Menu Editor.

Figure 4. Choose New from the pop-up menu.

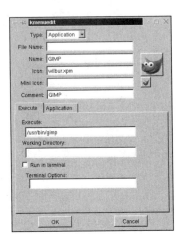

Figure 5. Use the kmenuedit dialog box to enter the command line information and select an icon.

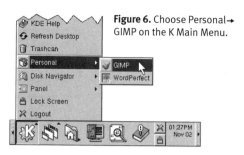

Figure 6. Choose Personal→ GIMP on the K Main Menu.

Figure 7. Choose Settings→Menu editor from the Gnome Main Menu.

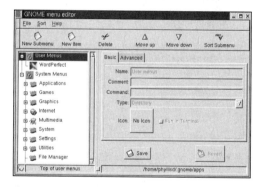

Figure 8. The GNOME menu editor dialog box opens with User Menus selected in the tree view window.

Figure 9. Use the Basic tab page to enter the program name, command line information, and select an icon.

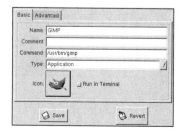

To put a menu item on the Gnome Main Menu:

1. Choose Settings→Menu editor from the Gnome Main Menu (**Figure 7**). The Gnome menu editor dialog box will open with User Menus selected in the tree view window (**Figure 8**).

2. On the Menu Bar, click New Item to add a new menu item under User Menus.

3. On the Basic tab page, type GIMP in the Name text box (**Figure 9**).

4. In the Command text box, type the full pathname of the location where the GIMP is installed plus the command to launch the GIMP. In **Figure 9** /usr/bin/gimp has been typed.

5. Click the Icon button to choose an appropriate icon. This is the icon that will appear on the menu.

6. Click Save.

7. Close the Gnome menu editor dialog box by clicking the Close button. The GIMP menu item will appear on the Gnome Main Menu (**Figure 10**).

✔ Tip

■ If you are logged on as root, you can add the GIMP menu item to the Graphics menu on the Gnome Main Menu. Once an icon is added to the Graphics menu, it is available to all users; whereas, an item added to the User menu is only available for that user.

PUT A MENU ITEM ON THE GNOME MAIN MENU

To put a shortcut on the Gnome Desktop:

1. Right-click on the Gnome Desktop. A pop-up menu will appear.

2. Choose New→Launcher from the pop-up menu (**Figure 11**). The Desktop entry properties dialog box will appear (**Figure 12**).

3. Type GIMP in the Name text box.

4. In the Command text box, type in the full path where the GIMP program is installed, including the program name itself (**Figure 13**). In **Figure 13**, /usr/bin/gimp has been entered.

5. Select Application from the Type drop-down list.

6. Click the Icon button to select an appropriate icon from the Choose an icon dialog box.

7. Click OK. The shortcut will appear on the Desktop (**Figure 14**).

Figure 10. The GIMP menu item appears as a user menu on the Gnome Main Menu.

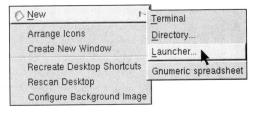

Figure 11. Right-click on the Gnome Desktop and choose New→Launcher from the pop-up menu.

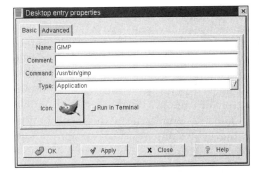

Figure 13. On the Basic tab page, enter the name of the program and the command line needed to launch it, then choose an icon.

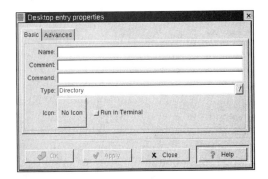

Figure 12. Use the Basic tab page of the Desktop entry properties dialog box to enter the information you need to create a shortcut.

Figure 14. The GIMP shortcut appears on the Gnome Desktop.

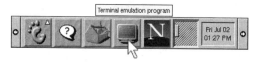

Figure 15. Click the Terminal emulation program button on the Gnome panel.

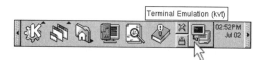

Figure 16. Click the Terminal Emulation button on the K panel.

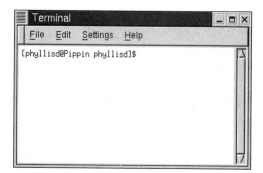

Figure 17. Use the Terminal window to move to the directory where the GIMP is installed, then enter the command to launch the GIMP.

To launch the GIMP using a menu item or shortcut:

If you are using the Gnome Desktop, choose User→GIMP from the Gnome Main Menu (**Figure 10**) or double-click the GIMP icon on your Desktop (**Figure 14**).

or

If you are using the K Desktop, choose Personal→GIMP from the the K Main Menu (**Figure 6**).

To launch the GIMP from the command line:

1. Open a terminal window. If you are using the Gnome desktop, click the Terminal emulation program button on the Gnome panel (**Figure 15**). If you are using the KDE desktop, click the Terminal Emulation button on the K panel (**Figure 16**). A Terminal window will open (**Figure 17**).

2. At the prompt, change directories to where the GIMP is installed. A typical installation places the GIMP in /usr/bin.

3. Type gimp (**Figure 18**), then press Enter on the keyboard to launch the GIMP.

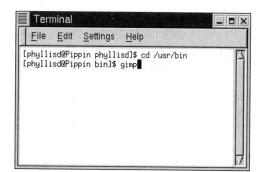

Figure 18. Change to the /usr/bin directory, then type gimp and press Enter on the keyboard to launch the GIMP.

Launching the GIMP for the First Time

When you launch the GIMP for the very first time, a GIMP Installation dialog box will appear (**Figure 19**). This box contains a bit about the GNU General Public License and tells about the personal files that need to be installed for you to use the GIMP. This dialog box will appear only once. You won't see it again after you have installed the personalization files.

To install GIMP personalization files:

1. Launch the GIMP for the first time. The GIMP Installation dialog box will open (**Figure 19**).

2. Click Install. The GIMP program will install the personalization files you need. When it is finished, an Installation Log dialog box will appear, confirming everything that has been installed (**Figure 20**).

3. Click Continue. The GIMP program will load (**Figure 21**). The GIMP Toolbox and GIMP Tip of the day dialog box will appear (**Figure 22**). This dialog box will display a handy tip every time you launch the GIMP. If you don't want to see tips, unselect the Show tip next time check button. (By the way, the cute dog with the beret on his head and the paintbrush in his mouth is Wilber, the GIMP mascot.)

4. Click Close. The GIMP Tip of the day dialog box will close, leaving the Toolbox ready for you to use (**Figure 1**).

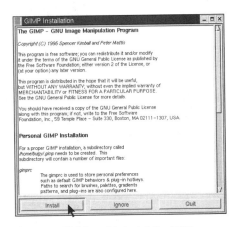

Figure 19. Click Install to install the GIMP personalization files.

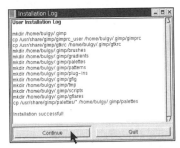

Figure 20. The Installation Log dialog box confirms that everything has been loaded.

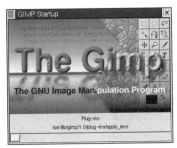

Figure 21. The GIMP Startup window appears as the GIMP loads.

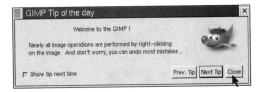

Figure 22. The friendly face of Wilber, the GIMP mascot, greets you on the GIMP Tip of the day dialog box.

Figure 23. Choose File→New in the GIMP Toolbox.

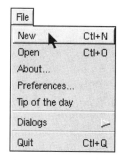

Figure 24. Right-click on an image window and choose File→New from the pop-up menu.

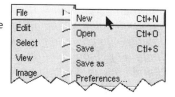

Figure 25. Use the New Image dialog box to set the size, color mode, and fill for the new image.

Starting a New Image

When the GIMP is launched, all that appears is a small toolbox (**Figure 1**). *Now what?* This unassuming little toolbox is your gateway to creating amazing images.

To start a new image:

1. Choose File→New in the GIMP Toolbox (**Figure 23**).

   or

   Press Ctrl+N on the keyboard.

   or

   If you already have an image window open, right-click on the image window and choose File→New from the pop-up menu (**Figure 24**).

   The New Image dialog box will open (**Figure 25**).

2. Use the Width and Height text boxes to set the dimensions of the new image. These dimensions are always set in *pixels*. Pixels are the tiny rectangular dots used to display an image on a computer screen.

(continued)

START A NEW IMAGE

How Big is a Pixel?

Pixels aren't absolute measurement units such as inches or centimeters are on a ruler. The size of a pixel depends upon the actual size of your computer monitor and its *resolution* setting. Resolution is the number of pixels displayed vertically and horizontally on the computer screen. Some typical resolution settings are 1024x768, 800x600, and 640x480. Normally, most monitors have between 50 and 100 pixels per inch (20 to 40 pixels per centimeter).

To summarize, pixels are not concrete in the way that inches and centimeters are. A pixel's actual real-world size depends upon a number of variables.

3. Select whether the image will be color or grayscale, by choosing either the RGB or Grayscale radio button in the Image Type area. (RGB and grayscale are discussed in detail in Chapter 3, *Color and the GIMP*.)

4. Use the Fill Type area to select the color for the background area of the image (**Figure 26**). Choose from the following:

- ◆ **Background** is the background color shown in the Color Selector on the Toolbox.

- ◆ **White** for a white background.

- ◆ **Transparent** is an invisible background.

- ◆ **Foreground** is the foreground color shown in the Color Selector on the Toolbox.

5. Click OK. A new, untitled image window will open, ready for you to use (**Figure 27**).

✔ Tips

- ■ For more information about the Color Selector on the Toolbox, turn to page 41.

- ■ To learn more about transparent backgrounds, take a look at page 39.

Figure 26. Select a color for the background area of the image.

Figure 27. The new image window opens, ready for you to begin.

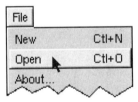

Figure 28. Choose File→Open in the GIMP Toolbox.

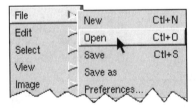

Figure 29. Right-click on an image window and choose File→Open from the pop-up menu.

How Many Image Windows Can I Open at Once?

You can have as many image windows open at one time as you like (depending upon the amount of memory in your computer). To see the GIMP with 800 image windows open (!), check out
`http://www.geocities.com/ResearchTriangle/8847/screen800.gif`

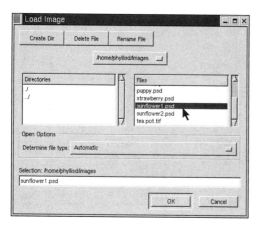

Figure 30. Use the Load Image dialog box to move to the directory where the file is stored and select it.

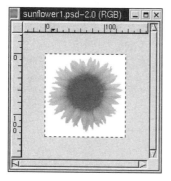

Figure 31. The image file opens in an image window.

To open an existing image:

1. Choose File→Open in the GIMP Toolbox (**Figure 28**).

   or

   If you have an image window already open, right-click on the image window and choose File→Open from the pop-up menu (**Figure 29**).

   or

   Press Ctrl+O on the keyboard.

   The Load Image dialog box will appear (**Figure 30**).

2. Use the Directories list box to move to the directory where the file is stored.

3. Use the Files list box to select the file you want to open.

4. Click OK. The image will appear in an image window (**Figure 31**).

File Types You Can Open with the GIMP

The GIMP can be used to open a whole kitchen sink's worth of different file types. You should use the GIMP's native file format, XCF, when you want to preserve layers, channels, and guides because most other file formats can't save these things. Some other formats the GIMP can open include:

BMP—Windows and OS/2 bitmap format
GIF—Graphics Interchange Format, commonly used for Web images
JPEG—Joint Photographic Experts Group format, typically used for full-color Web images
PSD—Photoshop's native file format
SGIX—Silicon Graphics image format

To save a new image:

1. Right-click on the image window and choose File→Save from the pop-up menu (**Figure 32**) or press Ctrl+S on the keyboard. The Save Image dialog box will open (**Figure 33**).

2. Use the Directories list box to move to the directory where you want to store the file.

   or

   Create a new directory for the image:

   A. Click Create Dir at the top left of the Save Image dialog box (**Figure 34**). The Create Directory dialog box will appear (**Figure 35**).

   B. Type a name for the new directory in the Directory name text box.

   C. Click Create. The Create Directory dialog box will close and the new directory will appear in the Directories list box.

3. Type the name for the image in the Selection text box. Be sure to add a file extension with the name. Otherwise, the GIMP won't know how to save it and will display an error message (**Figure 36**). For instance, in **Figure 33** the name of the image being saved is MyImage.xcf.

4. Click OK. The Save Image dialog box will close and the image will be saved.

To save an existing image:

Right-click on the image window and choose File→Save from the pop-up menu (**Figure 32**) or press Ctrl+S on the keyboard.

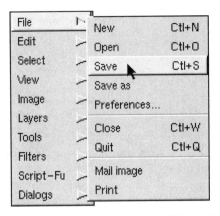

Figure 32. Right-click on the image window and choose File→Save from the pop-up menu.

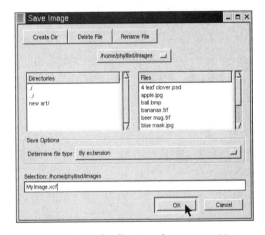

Figure 33. Move to the directory where you want to save the image, type its name in the Selection text box, then click OK.

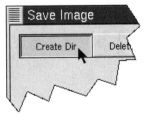

Figure 34. Click the Create Dir button at the upper left of the Save Image dialog box.

Figure 35. Type the name for the new directory in the Directory name text box, then click Create.

Figure 36. If you don't enter a file extension when you name a file, the GIMP won't know how to save the file and will open a GIMP Message dialog box saying the save failed. Click OK to close the dialog box and return to the Save Image dialog box.

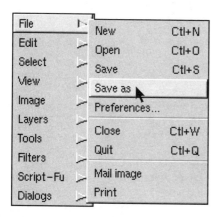

Figure 37. Right-click on the image window and choose File→Save as from the pop-up menu.

To save a copy of an image:

1. Right-click on the image window and choose File→Save as from the pop-up menu (**Figure 37**). The Save Image dialog box will open (**Figure 33**).

2. Use the Directories list box to move to the directory where you want to store the file.

   or

   Create a new directory:

   A. Click Create Dir at the top left of the Save Image dialog box (**Figure 34**). The Create Directory dialog box will appear (**Figure 35**).

   B. Type a name for the new directory in the Directory name text box.

   C. Click Create. The Create Directory dialog box will close and the new directory will appear in the Directories list box.

3. Type the name for the image copy in the Selection text box. Be sure to add a file extension with the name. Otherwise, the GIMP won't know how to save it and will display an error message (**Figure 36**).

4. Click OK. The new copy of the file will remain open while the original version is automatically closed.

✔ Tip

■ Save copies of an image while you work on it. That way, if you want to revert to a previous version of the image, it will be there waiting for you.

To save an image in another file format:

1. Right-click on the image window and choose File→Save as from the pop-up menu (**Figure 37**). The Save Image dialog box will open (**Figure 33**).

2. Use the Directories list box to move to the directory where you want to store the file.

3. Type the name of the file with its new file extension in the Selection text box (for instance, WebImage.png).

4. Click OK to save the file.

✔ **Tips**

■ In step 3, you can also select the file type from the Determine file type drop-down list found in the Save Options area (**Figure 38**). **By extension** is selected by default. This means that if you type in the file extension after the file name, the GIMP will automatically save it as that file type.

■ If you try to save a file using an *indexed color* format such as GIF and the GIMP says the save failed, chances are the file needs to be converted to Indexed color mode before it can be saved. To find out how to convert an image to another color mode, turn to page 36.

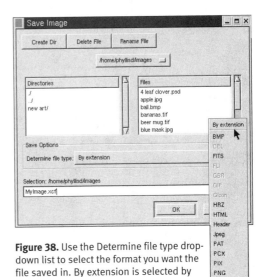

Figure 38. Use the Determine file type drop-down list to select the format you want the file saved in. By extension is selected by default.

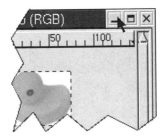

Figure 39. Click the Minimize button to get an image out of the way.

File Extensions and the GIMP

File extensions are the three or four letters that come after the period in a file name. In Linux/Unix there is no overall mechanism for associating file extensions with file types, though the GIMP needs a file extension in order to save a file correctly. If you try to save a file in the GIMP without a file extension, a GIMP Message dialog box appears, saying that the save failed (**Figure 36**).

Figure 40. Click the button on the Control Panel that corresponds to the image you want to view.

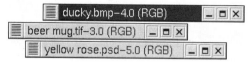

Figure 41. Image windows that are rolled up display only their Title Bars.

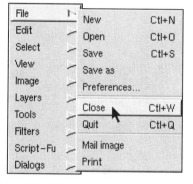

Figure 42. Right-click on the image window and choose File→Close from the pop-up menu.

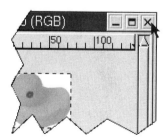

Figure 43. Click the Close button in the upper right-hand corner of the document window.

Getting Images Out of the Way

If you are working on several images at one time, you may want to get a few of the image windows out of the way but not close them. There are two ways to do this: you can minimize the window or roll it up.

To minimize an image window:

Click the Minimize button in the upper right-hand corner of the image window (**Figure 39**).

To view a minimized image window:

Depending upon the type of Linux/Unix distribution you are using, a minimized window will appear differently. For RedHat Linux or KDE, just click the button on the Control Panel to view a minimized window (**Figure 40**).

To roll up an image window:

Double-click on the Title Bar. The image window will roll up, displaying only the Title Bar (**Figure 41**).

✔ Tip

■ To unroll the image window, double-click on the Title Bar again.

To close an image window:

Right-click on the image window and choose File→Close from the pop-up menu (**Figure 42**).

or

Press Ctrl+W on the keyboard.

or

Click the Close button in the upper right-hand corner of the image window (**Figure 43**).

MINIMIZE, ROLL UP, OR CLOSE AN IMAGE WINDOW

To exit the GIMP:

Choose File→Quit in the GIMP Toolbox (**Figure 44**).

or

Click the Close button in the upper right-hand corner of the Toolbox (**Figure 45**).

or

Right-click on the image window and choose File→Quit from the pop-up menu (**Figure 46**).

or

Press Ctrl+Q on the keyboard.

Figure 44. Choose File→Quit in the GIMP Toolbox.

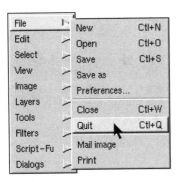

Figure 46. Right-click on an image window and choose File→Quit from the pop-up menu.

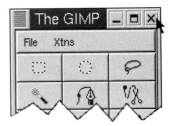

Figure 45. Click the Close button in the upper right-hand corner of the GIMP Toolbox.

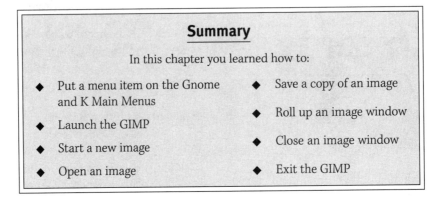

Summary

In this chapter you learned how to:

- Put a menu item on the Gnome and K Main Menus
- Launch the GIMP
- Start a new image
- Open an image
- Save a copy of an image
- Roll up an image window
- Close an image window
- Exit the GIMP

COLOR
AND THE GIMP

Figure 1. This vector image looks the same whether viewed close up or far away.

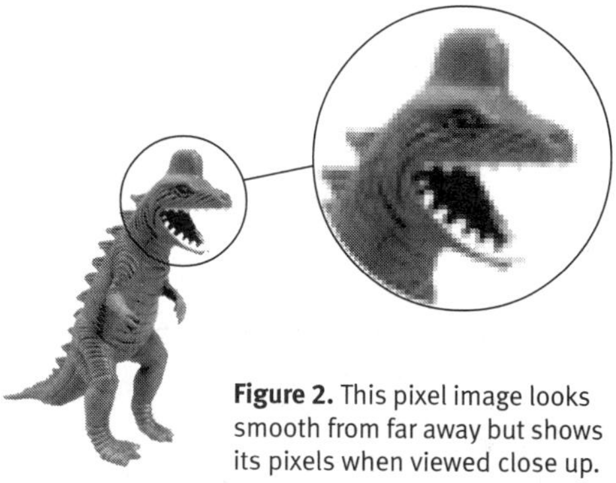

*T*his chapter covers the basics of how color works in the GIMP. You'll discover the difference between *vector-* and *pixel*-based programs, how *color models* work, and how *blending modes* affect colors in an image.

Vector- and Pixel-Based Imaging Programs

Computer imaging programs are either vector based or bitmap based.

In vector-based programs, such as CorelDraw and Adobe Illustrator, objects are created using drawing tools that make shapes defined by mathematical formulas. A vector object appears the same on the screen with smooth lines and continuous colors, whether you are looking at it from far away or up close (**Figure 1**). Vector drawings are *resolution independent*, meaning that the printed quality depends only on the resolution of the printer.

In bitmap-based programs, such as the GIMP, Corel PhotoPaint, and Adobe Photoshop, images are made up of tiny dots called *pixels* that are arranged and colored to form a pattern. The shape and color of a pixel image appear smooth from a distance, but if you were to view a pixel image close up, you would see tiny individual squares (**Figure 2**). Pixel images depend on the resolution at which they are saved for printout quality.

Figure 2. This pixel image looks smooth from far away but shows its pixels when viewed close up.

Color Models and Modes

A *color model* breaks colors down into their component primary parts. A color model is used to represent color in images in a standardized way. In the GIMP, color models are applied to images as *color modes*.

RGB Model

The Red, Green, Blue color model (normally called *RGB*) is used to display a color image on a computer monitor. RGB is an *additive* color model, meaning that every color can be created using red, green, and blue in varying degrees of brightness. (Brightness is expressed in a measurement called *value*.) Each of these three colors occupies its own *channel* within a pixel. This means that RGB color has three channels. Typically color information is saved in either 1-bit, 8-bit, or 24-bit color depth. Twenty-four-bit color saves the most color information per pixel, up to a value of 256 per channel. In each channel a value of 0 is the darkest (black) and a value of 255 is the lightest (white). **Figures 3a–b** show an RGB image and its three channels on the Channels tab page of the Layers & Channels dialog box.

CMYK Model

The Cyan, Magenta, Yellow, Black color model (known as *CMYK*—the K represents black) is used in high-quality offset color printing. Instead of using light to display color as with the RGB model, ink or toner is used. CMYK is a *subtractive* color model, meaning that as the colors are mixed darker colors are created. RGB at its highest value creates white; CMYK at its highest value creates black. CMYK color has four channels per pixel. Since the GIMP was originally designed for creating digital and Web images, it doesn't support the CMYK color model. You may be interested to know that the next released version of the GIMP will support this color model.

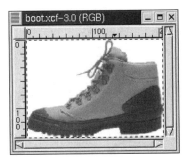

Figure 3a. This image is set in RGB mode (you'll have to use your imagination here since this figure isn't in color). Notice that the mode, RGB, appears in the title bar. This is a quick way to verify in which mode an image is set.

Figure 3b. The Channels tab page of the Layers & Channels dialog box shows the available channels.

Other Names for Pixel and Vector

Pixel-based programs are often referred to as *bitmap* or *raster* programs. Vector-based programs are also called *drawing* or *object-oriented* programs.

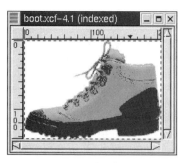

Figure 4. This image is set in Indexed color mode. Using the custom palettes, you can create interesting color effects.

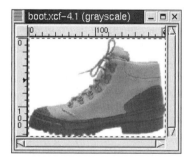

Figure 5. This image is set in grayscale mode.

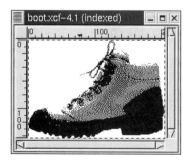

Figure 6. This image is set in bitmap mode. Notice that there are only black and white areas, no gray.

HSV Model

The Hue, Saturation, Value (*HSV*) model is used in combination with the RGB model in the GIMP. Hue represents the color in use— green, pink, orange, etc. Saturation refers to the intensity of the color and is measured as a percentage: at 100% saturation the color appears as the full color, whereas with 10% saturation the color appears very washed out. Value is the intensity of light on the color. This component is also expressed as a percentage. A value of 100% is white and a value of 0% is black. The color in use appears true at a value of 50%. HSV has three channels.

Indexed Mode

Indexed mode sets a specific number of colors used in an image from 1 to 256. Indexed color has one channel (**Figure 4**).

The GIMP comes with many custom color palettes that can be used with an indexed color image to create interesting effects. There are palettes that contain only desert-type tans and browns or sunset hues. There's even a Web palette that contains the 216 colors displayed in a browser. For more details about using color palettes, turn to page 47. To learn more about creating images for the Web, take a look at Chapter 17, *Creating Images for the Web*.

Grayscale Mode

An image set in *grayscale mode* contains no color, only varying shades of gray. There are 256 shades of gray from black (0) to white (255). The median shade of gray on the grayscale spectrum is set at a value of 128. Grayscale has one channel (**Figure 5**).

Bitmap Mode

Bitmap mode is the simplest of all. It contains only black or white pixels—no color or shades of gray (**Figure 6**).

Image Modes

Any GIMP image can be displayed in, edited in, and converted to any one of four image modes: bitmap, grayscale, indexed, or RGB.

To convert an image to a bitmap:

1. Open the image you want to convert (**Figure 7**).

2. Right-click on the image and choose Image→Indexed from the pop-up menu (**Figure 8**). The Indexed Color Conversion dialog box will open (**Figure 9**).

3. Select the Use black/white (1-bit) palette radio button in the Palette Options area (**Figure 10**).

4. Click OK. The Indexed Color Conversion dialog box will close, and the image will convert to a bitmap (**Figure 11**).

To convert an image to indexed mode:

1. Open the image you want to convert (**Figure 7**).

2. Right-click on the image and choose Image→Indexed from the pop-up menu (**Figure 8**). The Indexed Color Conversion dialog box will open (**Figure 9**).

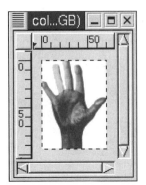

Figure 7. This is the original image set in RGB mode.

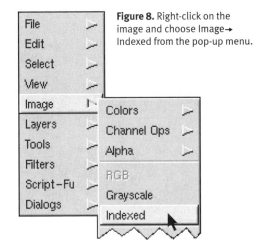

Figure 8. Right-click on the image and choose Image→ Indexed from the pop-up menu.

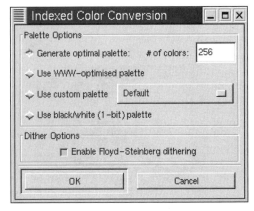

Figure 9. Use the Indexed Color Conversion dialog box to set images in indexed or bitmap mode.

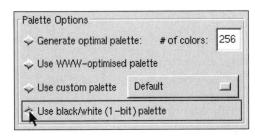

Figure 10. Select the Use black/white (1-bit) palette radio button, then click OK.

Figure 11. This is the same image shown in Figure 7, but it has been converted to bitmap mode.

Figure 12. Select the Use custom palette radio button in the Palette Options area, then choose a custom palette from the drop-down list.

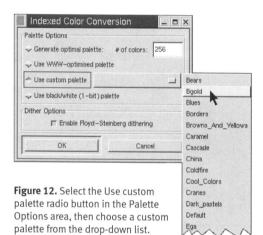

Figure 13. This is the same image shown in Figure 7, but it has been converted to indexed color mode.

3. In the Palette Options area, select a radio button next to one of the following:

   ◆ **Generate optimal palette** creates a palette of up to 256 colors based upon the colors currently present in the image. By default, 256 is entered in the # of colors text box. If you want to create a palette with fewer colors than this, type the number in the text box. (For Web images, the fewer colors the better since file size will be smaller.)

   ◆ **Use WWW-optimised palette** automatically changes the colors in the image to the closest matches available in the Web palette. The Web palette contains the 256 colors best displayed by Netscape Navigator.

   ◆ **Use custom palette** automatically changes the colors in the image to the closest matches available in the selected palette displayed on the drop-down list button. To select a different button, click the button and choose a palette from the drop-down list (**Figure 12**).

4. Click OK. The Indexed Color Conversion dialog box will close and the image will change (sometimes very noticeably) according to your selection (**Figure 13**).

✔ Tip

■ You can create custom palettes, as well as edit existing palette colors, and create new colors. For directions on how to do this, turn to pages 47–51.

To convert an image to RGB or grayscale:

1. Open the image you want to convert.

2. Right-click on the image and choose either Image→RGB or Image→Grayscale from the pop-up menu (**Figure 14**). The image will convert to RGB or grayscale depending upon the mode you selected.

✔ Tips

■ There will always be one color mode that is grayed out and unavailable for selection because that is the one currently in use.

■ If you change color modes and then realize that you made a mistake, you can always undo the change by pressing Ctrl+Z on the keyboard or by right clicking on the image and choosing Edit→Undo from the pop-up menu.

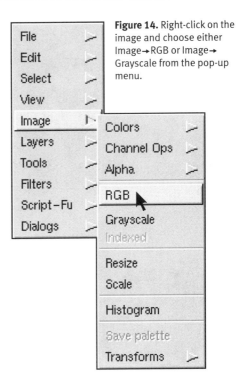

Figure 14. Right-click on the image and choose either Image→RGB or Image→Grayscale from the pop-up menu.

(Sidebar, vertical text: CONVERT AN IMAGE TO RGB OR GRAYSCALE)

Channels and File Size

While color modes do determine the number of colors displayed in an image, they also affect an image's file size and the number of channels it has. The more channels there are the greater the file size. For instance, in **Figures 15a–c** below, the same image is displayed as a bitmap, in grayscale, and RGB. Notice the difference in file sizes.

Figure 15a. This bitmap image has 1 channel and is 16K.

Figure 15b. This grayscale image has 1 channel and is 90K.

Figure 15c. This RGB image has 3 channels and is 290K.

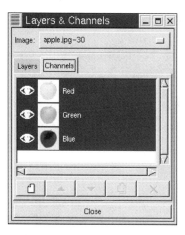

Figure 16. Channels show the information about the different color elements in an image. Every image in the GIMP has at least 1 channel. The RGB image whose channels are shown here has 3 channels.

Figure 17. Transparent areas in an image are shown with a checkerboard pattern.

Transparent area ⎯

How Many Channels are There?

The default number of channels for each image mode is as follows:

CHANNELS	MODES
1	Bitmap, Grayscale, Indexed
3	RGB, HSV
4	CMYK

Channels

Every GIMP image is made up of one or more channels. These channels show the information about the different color elements in an image. As discussed on page 34, RGB color has three channels and CMYK color has four.

Color tuning can be made to an individual channel using the Channels tab page on the Layers & Channels dialog box (**Figure 16**). But usually adjustments are made using the combined channels, affecting all the channels at once.

Special grayscale channels, called *alpha channels,* can be added to an image and are used to save a selected area as a *mask.* (Channels and masks are discussed in detail in Chapter 13, *Channels and Layer Masks.*)

Channels can be added to any type of image, RGB, Indexed, grayscale, or bitmap. An image in the GIMP can have as many channels as you want, though this does add considerably to the file size.

Transparency

When working on an image in the GIMP, any area of the image can be *transparent,* meaning that the pixels contain no color. A transparent area in the GIMP is shown with a light and dark gray checkerboard pattern (**Figure 17**).

Transparency is a wonderful and important feature when working with layers. Layers are like clear glass windows stacked one on top of the other. You can draw on one of these glass windows, then set whether the layer is completely visible, semi-transparent, or completely hidden. Layer transparency is set using a percentage of *opacity.* The more opaque a layer is, the less transparent it is. For a complete discussion of layers, turn to Chapter 7, *A Layer Primer.*

Blending modes

Blending modes work with layer transparency. A blending mode changes the way a layer's pixels blend with the pixels in the layer directly below it. Some of the blending modes are quite subtle, only changing a few colors or shifting hues, while others produce dramatic effects (**Figures 18a–c**). Blending modes are discussed in detail in Chapter 11, *Layer Techniques.*

Figure 18a. This is the original image before a layer is added using a blending mode.

Color and Web Images

When creating images for use on the Web, you need to keep in mind that the bigger the file, the longer the load time for those folks browsing your site. The best thing you can do is try to keep file size down without sacrificing too much of the image quality.

One way to cut image file size down is to convert the image to Indexed mode, selecting the Generate optimal palette radio button in the Indexed Color Conversion dialog box (**Figure 9**). In the # of colors box, enter the fewest number of colors you think would work, then click OK. If the results look okay, try converting the image using fewer colors. If the results look bad, undo the conversion by pressing Ctrl+Z on the keyboard and try again.

For details about images and the Web, turn to Chapter 17, *Creating Images for the Web.*

Figure 18b. A white semi-transparent layer using an Addition blending mode has been placed on top of the original object.

Figure 18c. A white semi-transparent layer using a Difference blending mode has been placed on top of the original object.

Summary

In this chapter you learned about:

◆ Vector- and pixel-based programs

◆ Color models and modes

◆ Converting images to bitmap or Indexed mode

◆ Converting images to RGB or grayscale

◆ Channels and transparency

◆ Blending modes

◆ Color and Web images

SELECTING COLORS

Figure 1. The color selector at the bottom of the GIMP Toolbox contains a foreground and background color.

Color Picker Tool

Color selector

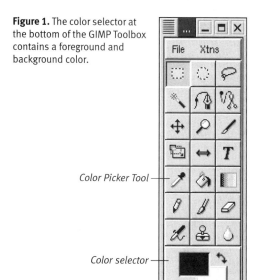

*N*ow that you've learned a bit about how color works in the GIMP, it's time to discover how to select colors for use in your images. There are several ways to select color in the GIMP. Three methods include using the *color selector* at the bottom of the Toolbox, using a predefined color palette, or picking colors from the image itself.

Using the Color Selector

The color selector is located at the bottom of the GIMP Toolbox (**Figure 1**). There you will see two large overlapping squares, two small overlapping squares, and a double-headed arrow (**Figure 2**).

The large overlapping squares are the *foreground* and *background colors*. By default, the foreground color is black and the background color is white. The foreground color is used in an image anytime you paint using the Pencil, Paintbrush, or Airbrush Tools, create type, or fill an area using the Bucket Fill Tool. When editing—erasing or cutting—an image, the hole that's left is filled with the background color.

The two small overlapping squares are used to reset the default foreground and background colors while the double-headed arrow is used to switch the foreground and background colors.

Foreground color square

Switch foreground and background colors

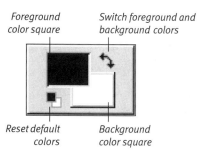

Reset default colors

Background color square

Figure 2. The color selector lets you set foreground and background colors.

To set the foreground or background color using the Color Selection dialog box:

1. Double-click either the foreground or background *color square* on the Toolbox (**Figure 2**). The Color Selection dialog box will open (**Figure 3**).

2. There are two ways to select a new color:

   A. If you want to use an RGB or HSV color and know the exact values for the color, select a radio button next to the color you want to set, then move the slider or type a value in the text box (**Figure 4**).

   B. Repeat step 2A above until you have entered all the values. As you enter values, the color you are creating will appear in the new color box.

   or

   A. Click on the color closest to the one you want to select in the long, thin *color field window* (**Figure 5**). The hue you selected will appear in the large *color box* on the left side of the dialog box.

   B. Click in the large color box on the color you want to select (you don't have to be too exact, you can adjust the color). Horizontal and vertical lines will appear where you clicked (**Figure 6**).

   C. Position the mouse pointer over the intersection of the two lines in the large color box.

   D. Press the left mouse button and drag the intersection until you see the color you want to use in the new color box (**Figure 4**).

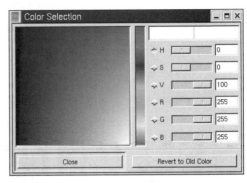

Figure 3. Use the Color Selection dialog box to set a new foreground or background color.

New color box   Old color box

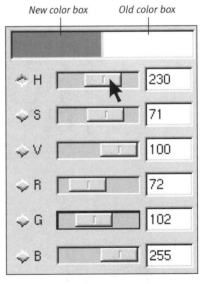

Figure 4. Select a radio button, then move the slider right or left, or type a value in the text box.

SET THE FOREGROUND OR BACKGROUND COLOR

Color box   Color field window

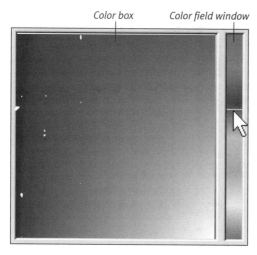

Figure 5. In the color field window, click on the color closest to the one you want to use. If you click on the wrong color, click again or drag the horizontal line up or down.

3. When you have selected the new color, click Close. The Color Selection dialog box will close and the color will be available in either the foreground or background color square on the Toolbox.

✔ Tips

■ To make colors appear washed out, select the V radio button and enter a new Value setting.

■ To make pastel colors, select the S radio button, enter a new Saturation, then slide the horizontal bar down the color field window (**Figure 5**).

■ If you decide you don't want to change to a new foreground or background color, click Revert to Old Color in the Color Selection dialog box. The dialog box will close and the original foreground or background color will be restored to its color square in the Toolbox.

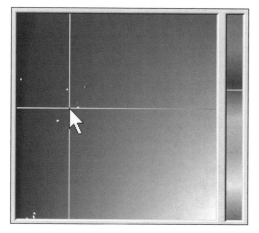

Figure 6. Position the mouse pointer at the intersection of the two lines and drag it around the color box until the color you want to use appears in the new color window.

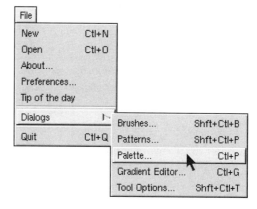

Figure 7. Choose Dialogs→Palette from the File menu in the Toolbox.

To set the foreground or background color using a color palette:

1. Click the foreground or background color square in the Toolbox to select the one you want to set.

2. Choose Dialogs→Palette from the File menu in the Toolbox (**Figure 7**).

   or

   Right-click on the image and choose Dialogs→Palette from the pop-up menu (**Figure 8**).

   or

   Press Ctrl+P on the keyboard.

   The Color Palette dialog box will appear (**Figure 9**).

3. Use the Color Palette drop-down list to select a color palette (**Figure 10**).

4. Click a color square in the palette window (**Figure 11**). The color will appear in either the foreground or background color square.

5. Click Close. The Color Palette dialog box will close.

   or

   If you want to select colors as you work, leave the Color Palette dialog box open.

✔ Tip

■ You can always adjust the color you selected using the Color Selection dialog box. To open the Color Selection dialog box, double-click on the color square containing the color you want to adjust.

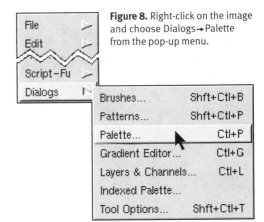

Figure 8. Right-click on the image and choose Dialogs→Palette from the pop-up menu.

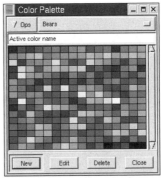

Figure 9. Using the Color Palette dialog box, you can select palettes and colors, and edit, create, and delete them as well.

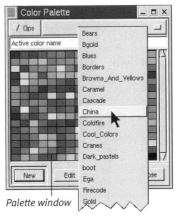

Figure 10. Select a palette from the Color Palette drop-down list.

Palette window

SET COLOR USING THE COLOR PALETTE

Figure 11. Click a color square in the palette window to select a foreground or background color.

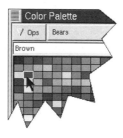

Figure 12. Position the Color Picker crosshair over the color you want to pick up, then click.

Figure 13a. If you select a color from an RGB image, the Red, Green, and Blue values of the color are displayed. If your image has an alpha channel, that value is shown as well. Otherwise, N/A (not applicable) is listed.

Figure 13b. If you select a color from an indexed image, the Index, Red, Green, and Blue values of the color are displayed. If your image has an alpha channel, that value is shown as well. Otherwise, N/A (not applicable) is listed.

To set the foreground or background color using the Color Picker Tool:

1. Click the foreground or background color square in the Toolbox to select the one you want to set.

2. Click the Color Picker Tool button in the Toolbox to select the tool or press O on the keyboard.

3. Position the mouse crosshair over the color in an image that you want to pick up (**Figure 12**).

4. Click to select the color directly under the crosshair.

   or

   Press the left mouse button and drag. As you drag the foreground or background color square in the color selector will display the different colors.

   The Color Picker dialog box will appear with information pertinent to the color mode your image is set in, telling you the exact color values (**Figures 13a–c**).

   (continued)

Figure 13c. If you select a color from a grayscale image, the Intensity value of the gray is shown. If your image has an alpha channel, that value is shown as well. Otherwise, N/A (not applicable) is listed.

SET COLOR WITH THE COLOR PICKER TOOL

5. Once you have found the color you want to use, click Close in the Color Picker dialog box. The color you picked up will be available in the foreground or background color square.

✔ Tip

■ By default, the Color Picker Tool picks up the color from the current layer. To pick up the blended colors from multiple, semi-transparent layers, double-click on the Color Picker button in the Toolbox and select the Sample Merged check button in the Tool Options dialog box (**Figure 14**).

To change back to the default foreground and background colors:

Click the small overlapping square icon on the color selector (**Figure 15**) or press D on the keyboard. The foreground color will change to black and the background color will change to white.

To switch the foreground and background colors:

Click the small double-headed arrow on the color selector (**Figure 16**) or press X on the keyboard.

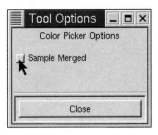

Figure 14. Select the Sample Merged check button in the Tool Options dialog box to pick up colors from multiple layers.

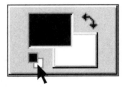

Figure 15. Click the small overlapping square icon to change back to the default colors.

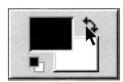

Figure 16. Click the double-headed arrow to switch the foreground and background colors.

Setting Web Page Color

To use a color you have selected for a Web page, use the Hex Triplet number found in the Color Picker dialog box (**Figures 13a–c**) and add it to your HTML code. To find out more about designing graphics for Web pages, turn to Chapter 17, *Creating Images for the Web*.

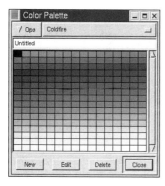

Figure 17. Open the Color Palette dialog box and select a palette from the Color Palette drop-down list. In this figure, Coldfire is selected.

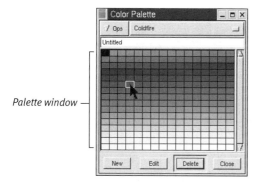

Palette window

Figure 18. In the palette window, click the color square that you want to change.

Color Palettes

When you want to work with a specific color or a group of colors, color palettes are the way to go. For instance, if you wanted to create buttons for a Web page and keep the colors consistent, you could create a color palette for that purpose. With the GIMP, you can edit existing palettes and create new ones.

To adjust a color in an existing palette:

1. Press Ctrl+P on the keyboard to open the Color Palette dialog box (**Figure 17**).

2. Use the Color Palette drop-down list to select a color palette (**Figure 10**).

3. In the palette window, click on the color square that you want to change (**Figure 18**).

4. Click Edit. The Color Selection dialog box will appear (**Figure 3**).

5. Use the Color Selection dialog box to adjust the color. (For directions on how to do this, take a look at step 2 on page 42.)

6. Click OK in the Color Selection dialog box to close it and return to the Color Palette dialog box. The selected color square will change to the new color.

7. When you are finished changing colors, click Close to close the Color Palette dialog box.

Why Don't My Keyboard Shortcuts Work?

If the GIMP Toolbox or any other desktop window or icon (besides a GIMP image window) has *focus* (is selected), GIMP keyboard shortcuts won't work. To make them work, just click on a GIMP image window to select it, then press the keyboard shortcut you want to use.

To add a color to a palette:

1. Choose Dialogs→Palette in the GIMP Toolbox (**Figure 19**).

   or

   Right-click on an image window and choose Dialogs→Palette from the pop-up menu (**Figure 20**).

   or

   Press Ctrl+P on the keyboard.

   The Color Palette dialog box will open (**Figure 21**).

2. Use the Color Palette drop-down list to select a color palette (**Figure 22**).

3. Use the Color Picker Tool or the Color Selection dialog box to select a color. The color will appear in either the foreground or background color square on the Toolbox. (For details on using the Color Picker Tool, see steps 2–4 on page 45. To find out how to use the Color Selection dialog box, see steps 1–2 on page 42.)

4. Click New in the Color Palette dialog box (**Figure 23**). The color will appear in the palette window.

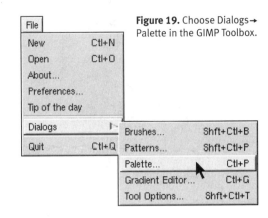

Figure 19. Choose Dialogs→Palette in the GIMP Toolbox.

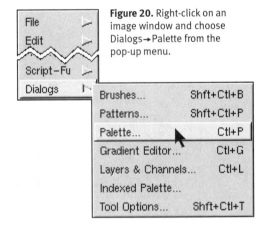

Figure 20. Right-click on an image window and choose Dialogs→Palette from the pop-up menu.

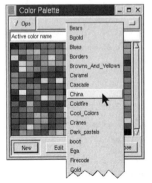

Figure 22. Select a color palette from the Color Palette drop-down list.

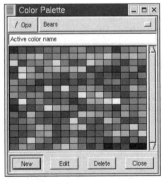

Figure 21. You can create new colors and add them to existing palettes.

ADD A COLOR TO AN EXISTING PALETTE

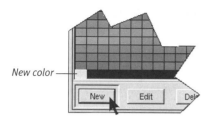

New color

Figure 23. When you click New, the new color appears at the end of the palette in the palette window.

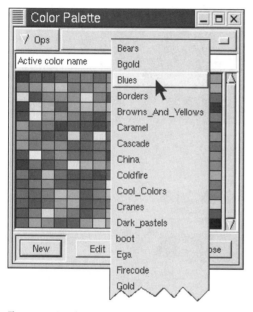

Figure 24. Use the Color Palette drop-down list to select the palette from which you want to delete a color.

To delete a color from a palette:

1. Choose Dialogs→Palette in the GIMP Toolbox (**Figure 19**).

   or

   Right-click on an image window and choose Dialogs→Palette from the pop-up menu (**Figure 20**).

   or

   Press Ctrl+P on the keyboard.

   The Color Palette dialog box will open (**Figure 21**).

2. Use the Color Palette drop-down list to select a color palette (**Figure 24**).

3. In the palette window, click on the color you want to delete (**Figure 25**).

4. Click Delete. The color will be removed from the color palette.

Figure 25. Click the color that you want to remove from the palette, then click Delete.

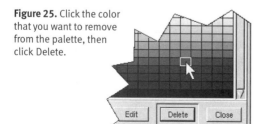

Figure 26. Choose New Palette from the Ops drop-down list in the Color Palette dialog box.

DELETE A COLOR FROM A PALETTE

To create a new color palette:

1. Press Ctrl+P on the keyboard to open the Color Palette dialog box (**Figure 21**).

2. Choose Ops→New Palette in the Color Palette dialog box (**Figure 26**). The New Palette dialog box will appear (**Figure 27**).

3. Type a name for the palette in the text box.

4. Click OK. The New Palette dialog box will close and the new palette's name will appear on the Color Palette drop-down list button (**Figure 28**). Since there are no colors in the palette yet, the palette window will be empty (completely black).

5. Use the Color Picker Tool or the Color Selection dialog box to select a color. The color will appear in either the foreground or background color square on the Toolbox. (For details on using the Color Picker Tool, see steps 2–4 on page 45. To find out how to use the Color Selection dialog box, see steps 1–2 on page 42.)

6. In the Color Palette dialog box, click New. The color will appear in the palette window (**Figure 29**). Continue adding colors to the new palette, following step 5.

To create a saved palette from an indexed image:

1. If you haven't already done so, convert the image to indexed mode (see page 36 for directions on how to do this).

2. Right-click on the image and choose Image→Save palette from the pop-up menu (**Figure 30**). The Export GIMP Palette dialog box will open, with your personal palette directory selected (**Figure 31**).

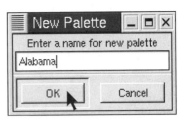

Figure 27. Type a name for the new palette in the text box, then click OK.

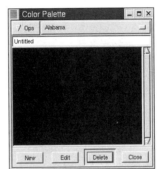

Figure 28. In the Color Palette dialog box, the new palette name appears on the drop-down list button and an empty, black palette appears in the palette window.

Figure 29. In the Color Palette dialog box, the color appears in the palette window. Continue adding colors until you have the palette you need.

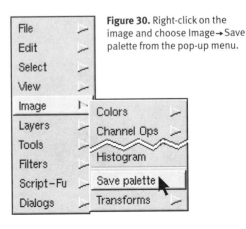

Figure 30. Right-click on the image and choose Image→Save palette from the pop-up menu.

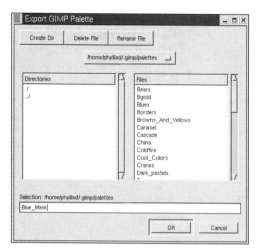

Figure 31. In the Export GIMP Palette dialog box, type a name for the palette in the Selection text box, then click OK.

Figure 32. In the Color Palette dialog box, choose Refresh Palettes from the Ops drop-down list.

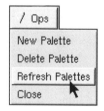

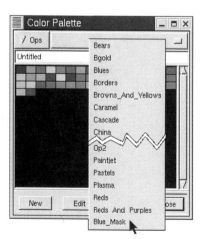

Figure 33. The new palette name appears at the bottom of the Color Palettes drop-down list.

3. Type a name for the palette in the Selection text box.

4. Click OK. The Export GIMP Palette dialog box will close.

5. Press Ctrl+P on the keyboard to open the Color Palette dialog box (**Figure 21**).

6. Choose Refresh Palettes from the Ops drop-down list (**Figure 32**). Your new palette will appear at the bottom of the Color Palettes drop-down list (**Figure 33**).

To use a temporary palette created from an indexed image:

1. Click the foreground or background color square in the Toolbox to select the one you want to set.

2. Right-click on the image and choose Dialogs→Indexed Palette from the pop-up menu (**Figure 34**). An Indexed Color Palette will appear (**Figure 35**).

3. Click a color square to select the color. The color will appear in either the foreground or background color square.

✔ Tips

■ You can adjust the colors in this temporary palette. Right-click on a color square to open the Color Selection dialog box, then adjust the color following the directions in step 2 on page 42. If you adjust a color in this temporary palette, though, that color will also change in the indexed image, altering its appearance.

■ This is a temporary, custom palette that is handy for adjusting the color in an indexed image. It will only be available while the indexed image is open. When the image is closed, the palette is gone.

CREATE AN INDEXED COLOR PALETTE

To delete a palette:

1. Press Ctrl+P on the keyboard to open the Color Palette dialog box (**Figure 21**).

2. Select the palette you want to delete from the Color Palette drop-down list.

3. Choose Delete Palette from the Ops drop-down list (**Figure 36**). The palette will be deleted and disappears from the palette window and the Color Palette drop-down list.

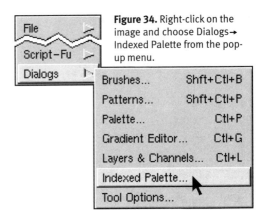

Figure 34. Right-click on the image and choose Dialogs→ Indexed Palette from the pop-up menu.

Figure 36. In the Color Palette dialog box, choose Delete Palette from the Ops drop-down list.

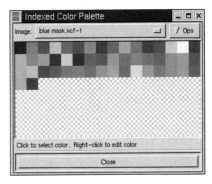

Figure 35. The Indexed Color Palette dialog box contains a temporary palette made up of colors from the indexed image.

Summary

In this chapter you learned how to:

- Use the color selector
- Set color using the Color Selection dialog box
- Set color using a color palette
- Set color using the Color Picker Tool
- Change back to the default foreground and background colors

- Switch the foreground and background colors
- Adjust a color in a color palette
- Add and delete colors from a palette
- Create a new color palette
- Create an indexed color palette
- Delete a palette

DELETE A PALETTE

MOVING ABOUT

*B*eing able to view your images up close is very important. If you want to do any type of detailed work, *zooming in* on the area you want to change is the way to go. After making changes, you can view the entire image again by *zooming out*. In fact, with the GIMP you can view the same image in two image windows at the same time—one window zoomed in to work on the detail, the other zoomed out to see the entire image and the changes you have made.

This chapter takes you through the ins and outs of viewing images in the GIMP. You'll discover how to change the viewing size, zoom to a specific scale, and zoom in on a specific area. Next, you'll find out how to set an image window to resize as you zoom. Finally, you'll learn how to show the same image in two (or more) windows and create duplicate images.

There are several ways to zoom in and out in the GIMP. You can use the Magnify Tool found in the Toolbox (**Figure 1**), choose magnifications using a menu, or use keyboard shortcuts. When you zoom in or out to view an image, the image itself is not affected, only your view of it.

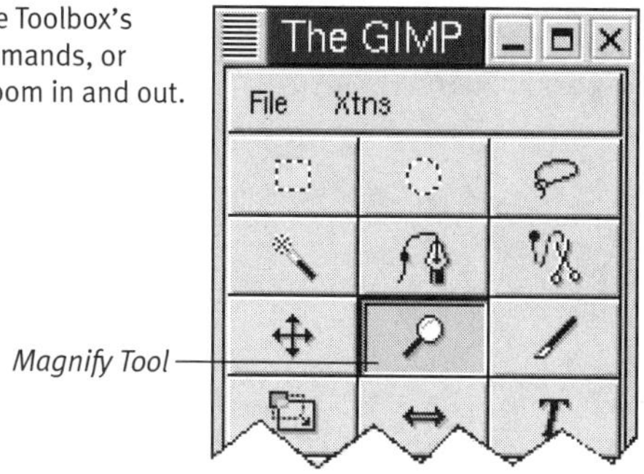

Figure 1. You can use the Toolbox's Magnify Tool, menu commands, or keyboard shortcuts to zoom in and out.

Magnify Tool

To zoom in:

1. Select the Magnify Tool from the Toolbox or press Shift+M on the keyboard.

2. Click in the image window.

or

Right-click on the image and choose View→Zoom In from the pop-up menu (**Figure 2**).

or

Press the = (equals) key on the keyboard.

✔ Tip

■ To quickly view the image at its actual size, press 1 on the keyboard.

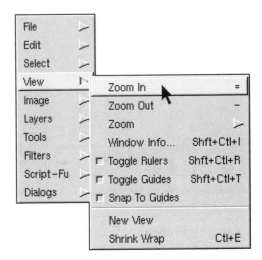

Figure 2. Choose View→Zoom In from the pop-up menu.

To zoom out:

1. Select the Magnify Tool from the Toolbox or press Shift+M on the keyboard.

2. Press down the Shift key on the keyboard, then click in the image window.

or

Right-click on the image and choose View→Zoom Out from the pop-up menu (**Figure 3**).

or

Press the – (hyphen) key on the keyboard.

✔ Tip

■ To quickly view the image at its actual size, press 1 on the keyboard.

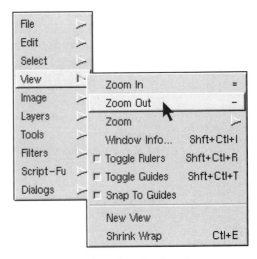

Figure 3. Choose View→Zoom Out from the pop-up menu.

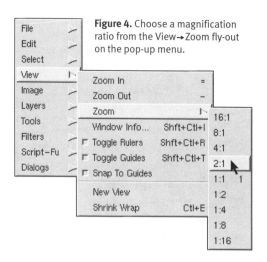

Figure 4. Choose a magnification ratio from the View→Zoom fly-out on the pop-up menu.

To zoom to a specific magnification:

Right-click on an image and choose a magnification ratio from the View→Zoom fly-out on the pop-up menu (**Figure 4**). 16:1 is the closest you can zoom in. 1:16 is the farthest you can zoom out.

To zoom to a specific area:

1. Select the Magnify Tool from the Toolbox or press Shift+M on the keyboard.

2. Position the mouse crosshair at the top left of the area you want to zoom in to (**Figure 5**).

3. Press the left mouse button and drag diagonally down and to the right (**Figure 6**). As you drag, a dashed rectangle, or *marquee*, will appear.

4. When the dashed rectangle completely encompasses the area you want to zoom in on, release the left mouse button. The image view will zoom in to that area (**Figure 7**).

Mouse crosshair

Figure 5. Position the mouse crosshair at the upper left of the area that you want to zoom in on.

Figure 6. Drag the mouse diagonally down to the right until the rectangle encompasses the area you want to zoom in on.

Figure 7. When the mouse button is released, the view zooms in to the area you selected.

ZOOM TO A SPECIFIC AREA

Resizing the Image Window as You Zoom

Many times when zooming in or out, an image window will become smaller than the image—blocking view of the entire image—or larger than the image—using up precious screen real estate. With the GIMP, you can quickly resize an image window using the *Shrink Wrap* command or you can set the image window to automatically resize.

To resize an image window using Shrink Wrap:

Right-click on the image and choose View→ Shrink Wrap from the pop-up menu (**Figure 8**) or press Ctrl+E on the keyboard.

To automatically resize image windows when zooming:

1. Double-click on the Magnify Tool button in the Toolbox. The Tool Options dialog box will open (**Figure 9**).

2. Select the Allow Window Resizing check button.

3. Click Close. The next time you zoom in or out to view an image, the image window will automatically resize to accommodate the new view size.

✔ Tip

■ When you zoom in or out to view an image, the image itself is not affected, only your view of it.

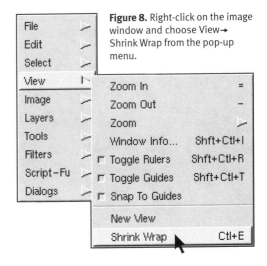

Figure 8. Right-click on the image window and choose View→ Shrink Wrap from the pop-up menu.

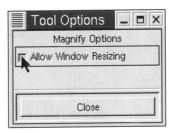

Figure 9. Select the Allow Window Resizing check button, then click Close.

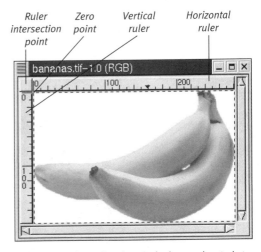

Figure 10. Horizontal and vertical rulers are located at the top and left of the image window.

RESIZE THE IMAGE WINDOW AS YOU ZOOM

Guides

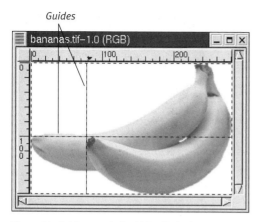

Figure 11. Guides are dashed blue lines that can be positioned anywhere in the image window.

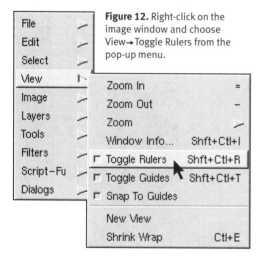

Figure 12. Right-click on the image window and choose View→Toggle Rulers from the pop-up menu.

Figure 13. Drag the guide to its position in the image window.

Rulers and Guides

The horizontal and vertical rulers are located at the top and left of the image window (**Figure 10**). The two rulers meet at a small square called the *ruler intersection point*. The rulers monitor the location of the mouse using small triangles on the rulers. All measurements are made from the *zero point*. This is the point where both the vertical and horizontal rulers show a value of 0. In the GIMP all images are measured in pixels. Therefore, the rulers' unit of measure is pixels. (To find out more about pixels, turn to page 25.)

Guides (also known as *guidelines*) are an extension of rulers that can be positioned anywhere in the image window (**Figure 11**). They are very useful for setting up exact areas where you are going to draw or paint and for helping position and shape selections. A guide consists of a dashed blue line. When the mouse pointer is positioned close to a guide, the guide turns red and the mouse pointer changes to a tiny pointing hand.

To view/hide rulers:

Right-click on an image and choose View→ Toggle Rulers from the pop-up menu (**Figure 12**) or press Shift+Ctrl+R on the keyboard.

To add guides to an image window:

1. Position the mouse over one of the rulers. Use the horizontal ruler to create horizontal guides and the vertical ruler to create vertical guides.

2. Press the left mouse button and drag. A guide will appear under the mouse pointer (**Figure 13**).

3. Release the mouse button when you are happy with the guide's position.

VIEW/HIDE RULERS; ADD GUIDES

To move a guide:

1. Select the Move Tool from the Toolbox.

2. Position the mouse over the guide you want to move. The mouse pointer will change to a tiny pointing hand.

3. Press the left mouse button and drag the guide to its new position (**Figure 14**).

Figure 14. Using the Move Tool, drag the guide to its new position.

To view/hide guides:

Right-click on an image and choose View→ Toggle Guides from the pop-up menu (**Figure 15**) or press Shift+Ctrl+T on the keyboard.

To remove a guide:

1. Select the Move Tool from the Toolbox.

2. Position the mouse over the guide you want to remove. The mouse pointer will change to a tiny pointing hand.

3. Press the left mouse button and drag the guide back to the ruler it came from.

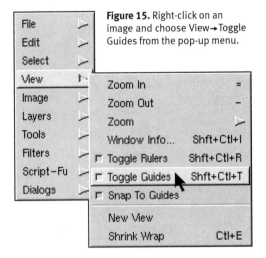

Figure 15. Right-click on an image and choose View→Toggle Guides from the pop-up menu.

Snap To Guides

An important guide feature is *Snap To Guides* which makes precise alignment easy by forcing a selection to line up with a guide.

To turn on Snap To Guides:

Right-click on an image and choose View→Snap To Guides from the pop-up menu (**Figure 16**). The next time you create a selection or paint a line, the selection or line will snap to the closest guide.

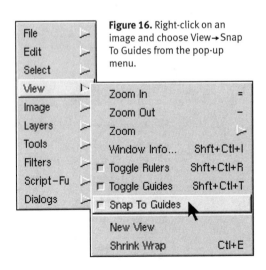

Figure 16. Right-click on an image and choose View→Snap To Guides from the pop-up menu.

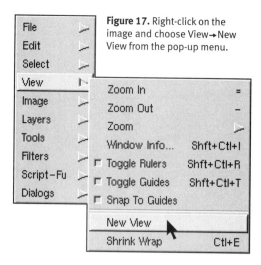

Figure 17. Right-click on the image and choose View→New View from the pop-up menu.

Viewing an Image in Two Image Windows

Using *New View*, an image can be opened in two or more image windows at the same time. This can be very helpful. One image window could be in a large display size to edit the detail while the other image window could be in a smaller view size to see the changes made to the entire image. Changes made in one window appear in the other and vice versa. This is because it is the same image viewed in two windows. The two image windows are *linked*.

To view the same image in two image windows:

1. Open an image or get one started in a new image window.

2. Right-click on the image and choose View→New View from the pop-up menu (**Figure 17**). A new image window will appear next to the original (**Figure 18**).

✔ Tip

■ If you look at the title bars of the two image windows, you will notice that the original file name has –1.0 appended to it and the new image window has –1.1 appended to it. If you opened another image window –1.2 would be appended the file name.

Figure 18. A new image window displaying the image appears next to the original image window. These two image windows are *linked*. Any changes made to the image in either window appear in both windows.

Duplicating an Image

Suppose that you want to try out some different effects and don't want to change the original image. If you used New View to open several image windows, any changes made to the image in any of the image windows would change the rest, too. This is where *Duplicate* comes in handy. Duplicate image windows are separate copies of an original image. Changes made in a duplicate image window won't appear in the original image window. The copies are completely separate images.

Figure 19. Open the image you want to duplicate.

To duplicate an image:

1. Open the image you want to duplicate (**Figure 19**).

2. Press Ctrl+D on the keyboard. A duplicate image will appear next to the original (**Figure 20**).

✔ Tip

■ If you look at the title bar of the duplicate image, you'll notice that it's an unsaved, untitled image.

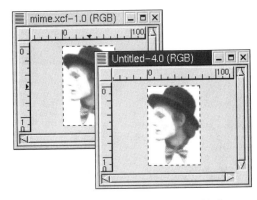

Figure 20. The duplicate image appears next to the original. Notice that the duplicate is untitled and unsaved. The two images are not linked in any way. Changes made in one window will not affect the other.

DUPLICATE AN IMAGE

Summary

In this chapter you learned how to:

◆ Zoom in and out

◆ Zoom to a specific magnification

◆ Zoom to a specific area

◆ Resize the image window as you zoom

◆ View rulers

◆ Add and move guides

◆ View an image in two windows

◆ Duplicate an image

MAKING SELECTIONS

Elliptical Selection Tool

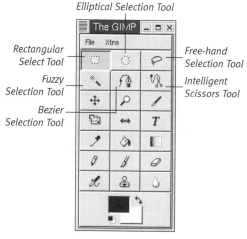

Rectangular Select Tool

Free-hand Selection Tool

Fuzzy Selection Tool

Intelligent Scissors Tool

Bezier Selection Tool

Figure 1. There are six selection tools you can use to select areas of an image for editing.

When you want to edit an area of an image, the GIMP needs to know which section it is that you want to change. The way to tell the GIMP is to *select* the area. Selections are made using one of six selection tools found at the top of the GIMP Toolbox (**Figure 1**). A selection consists of the portion of the image inside a *selection boundary*—a moving dashed line (**Figure 2**). (The moving dashed line is often described as "marching ants.")

Once a selection is made, only the area inside the selection boundary can be edited. A selection contains the pixels from the *currently active layer*. Any area outside of the boundary or on other layers will not be effected by changes made to the selected area. (To learn more about layers, turn to Chapter 7, *A Layer Primer*.)

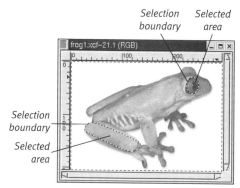

Selection boundary   Selected area

Selection boundary

Selected area

Figure 2. A selected area is surrounded by a dashed, moving selection boundary. In this figure, the eye and leg of the frog are selected.

Selection Tool Options

Before using the selection tools, you should know that they have various options that can be turned on or off. Each of the six selection tools can be set to *feather* and/or *antialias*. (The exception to this is the Rectangular Select Tool which only supports feathering.) These two options set how a selection reacts with the surrounding, unselected area.

◆ **Feather**—this option makes the transition from the selection to the surrounding area smoother (**Figure 3**). If you apply a filter to a selected area and feather the edges, the change from the filtered area to the non-filtered area will be less abrupt.

◆ **Antialias**—like feathering, anitaliasing creates a smooth transition from the selected area to the unselected area. While feathering blends pixels from the edge of the selection out into the unselected area, antialiasing blends pixels only along the edge of the selection (**Figure 4**). Antialiasing is especially useful when you are working with type and want to create smooth edges.

It's easy to turn these options on using the Tool Options dialog box.

To turn feathering or antialiasing on:

1. In the GIMP Toolbox, double-click on the selection tool whose options you want to change. The Tool Options dialog box will open, displaying the options available for that tool (**Figure 5**).

    or

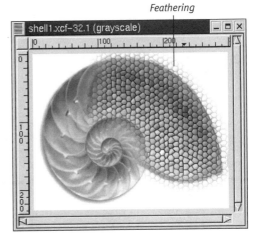

Feathering

Figure 3. Feathering makes the transition from one area to another smoother. In this figure, the mosaic filter was applied to the large area of the shell on the right and feathering was set to 15 pixels. Notice how the mosaic effect extends beyond the shell as it fades into the white area of the image. This is the feathered edge.

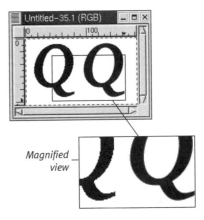

Magnified view

Figure 4. The Q on the left is not antialiased. Notice the jaggy edges in the magnified view. The Q on the right is antialiased. In the magnified view, you can see the blended edges that create a smoother line.

Figure 5. In the Tool Options dialog box, select the Antialiasing and/or Feather check buttons. Use the Feather Radius slider to set the depth of the feathering.

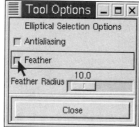

Choose File→Dialogs→Tool Options in the GIMP Toolbox (**Figure 6**), then click the selection tool in the Toolbox whose options you want to change.

or

Right-click on an image and choose Dialogs→Tool Options from the pop-up menu (**Figure 7**), then click the selection tool in the Toolbox whose options you want to change.

or

Press Shift+Ctrl+T on the keyboard, then click the selection tool in the Toolbox whose options you want to change.

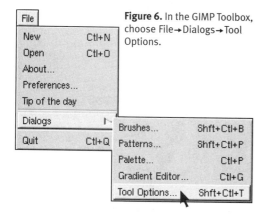

Figure 6. In the GIMP Toolbox, choose File→Dialogs→Tool Options.

2. To turn feathering on:

   A. Select the Feather check button.

   B. Move the Feather Radius slider left or right for less or more feathering. A higher feather radius setting makes for more feathering: the pixels from the edge of the selection will spread out further into the unselected area, blending more.

3. Select the Antialiasing check button to turn that option on. (This option is not available for the Rectangular Select Tool.)

4. Click Close. The Tool Options dialog box will close.

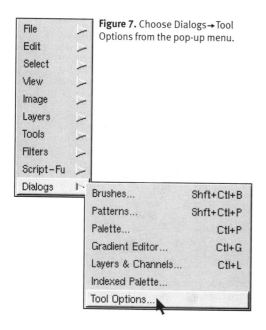

Figure 7. Choose Dialogs→Tool Options from the pop-up menu.

✔ Tips

■ The feathering and antialiasing options will remain on until you deselect the Antialiasing and Feather check buttons.

■ You can also add feathering to a specific selection using Select→Feather on the pop-up menu. For details about using this command, turn to page 82.

SELECTION TOOL OPTIONS

The Rectangular Select Tool

With the Rectangular Select Tool you can select rectangular and square areas. This tool works by clicking and dragging a selection boundary or *marquee* around a specific area of an image.

To select a rectangular area:

1. Use the Layers & Channels dialog box to set which layer is active. (This is the layer whose pixels will be selected.)

2. Click the Rectangular Select Tool in the GIMP Toolbox or press R on the keyboard.

3. Position the mouse crosshair at the upper-left corner of the area you want to select (**Figure 8**).

4. Press the left mouse button and drag diagonally down and to the right (**Figure 9**). As you drag a rectangle will appear.

5. Release the left mouse button when the entire area you want selected is encompassed by the rectangle. The selection will become activated and the rectangle's edge will change to a moving, dashed selection boundary (**Figure 10**).

✔ Tips

- To select an area that is an exact square, hold down the Shift key on the keyboard while dragging the mouse. Be sure to release the left mouse button first, before releasing the Shift key or the selection will spring to a rectangular shape.

- This tool supports feathering. To learn more about this option and turn it on, take a look at page 62.

- If you're not happy with a selection, you can make a new one. When you make a new selection, the first one disappears.

Figure 8. Position the mouse crosshair at the upper-left corner of the area you want to select.

Figure 9. As you drag the mouse a rectangle appears indicating the area that will be selected.

Figure 10. When you release the mouse button, the selection becomes active and the edge of the rectangle changes to a dashed, moving line.

Figure 11. Position the mouse crosshair at the upper-left corner of the area you want to select.

Figure 12. As you drag the mouse an ellipse appears indicating the area that will be selected.

Figure 13. When you release the mouse button, the selection becomes active and the edge of the ellipse changes to a dashed, moving line.

The Elliptical Selection Tool

The Elliptical Selection Tool works just like the Rectangular Select Tool—click and drag.

To select an elliptical area:

1. Use the Layers & Channels dialog box to set which layer is active. (This is the layer whose pixels will be selected.)

2. Click the Elliptical Selection Tool in the GIMP Toolbox or press E on the keyboard.

3. Position the mouse crosshair at the upper left of the area you want to select (**Figure 11**).

4. Press the left mouse button and drag diagonally down and to the right (**Figure 12**). As you drag an ellipse will appear.

5. Release the left mouse button when the entire area you want selected is encompassed by the ellipse. The selection will become activated and the ellipse's edge will change to a moving, dashed selection boundary (**Figure 13**).

✔ Tips

■ To select an area that is an exact circle, hold down the Shift key on the keyboard while dragging the mouse. Be sure to release the left mouse button first, before releasing the Shift key or the selection will spring to an elliptical shape.

■ This tool supports antialiasing and feathering. To learn more about these options and turn them on, take a look at page 62.

■ You can add to, subtract from, or intersect a selection. For details about how to do this turn to pages 77–79.

ELLIPTICAL SELECTION TOOL

The Free-hand Selection Tool

The Free-hand Selection Tool (also called the lasso) works like a pencil on paper. As you press the mouse and drag, a selection boundary appears. Wherever you stop dragging and release the mouse, the GIMP will automatically close the boundary you have drawn, creating a closed selection area.

To create a freehand selection:

1. Use the Layers & Channels dialog box to set which layer is active. (This is the layer whose pixels will be selected.)

2. Click the Free-hand Selection Tool in the Toolbox or press F on the keyboard.

3. Position the mouse crosshair where you would like to start the selection (**Figure 14**).

4. Press the left mouse button and drag. As you drag, a selection boundary will appear (**Figure 15**).

5. When you have encompassed the area you want to select, release the left mouse button. The GIMP will automatically close the selection boundary and it will become active (**Figure 16**).

✔ Tips

- This tool supports antialiasing and feathering. To learn more about these options and turn them on, take a look at page 62.

- You can add to, subtract from, or intersect a selection. For details about how to do this turn to pages 77–79.

Figure 14. Position the mouse crosshair where you would like the selection to start.

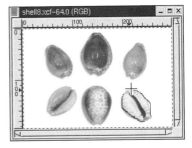

Figure 15. Press the left mouse button and drag to create the selection.

Figure 16. When you release the left mouse button, the selection is activated.

Figure 17. Position the mouse crosshair over the pixel containing the color you want to select. (You may need to zoom in to see the exact pixel.)

Figure 18. When you click, the area containing similar colored pixels is selected.

The Fuzzy Selection Tool

The Fuzzy Selection Tool creates a selection using color. When you click on a pixel in an image, any touching or adjacent pixels that are similar in hue and value to that pixel are selected. This tool can be useful for selecting areas filled with one color, such as backgrounds. The Fuzzy Selection Tool supports the feather and antialias options, as well as a Sample Merged option. When Sample Merged is turned on, the colors created by the blending of two or more layers are selected.

To select an area using the Fuzzy Selection Tool:

1. Use the Layers & Channels dialog box to set which layer is active. (This is the layer whose pixels will be selected.) If you turn the Sample Merged option on, the blended color from all layers will be used to create the selection. (The Sample Merged option is described on page 68.)

2. Click the Fuzzy Selection Tool in the Toolbox or press Z on the keyboard.

3. Position the mouse crosshair over the color that you want to select (you may need to zoom in to select an exact pixel) (**Figure 17**).

4. Click. The area surrounding colors similar to the pixel you clicked on will be selected (**Figure 18**).

✔ Tip

■ To select a wider range of colors, don't click in step 4. Instead, press the left mouse button and drag the mouse crosshair over all the colors you want to select, then release the mouse.

To turn on the Sample Merged option:

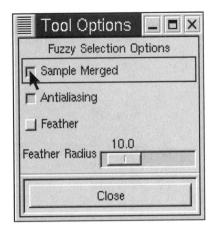

Figure 19. Choose the Sample Merged check button, then click Close.

1. In the GIMP Toolbox, double-click on the Fuzzy Selection Tool. The Tool Options dialog box will open, displaying the Fuzzy Selection Tool options (**Figure 19**).

2. Select the Sample Merged check button.

3. Click Close. The Tool Options dialog box will close.

✔ Tip

■ The Sample Merged option will remain on until its check button is unselected.

If You Make a Mistake, Don't Panic!

If you select and edit an area you didn't mean to or deactivate a selection before you meant to, don't worry! Just press Ctrl+Z on the keyboard or right click on the image and choose Edit→Undo from the pop-up menu to undo the change. (Remember, by default, you can undo up to five actions. To find out how to change the default number of undo actions, turn to page 14.)

Who was Bézier Anyhow?

The Bezier curve—the curve representation used most frequently in computer graphics—is named after Pierre Bézier, a French engineer who worked for the car manufacturer Renault. In the 1960s, in an attempt to draw car parts, he developed the mathematical equations that represent a curve geometrically.

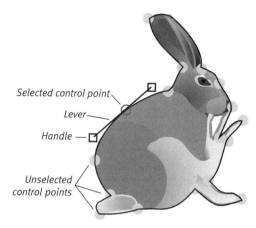

Selected control point

Lever

Handle

Unselected control points

Figure 20. The control points and handles control the shape of a bezier selection boundary. In this figure, a bezier selection boundary has been shaped around the outer edge of the jackrabbit.

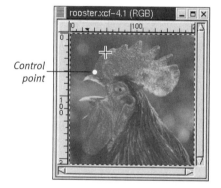

Control point

Figure 21. A circular control point appears where you click the mouse.

Closing an Image while a Selection is Active

If you are working on an image saved in the native GIMP file format, .xcf, and close it while a selection is active, that selection will still be active and available the next time you open the file.

The Bezier Selection Tool

The Bezier Selection Tool creates selections using *control points*, *levers*, and *handles* (**Figure 20**). The handles determine the curvature of segments of the selection boundary. The levers are just a visual representation of which handle goes with which control point.

With the Bezier Selection Tool, you can create straight selection segments and curvy selection segments. After you have created a bezier selection, you can edit it, using the control points and handles to change the shape of the selection segments.

When creating a selection with the Bezier Selection Tool, it's easiest to use the following steps:

◆ Create a basic, straight segment selection;

◆ Move any control points that are out of place; and then

◆ Edit the control points to add curves and sharp bends.

To create the basic, straight segment selection:

1. Use the Layers & Channels dialog box to set which layer is active. (This is the layer whose pixels will be selected.)

2. Click the Bezier Selection Tool in the Toolbox or press B on the keyboard.

3. Position the mouse crosshair over the image where you would like the first segment to start.

4. Click. A circular control point will appear where you clicked (**Figure 21**).

(continued)

5. Move the mouse crosshair to a new position and click again. A second control point will appear where you clicked and a straight selection boundary segment will appear between the two control points (**Figure 22**).

6. Repeat step 5 until you have created a basic, straight segment selection around the area you want to select (**Figure 23**). If a control point is not in the correct position, don't worry! You can move it using the following directions.

✔ Tip

■ Take some care when placing control points. While you can move them, you can't add or delete them.

To move a control point:

1. Position the mouse crosshair over the control point you want to move.

2. Press and hold down the Ctrl key on the keyboard.

3. Press the left mouse button and drag the control point to a new position.

4. When the control point is in the correct position, release both the left mouse button and the Ctrl key on the keyboard. Now that you have created the basic outline, it's time to add some curves and sharp bends to the bezier selection.

Figure 22. When you click, a second control point appears under the mouse crosshair and a selection boundary segment appears, joining the two control points.

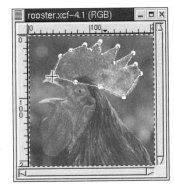

Figure 23. Continue adding control points until the entire area is encompassed by selection boundary segments.

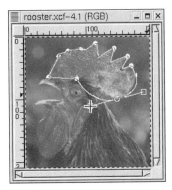

Figure 24. When you press the left mouse button and drag, the selection boundary segment becomes curved and two handles appear.

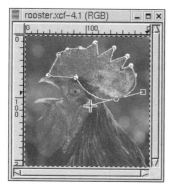

Figure 25. Position the mouse crosshair over the handle you want to move.

Figure 26. Press the left mouse button and drag the handle to change the shape of the boundary segment curve.

To add curves and corners to the straight segments:

1. With the Bezier Selection Tool still active, position the mouse crosshair over a control point, press the left mouse button and drag. Two handles will appear and the straight line will become curved (**Figure 24**).

2. Release the left mouse button when the curved segment is closer to the shape you want. The control point will remain selected with the handles visible. You can now manipulate the handles individually to create smooth curves or sharp corners.

3. To create a smooth curve:

   A. Position the mouse crosshair over a handle (**Figure 25**).

   B. Press the left mouse button and drag the handle to a new position (**Figure 26**). Notice that you can drag a handle far away from or place it directly on top of its control point.

   C. Release the left mouse button when you are happy with the shape of the curve (**Figure 27**).

(continued)

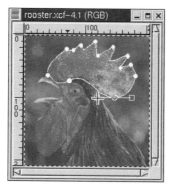

Figure 27. Release the left mouse button when you are happy with the shape of the curve.

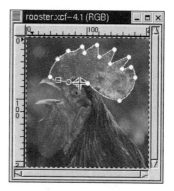

Figure 28. Position the mouse crosshair over the handle you want to move.

BEZIER SELECTION TOOL: ADD CURVES

4. To create a sharp corner at a control point:

A. Position the mouse crosshair over a handle (**Figure 28**).

B. Press and hold down the Shift key.

C. Press the left mouse button and drag the handle to a new position (**Figure 29**). Notice that instead of curving, a sharp bend appears in the selection segment at the control point.

D. Release the left mouse button and Shift key when you are happy with the shape of the bend (**Figure 30**). Once you are satisfied with the shape of the selection segments, the final step is to activate the bezier selection.

To activate the bezier selection:

Click inside the bezier selection area to activate the selection. The control points will disappear and the selection segments will change to a dashed, moving boundary (**Figure 31**).

✔ Tips

■ Bezier selections are complicated and time consuming to create. Once you've created one, you'll probably want to use it again in the future, so save it. Turn to page 86 for directions on how to do this.

■ The Bezier Selection Tool supports both antialiasing and feathering. To learn more about these options and turn them on, turn to page 62.

■ You can add to, subtract from, or intersect a selection. For details about how to do this turn to pages 77–79.

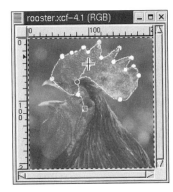

Figure 29. Press the left mouse button and drag the handle to a new position. As you drag, a bend forms at the control point.

Figure 30. Release the mouse button and Shift key when you are happy with the curve.

Figure 31. Click inside the bezier selection boundary to activate the selection.

BEZIER SELECTION TOOL: ACTIVATE THE SELECTION

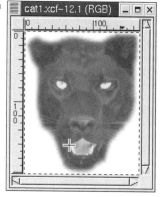

Figure 32. Position the mouse crosshair where you would like to start the selection. In this figure, the panther's mouth will be selected.

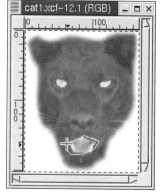

Figure 33. As you drag the mouse, a rough selection boundary appears around the area.

Figure 34. When you release the mouse button, the Intelligent Scissors Tool shapes the selection boundary, smoothing it out.

The Intelligent Scissors Tool

The Intelligent Scissors Tool works like the Free-hand Selection Tool in that clicking and dragging creates a selection boundary. However, this tool does have a mind of its own. When you make a selection, this tool tries to guess exactly which edge you are trying to select using the colors you select. The Intelligent Scissors Tool supports several options. Along with antialiasing and feathering, you can set *curve resolution*, *edge detect threshold*, and *elasticity*. In addition, if the Intelligent Scissors Tool does not create the exact selection you want, you can convert the Intelligent Scissors selection to a Bezier Curve Selection and edit the curves as described on pages 70–72.

To create an Intelligent Scissors selection:

1. Use the Layers & Channels dialog box to set which layer is active. (This is the layer whose pixels will be selected.)

2. Click the Intelligent Scissors Tool in the Toolbox or press I on the keyboard.

3. Position the mouse crosshair where you would like to start the selection (**Figure 32**).

4. Press the left mouse button and drag. As you drag, a selection boundary will appear (**Figure 33**).

5. When you have encompassed the area you want to select, release the left mouse button. The Intelligent Scissors Tool will make its best guess and shape the selection boundary accordingly (**Figure 34**). If the selection boundary is not exactly the way you want it, you should convert the boundary to a bezier selection boundary and reshape it. If you like the shape of the selection, skip to step 8.

(continued)

INTELLIGENT SCISSORS TOOL

6. To convert the Intelligent Scissors boundary to a Bezier Selection Tool boundary:

A. Double-click the Intelligent Scissors Tool in the Toolbox. The Tool Options dialog box will open, showing Intelligent Scissors Tool options (**Figure 35**).

B. Click the Convert to Bezier Curve button. Control points will appear around the selection boundary (**Figure 36**) and the Tool Options dialog box will change to display Bezier Selection Tool options (**Figure 37**).

7. Manipulate the bezier control points and handles as you would any bezier selection. (See pages 70–72 for details about how to do this.)

8. When you are happy with the selection boundary shape, click inside the selection boundary to activate the selection. The selection boundary will change to a dashed, moving boundary (**Figure 38**).

✔ Tips

■ This tool works best on an image with high contrast areas.

■ This tool supports antialiasing and feathering. To learn more about these options and turn them on, take a look at page 62.

■ You can add to, subtract from, or intersect a selection. For details about how to do this turn to pages 77–79.

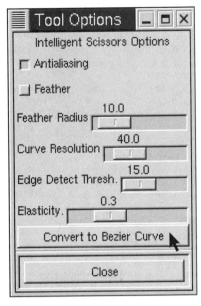

Figure 35. Use the Tool Options dialog box to change the Intelligent Scissors selection to a bezier curve selection.

Figure 36. Control points appear around the selection boundary. To access the handles and change the shape of the curve, click a control point.

INTELLIGENT SCISSORS TOOL

Figure 37. When the bezier control points appear around the selection boundary, the Tool Options dialog box changes to display Bezier Selection Options.

Figure 38. Click inside the selection boundary to activate the selection.

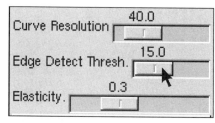

Figure 39. Use the slider bars to set the sensitivity of the Intelligent Scissors Tool.

Intelligent Scissors Tool Options

Along with feathering and antialiasing, the Intelligent Scissors Tool also supports three other options. They are:

◆ **Curve Resolution**—this option controls how smooth a selection is. The higher the setting, the smoother the curve.

◆ **Edge Detect Threshold**—sets how sensitive the Intelligent Scissors Tool is to edges in an image. The higher the setting, the more sensitive the tool becomes.

◆ **Elasticity**—this option sets the tool's ability to move away from the boundary you have outlined when it tries to find an edge in an image. If elasticity is set low, the Intelligent Scissors Tool will keep the selection boundary it sets closer to the one you drew with the tool. If the elasticity is set high, the tool will move the selection boundary further away from the one you drew. In fact, if elasticity is set very high, the tool may even snap the selection boundary to a color area nearby that you did not intend to select.

To set Intelligent Scissors Tool options:

1. In the GIMP Toolbox, double-click on the Intelligent Scissors Tool. The Tool Options dialog box will open, displaying the options available for that tool (**Figure 35**).

2. Use the slider bars to the right of Curve Resolution, Edge Detect Threshold, and Elasticity to set those options (**Figure 39**).

3. Click Close. The Tool Options dialog box will close.

Creating Multiple Selections

Suppose you want to add a filter effect to several areas of an image. Instead of selecting one area, applying the filter, then selecting another area and applying the filter again, you can select several areas at once and apply the filter once.

To create multiple selections:

1. Create the first selection using the selection tool of your choice (**Figure 40**).

2. Press and hold down the Shift key on the keyboard.

3. Make a second selection (**Figure 41**).

4. Repeat steps 2–3 to create additional selections.

✔ Tips

- So long as the extra selections do not touch or overlap, the selections will remain separate.

- If you release the Shift key before you release the mouse button, the first selection will disappear, leaving only the second selection.

- You can change selection tools while making selections in order to select different shaped areas (**Figure 42**).

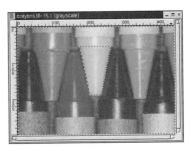

Figure 40. Create the first selection using the selection tool of your choice. In this figure, the Bezier Selection Tool was used to select the tip of the crayon.

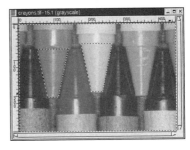

Figure 41. Hold down the Shift key and make a second selection. Be sure to release the mouse button before releasing the Shift key. Otherwise, the first selection will disappear.

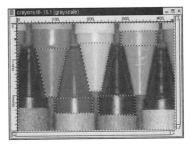

Figure 42. Use the different selection tools to select the areas that you need. In this figure both the Rectangular Select and the Bezier Selection Tools were used.

Figure 43. Create the first selection using the selection tool of your choice.

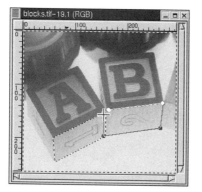

Figure 44. Hold down the Shift key as you make the second selection. Be sure the two selection areas overlap.

Figure 45. Release the mouse button, and then the Shift key. The two selections will merge, creating a larger, single selection.

Adding to a Selection

If you want to extend the area of a selection you have made, you can do so using any of the selection tools.

To add to a selection:

1. Create the first selection using the selection tool of your choice (**Figure 43**).

2. Press and hold down the Shift key on the keyboard.

3. Using the selection tool of your choice, create a second selection that overlaps the first selection (**Figure 44**).

4. Release the mouse button and then the Shift key. The two selections will merge to become a single selection (**Figure 45**).

✔ Tips

■ You can change selection tools while making selections in order to select different shaped areas.

■ If you release the Shift key before you release the mouse button, the first selection will disappear, leaving only the second selection.

ADD TO A SELECTION

Subtracting from a Selection

If you want to remove part of a selection after you have made it, all you need to do is subtract that area from the selection using any one of the selection tools.

To subtract from a selection:

1. Create the first selection using the selection tool of your choice (**Figure 46**).

2. Press and hold down the Ctrl key on the keyboard.

3. Using the selection tool of your choice, create a second selection that overlaps the first selection, covering the selection area that you want to remove (**Figure 47**).

4. Release the mouse button and then the Ctrl key. The area where the second selection overlapped the first will be subtracted from the first selection (**Figure 48**).

✔ Tips

- You can change selection tools while making selections in order to subtract different shaped areas.

- If you release the Ctrl key before you release the mouse button, the first selection will disappear, leaving only the second selection.

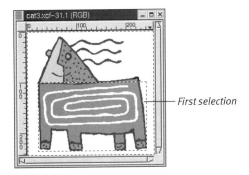

Figure 46. Create the first selection using the selection tool of your choice.

First selection

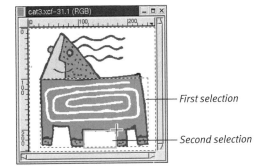

Figure 47. Hold down the Ctrl key while making the second selection.

First selection

Second selection

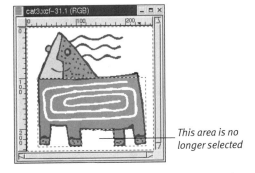

Figure 48. When you release the mouse button and then the Ctrl key, the area covered by the second selection disappears from the first selection.

This area is no longer selected

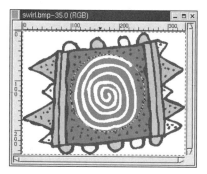

Figure 49. Create the first selection using the selection tool of your choice.

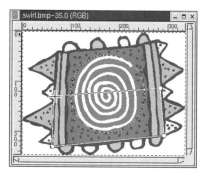

Figure 50. Hold down the Shift and Ctrl keys while making the second selection.

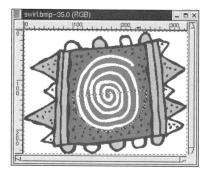

Figure 51. When you release the mouse button and then the Ctrl and Shift keys, only the intersection of the overlapping selection areas remains.

Intersecting Two or More Selections

You can also create a selection from the overlapping areas of two selections. This is called an *intersection*.

To intersect two selections:

1. Create the first selection using the selection tool of your choice (**Figure 49**).

2. Press and hold down the Shift and Ctrl keys on the keyboard.

3. Using the selection tool of your choice, make a second selection that overlaps the first selection, covering the intersecting selection area that you want to create (**Figure 50**).

4. Release the mouse button, and then the Shift and Ctrl keys. The area where the two selections overlapped will remain as the active selection (**Figure 51**).

✔ Tips

■ You can change selection tools while making the intersection in order to select different shaped areas.

■ If you release the Shift and Ctrl keys before you release the mouse button, the first selection will disappear, leaving only the second selection.

Growing or Shrinking a Selection

As you know, each selection tool comes with special options. But sometimes you'll need to fine tune a selection to make it work better with the effect you have in mind. One way to fine tune a selection is to expand or shrink an entire selection boundary by a set number of pixels.

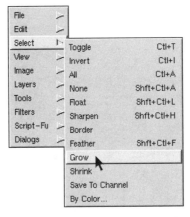

Figure 52.
You can make the active selection uniformly larger using the Grow command.

To grow a selection:

1. Create the selection (**Figure 52**).

2. Right-click on the image and choose Select→Grow from the pop-up menu (**Figure 53**). The Grow Selection dialog box will open (**Figure 54**).

3. Enter the number of pixels by which you want the selection to expand in the Grow selection by text box.

4. Click OK. The Grow Selection dialog box will close and the selection will expand by the number of pixels you entered (**Figure 55**).

Figure 53. Choose Select→Grow from the pop-up menu.

To shrink a selection:

1. Create the selection (**Figure 52**).

2. Right-click on the image and choose Select→Shrink from the pop-up menu (**Figure 56**). The Shrink Selection dialog box will appear (**Figure 57**).

3. Enter the number of pixels by which you want the selection to shrink in the Shrink selection by text box.

4. Click OK. The Shrink Selection dialog box will close and the selection will shrink by the number of pixels you entered (**Figure 58**).

Figure 54.
In the Grow Selection dialog box, enter the number of pixels by which you want to expand the selection.

Figure 55.
The selection uniformly expands by the number of pixels you entered in the Grow Selection dialog box.

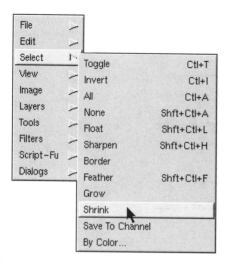

Figure 56. Right-click on the image and choose Select→Shrink from the pop-up menu.

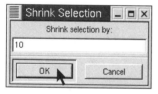

Figure 57. In the Shrink Selection dialog box, enter the number of pixels you want to shrink the selection.

Figure 58. The selection uniformly shrinks by the number of pixels you entered in the Shrink Selection dialog box.

Sharpening a Selection

The Sharpen command removes pixels from the edge of an antialiased or feathered selection, making the edge less fuzzy and more distinct.

To sharpen a selection:

1. Create the selection you want to sharpen using the selection tool of your choice.

2. Right-click on the image and choose Select→Sharpen from the pop-up menu (**Figure 59**) or press Shift+Ctrl+H on the keyboard. The edges of the selection will be sharper when an effect is applied to the selected area.

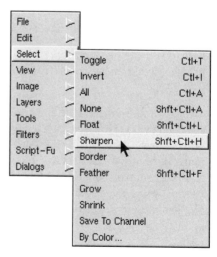

Figure 59. Right-click on the image and choose Select→Sharpen from the pop-up menu.

Feathering a Selection

As discussed on page 62, feathering makes the transition from the selection to the surrounding area smoother. If you've made a selection and want to set more feathering, use the Feather command on the Select fly-out.

To feather a selection:

1. Create the selection you want to feather using the selection tool of your choice.

2. Right-click on the image and choose Select→Feather from the pop-up menu (**Figure 60**) or press Shift+Ctrl+F on the keyboard. The Feather Selection dialog box will appear (**Figure 61**).

3. In the Feather selection by text box, enter the number of pixels by which you want to feather the edge of the selection.

4. Click OK. The Feather Selection dialog box will close and any effect applied to the area of the selection will be feathered (**Figure 3**).

✔ Tips

■ You can also set any of the selection tools to feather using the Tool Options dialog box. For details on how to do this, turn to page 62.

■ A high number entered in the Feather selection by text box will create a selection with a very fuzzy edge. To make an edge more distinct, use the Sharpen command as described on the previous page. You can also apply the Sharpen filter to a specific area. For details about applying a filter, turn to page 231.

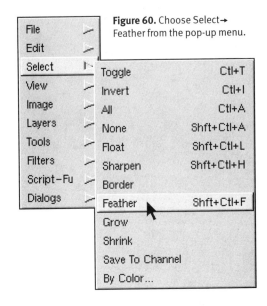

Figure 60. Choose Select→ Feather from the pop-up menu.

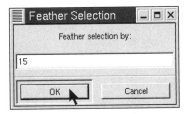

Figure 61. In the Feather Selection dialog box, enter the number of pixels by which you want to feather the selection.

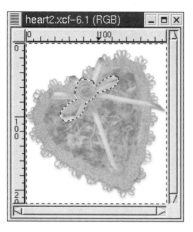

Figure 62. You can move any selection to a new position using the Move Tool.

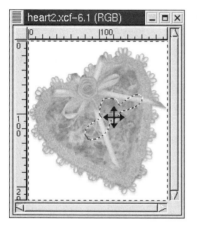

Figure 63. Press and hold down the Ctrl and Alt keys, press the left mouse button, and then drag the selection to a new position.

Moving Selection Boundaries

If you use the Move Tool to move a selection boundary and don't hold down the Ctrl and Alt keys, the entire image will move in the image window.

Moving Selections

If you move the mouse crosshair over the selected area right after making the selection, the mouse cursor changes to the Move Tool's double-headed arrows even though the Move Tool has not been selected. This lets you move either the image contained within the selected area, creating a *floating* selection, or move the selection boundary itself.

A floating selection is an area of an image that is unattached to any layer. To learn more about floating selections and what you can do with them, turn to page 99.

Moving the selection boundary without moving the contents is very handy for fine tuning a selection.

To move a selection boundary:

1. Create a selection using the selection tool of your choice (**Figure 62**).

2. If you have just created the selection, position the mouse inside the boundary. The mouse crosshair will change to double-headed arrows.

   or

   If you have edited the area within the selection boundary and want to move only the boundary, click the Move Tool in the Toolbox.

3. Press and hold down the Ctrl and Alt keys on the keyboard.

4. Press the left mouse button and drag the selection boundary to its new position (**Figure 63**).

5. Release the left mouse button, and then the Ctrl and Alt keys when you are happy with the boundary's position.

Inverting a Selection

If you want to select a large, complex section of an image, but don't want to take the time going around every corner and curve with a selection boundary, you can select the area you *don't* want selected, then use the Invert command. This switches the selected and unselected areas.

Figure 64. Select the area that you don't want selected. In this figure, the back of the lizard is selected.

To invert a selection:

1. Create the selection that you want to invert (**Figure 64**). (In other words, you are selecting the area you *don't* ultimately want selected.)

2. Right-click on the image and choose Select→Invert from the pop-up menu (**Figure 65**) or press Ctrl+I on the keyboard. The selected and unselected areas will switch (**Figure 66**).

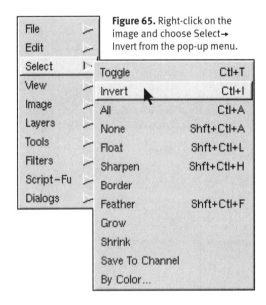

Figure 65. Right-click on the image and choose Select→Invert from the pop-up menu.

Selecting an Entire Layer

Using the Select All command, it's easy to select an entire layer.

To select an entire layer:

1. Use the Layers & Channels dialog box to set which layer is active. (This is the layer whose pixels will be selected. If the image only has one layer, the entire image will, of course, be selected.)

2. Right-click on an image and choose Select→All from the pop-up menu (**Figure 67**) or press Ctrl+A on the keyboard. An active selection boundary will appear around the entire image (**Figure 68**).

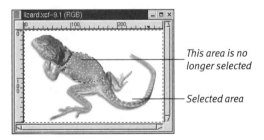

Figure 66. With the selection inverted, everything that wasn't selected becomes selected. In this figure, everything in the image except for the lizard's back is selected.

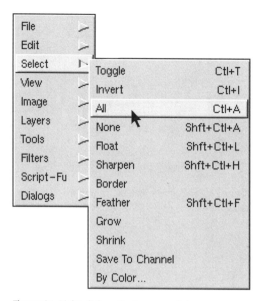

Figure 67. Right-click on the image and choose Select→All from the pop-up menu.

Hiding a Selection Boundary

Sometimes, when working on an image, the "marching ants" selection boundary can become distracting. You can hide the boundary to view the image without the moving dashed lines.

To hide/view a selection boundary:

Right-click on an image that contains a selection and choose Select→Toggle from the pop-up menu (**Figure 69**) or press Ctl+T on the keyboard.

✔ Tip

■ The Toggle command only hides the selection boundary, it doesn't remove the boundary.

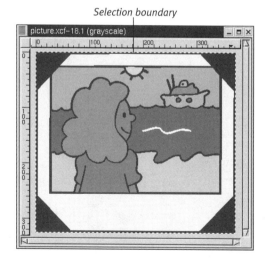

Figure 68. When you choose Select→All from the pop-up menu, the entire layer is selected. In this figure, the dashed, moving selection boundary surrounds the entire, one layer image.

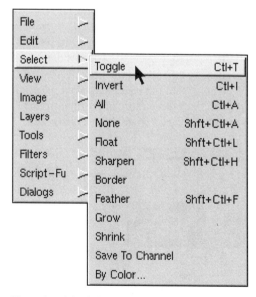

Figure 69. Right-click on the image and choose Select→Toggle from the pop-up menu.

HIDE/VIEW A SELECTION BOUNDARY

Saving Your Selections

When you make a complicated selection, chances are that you will want to use it again. You can save any selection you create to a *channel*. This saves the selection to an *alpha channel* which saves the selection's shape and transparency. You can then use the selection again at any time by activating the channel. For details on activating a channel and using a saved selection, turn to page 199 in Chapter 13, *Channels and Layer Masks*.

To save a selection to a channel:

1. Create the selection you want to save using the selection tool of your choice (**Figure 70**).

2. Right-click on the image and choose Select→Save To Channel (**Figure 71**). The selection will be saved to a channel. It will automatically be named "Selection Mask copy."

✔ Tip

■ To see the selection you have saved to a channel, right-click on the image, choose Layers→Layers & Channels (**Figure 72**) to open the Layers & Channels dialog box, and then click the Channels tab to display that tab page. The saved selection will be at the bottom of the channel list on the Channels tab page (**Figure 73**).

Figure 70. You can use channels to save any selection you make. In this figure the middle and right shells are selected.

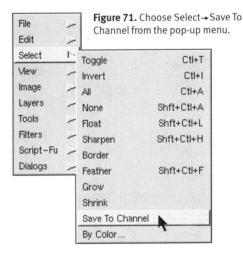

Figure 71. Choose Select→Save To Channel from the pop-up menu.

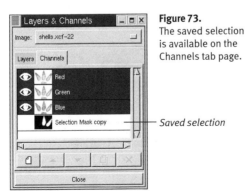

Figure 73. The saved selection is available on the Channels tab page.

Saved selection

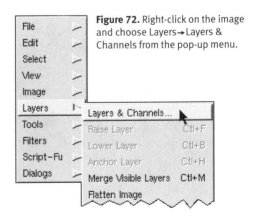

Figure 72. Right-click on the image and choose Layers→Layers & Channels from the pop-up menu.

SAVE A SELECTION TO A CHANNEL

Figure 74. Create the selection to which you want to add the border.

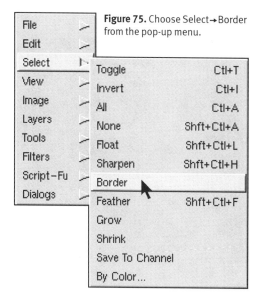

Figure 75. Choose Select→Border from the pop-up menu.

Making Border Selections

With the GIMP, it's easy to create a border selection. This can be very handy when creating a vignette from a photograph, for instance, or adding an outline.

To make a border selection:

1. Create the selection that will become the inside selection boundary of the border (**Figure 74**).

2. Right-click on the image and choose Select→Border from the pop-up menu (**Figure 75**). The Border Selection dialog box will appear (**Figure 76**).

3. Set the width of the border selection by entering the number of pixels in the Border selection by text box.

4. Click OK. The Border Selection dialog box will close and the outside selection boundary will appear around the edge of the original selection (**Figure 77**).

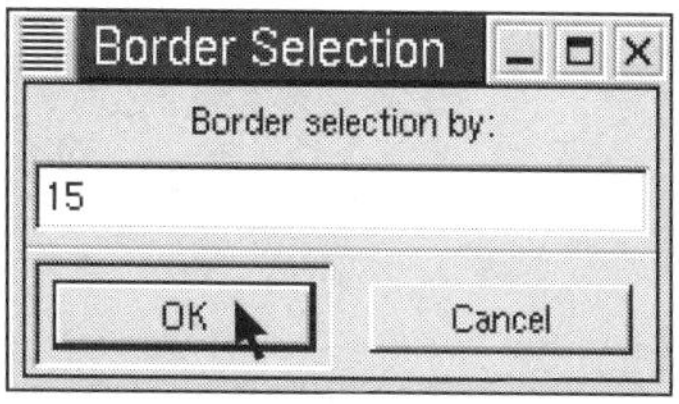

Figure 76. In the Border Selection dialog box, set the border's width in pixels by entering a number in the text box.

Figure 77. A border appears around the original selection.

MAKE A BORDER SELECTION

Deleting a Selected Area

When you delete the area within a selection (**Figure 78**), that portion of the image will disappear. In its place one of two things will appear:

◆ If the image is made up of only one layer (the *background layer*), the active background color in the color selector on the Toolbox will become visible (**Figure 79**); or

◆ If the image contains more than one layer or an alpha channel, the checker-board background, denoting transparency, will become visible (**Figure 80**).

To delete a selected area:

Right-click on the selected area and choose Edit→Clear from the pop-up menu (**Figure 81**) or press Ctrl+K on the keyboard.

✔ Tips

■ For information about alpha channels, what they are used for, and how to add one to an image, turn to page 194.

■ To learn about layers and the background layer, turn to page 91.

Figure 78. Select the area of the image you want to remove. In this figure, the dark gray background around the baby's head has been selected.

Figure 79. When an area of a one layer image is deleted, the background color remains. In this figure, a white background replaces the dark gray because the background color in the color selector is set to white.

Figure 80. When an area of an image with more than one layer or an alpha channel is deleted, the area becomes transparent.

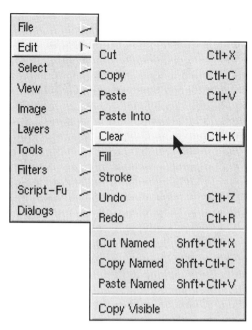

Figure 81. Right-click on the selected area and choose Edit→Clear from the pop-up menu.

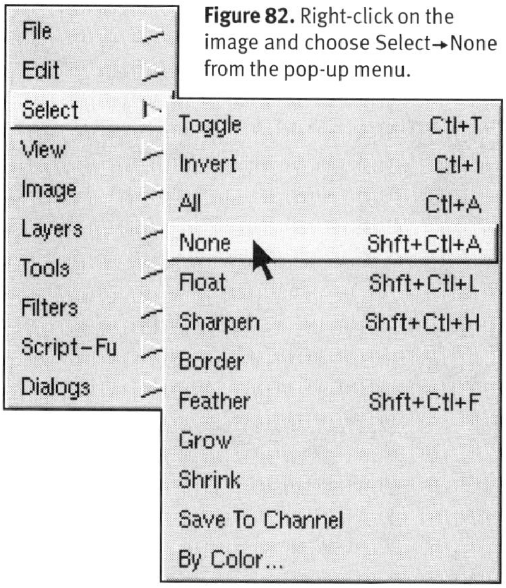

Deactivating and Restoring a Selection

It's easy to deactivate and restore selections with a few clicks of the mouse or key presses on the keyboard.

To deactivate a selection:

Right-click on the image and choose Select→None from the pop-up menu (**Figure 82**).

or

Press Shift+Ctrl+A on the keyboard.

or

Select the Rectangular, Elliptical, or Free-hand Selection Tools from the GIMP Toolbox and click on the image.

✔ Tip

■   If you start a new selection, the current selection will automatically deactivate and disappear.

Figure 82. Right-click on the image and choose Select→None from the pop-up menu.

Removing a Selection Before You Finish It

If you are making a selection and realize you didn't want to create it, there's a way out. Before releasing the left mouse button (which is pressed when dragging a selection boundary), press and hold down the right mouse button. Next, release the left mouse button and then the right mouse button. The selection you were making will disappear.

While the finger coordination is a bit tricky, this can be useful when dealing with complex, multiple selections.

To restore the last selection:

Right-click on the image and choose
Edit→Undo from the pop-up menu
(**Figure 83**) or press Ctrl+Z on the
keyboard. The last selection you made
will appear active (with a dashed moving
border) in the image window.

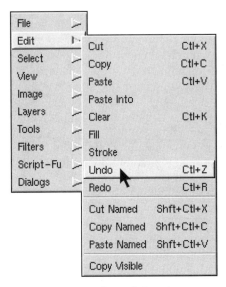

Figure 83. Choose Edit→Undo from the pop-up menu.

Summary

In this chapter you learned how to:

- Turn on selection tool options

- Use the Rectangular Select Tool

- Use the Elliptical Selection Tool

- Use the Free-hand Selection Tool

- Use the Fuzzy Selection Tool and the
  Sample Merged option

- Create a bezier selection using the
  Bezier Selection Tool

- Use the Intelligent Scissors Tool

- Set Intelligent Scissors Tool options

- Make multiple selections

- Add to and subtract from a selection

- Intersect selections

- Grow and shrink selections

- Sharpen and feather selections

- Move a selection boundary

- Invert a selection

- Select an entire layer

- Hide/view a selection boundary

- Save a selection to an alpha channel

- Make a border selection

- Delete the area within a selection

- Deactivate a selection

- Restore the last selection

A Layer Primer

7

When you start a new image in the GIMP, it consists of a *background layer*. You can think of this layer as the canvas under a painting. One or more layers can be added on top of the background layer. Layers are like clear glass windows stacked one on top of the other. You can draw (or paste an image) on one of the glass windows, then set how the layer blends with those below it using *opacity* and *modes*. You can edit an area on one layer without affecting image elements on other layers.

Figure 1 shows an image with four layers. Each item—flowers, palette, and pencils—is on its own layer. The fourth layer is the background layer. These four layers are shown in the Layers & Channels dialog box. The layers are shown from top to bottom with the textured background layer (which is behind the three layers) at the bottom of the list. This is the *stacking order*.

The flowers layer is on top

Stacking order

Figure 1. The Layers & Channels dialog box shows an image's layers. In this image there are four layers— flowers, palette, pencils, and Background.

The Layers & Channels Dialog Box

When working with layers, you'll use the Layers & Channels dialog box (**Figure 2**). To open the dialog box, right-click on an image and choose Layers→Layers & Channels from the pop-up menu (**Figure 3**).

In this chapter, you'll discover how to use the layer window to set the *active layer* and edit layer properties. Also, you'll use the buttons at the bottom of the dialog box to create new and duplicate layers, move layers up and down the stacking order, delete layers, and anchor a floating layer. We'll discuss the other items available on the Layers tab page—the Mode drop-down list, Keep Trans check button, and Opacity slider—in Chapter 11, *Layer Techniques*.

The Active Layer

When the Layers & Channels dialog box is open, you'll notice that one of the layers is highlighted in blue (**Figure 2**). The highlighted layer is the active layer. In the image window, the active layer has a dashed yellow rectangle around it. Any changes you make using GIMP tools and filters will affect the active layer. Other layers will not be affected. With just the click of a mouse, you can set which layer is the active layer.

To make a layer the active layer:

1. Right-click on the image and choose Layers→Layers & Channels from the pop-up menu (**Figure 3**). The Layers & Channels dialog box will open displaying the Layers tab page (**Figure 2**).

2. Click on the name of the layer you want to be the active layer. That layer will become highlighted and active.

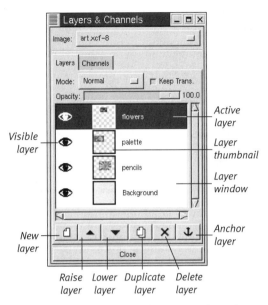

Figure 2. The Layers tab page in the Layers & Channels dialog box is used to manipulate your image layer by layer.

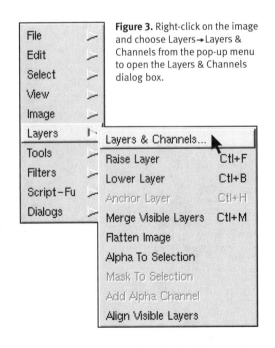

Figure 3. Right-click on the image and choose Layers→Layers & Channels from the pop-up menu to open the Layers & Channels dialog box.

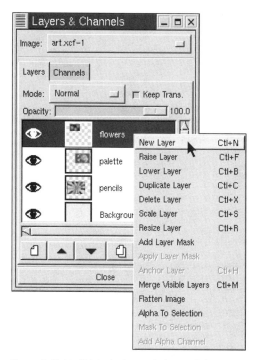

Figure 4. Right-click in the layer window and choose New Layer from the pop-up menu.

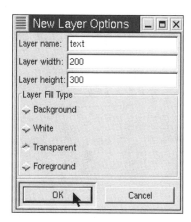

Figure 5. Use the New Layer Options dialog box to set the layer's name, its size, and fill type.

Manipulating Layers

It's easy to work with layers in an image. You can create new layers, duplicate existing ones, or turn a *floating selection* into a layer. Layers can be renamed, deleted, and hidden from view. Layers can also be scaled and resized. In fact, there are many more ways to manipulate layers. To find out more about using layers, turn to Chapter 11, *Layer Techniques*.

To create a new layer:

1. Right-click on the image and choose Layers→Layers & Channels from the pop-up menu (**Figure 3**). The Layers & Channels dialog box will open displaying the Layers tab page (**Figure 2**).

2. Click the New Layer button at the bottom left of the dialog box.

   or

   Right-click in the layer window and choose New Layer from the pop-up menu (**Figure 4**).

   or

   With the Layers & Channels dialog box active (the title bar will be highlighted), press Ctrl+N on the keyboard.

   The New Layer Options dialog box will appear (**Figure 5**).

3. Type a name for the new layer in the Layer name text box.

4. Enter the layer's width and height in pixels using the Layer width and Layer height text boxes.

   (continued)

5. In the Layer Fill Type area, select the radio button next to the type of fill you would like for the new layer:

♦ **Background** fills the new layer with the current background color selected in the Toolbox.

♦ **White** fills the new layer with (of course) white.

♦ **Transparent** leaves the layer completely transparent.

♦ **Foreground** fills the new layer with the current foreground color selected in the Toolbox.

6. Click OK. The new layer will appear highlighted (active) in the layer window in the Layers & Channels dialog box (**Figure 6**).

To duplicate a layer:

1. Open the Layers & Channels dialog box by right clicking on the image and choosing Layers→Layers & Channels from the pop-up menu (**Figure 3**).

2. In the layer window, click the name of the layer you want to duplicate. The layer will become highlighted and active.

3. Click the Duplicate Layer button or press Ctrl+C on the keyboard.

or

In the layer window, right-click on the name of the layer you want to duplicate and choose Duplicate Layer from the pop-up menu (**Figure 7**).

The duplicate layer will appear in the layer window with the word "copy" after the original layer's name (**Figure 8**).

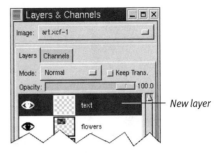

Figure 6. The new layer appears in the layer window.

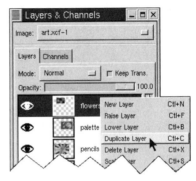

Figure 7. Right-click on the layer you want to duplicate, then choose Duplicate Layer from the pop-up menu.

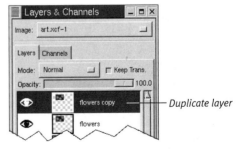

Figure 8. The duplicate layer appears above the original layer with the word "copy" appended to the original name.

Figure 9. Double click on the layer you want to rename.

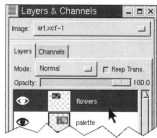

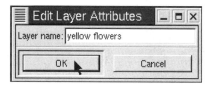

Figure 10. Type a new name in the Layer name text box.

Figure 11. The new layer name appears in the layer window.

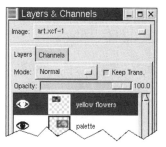

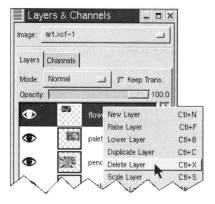

Figure 12. Right-click on the layer you want to delete, then choose Delete Layer from the pop-up menu.

To rename a layer:

1. Double-click on the name of the layer you want to change (**Figure 9**). The Edit Layer Attributes dialog box will open (**Figure 10**).

2. Type a new name in the Layer name text box.

3. Click OK. The Edit Layer Attributes dialog box will close and the layer name will change in the layer window (**Figure 11**).

To delete a layer:

1. In the Layers & Channels dialog box, highlight the layer you want to delete.

2. Click the Delete Layer button near the bottom right of the dialog box or press Ctrl+X on the keyboard. The layer will be deleted and disappear from the layer window.

    or

    Right-click on the name of the layer you want to delete and choose Delete Layer from the pop-up menu (**Figure 12**). The layer will be deleted and disappear from the layer window.

✔ Tip

■   If you delete a layer and realize you made a mistake, here's how to get the layer back. Click on the image window to make it active, then press Ctrl+Z on the keyboard. The layer will reappear.

Scaling and Resizing Layers

Scaling and resizing each change the size of a layer but with different consequences. Scaling changes both the size of a layer *and* its contents. Resizing changes the size of the layer, but doesn't alter the contents.

To scale a layer:

1. Open the Layers & Channels dialog box by right clicking on the image and choosing Layers→Layers & Channels from the pop-up menu (**Figure 3**).

2. Right-click on the name of the layer you want to scale and choose Scale Layer from the pop-up menu (**Figure 13**).

   or

   Highlight the layer you want to scale, then press Ctrl+S on the keyboard.

   The Scale Layer dialog box will open (**Figure 14**).

3. Use the New width and New height text boxes to enter the layer's new dimensions in pixels. If the Constrain Ratio check button is selected, the horizontal and vertical proportions of the layer will remain the same.

4. Click OK. The Scale Layer dialog box will close and the layer will scale to its new size.

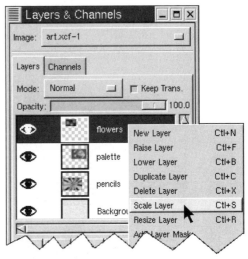

Figure 13. Right-click on the layer you want to scale, then choose Scale Layer from the pop-up menu.

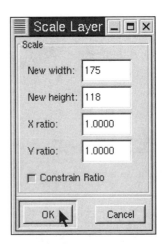

Figure 14. Use the New width and New height text boxes to enter the layer's new size in pixels. If the Constrain Ratio check button is selected, the width and height remain proportionally the same.

SCALE A LAYER

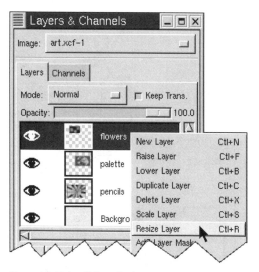

Figure 15. Right-click on the layer you want to resize, then choose Resize Layer from the pop-up menu.

Figure 16. Use the New width and New height text boxes to set the layer's new size in pixels. If the Constrain Ratio check button is selected, the width and height remain proportionally the same.

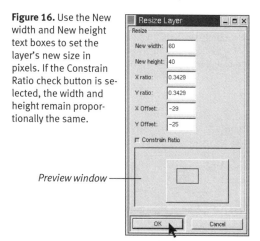

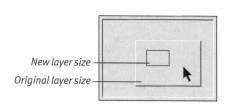

Figure 17. Move the original layer size box around until the new layer size box is positioned where you want it.

To resize a layer:

1. Open the Layers & Channels dialog box by right clicking on the image and choosing Layers→Layers & Channels from the pop-up menu (**Figure 3**).

2. Right-click on the name of the layer you want to resize and choose Resize Layer from the pop-up menu (**Figure 15**).

    or

    Highlight the layer you want to scale, then press Ctrl+R on the keyboard.

    The Resize Layer dialog box will open (**Figure 16**).

3. Use the New width and New height text boxes to enter the layer's new dimensions in pixels. If the Constrain Ratio check button is selected, the horizontal and vertical proportions of the layer will remain the same.

4. If the layer's new size will be smaller than it originally was, you can set where the newly sized layer will be positioned using the X and Y Offset text boxes or the preview window (**Figure 17**). Enter pixel amounts in the text boxes or position the mouse pointer over the original layer rectangle, press the left mouse button, and drag the rectangle to a new position.

5. Click OK. The Resize Layer dialog box will close and the layer will resize.

✔ Tip

■ If the layer's contents are bigger than the layer's new size, the contents will be cropped to fit the new size.

SHOW/HIDE A LAYER

Showing and Hiding Layers

If you're working on a complicated image, it can be useful to hide any layers you are not currently working on.

To hide or view a layer:

1. Open the Layers & Channels dialog box by right clicking on the image and choosing Layers→Layers & Channels from the pop-up menu (**Figure 3**).

2. To hide the layer, in the layer window, click the eye icon that corresponds to the layer you want to hide. The eye will disappear and the layer will disappear from your image (**Figure 18**). To view the layer, click the area where the eye icon was. The eye will reappear and the layer will be visible (**Figure 19**).

✔ Tips

■ Even if a layer is hidden, it can still be the active layer. So be careful! If your hidden layer is active, you may make changes to the layer that you did not intend.

■ If you want to hide all layers except one, here's how. Position the mouse cursor over the eye icon of the layer you want to see, press the Shift key on the keyboard, and then click the eye icon. All layers except that one will be hidden. To view all the layers again, press the Shift key when clicking the eye icon.

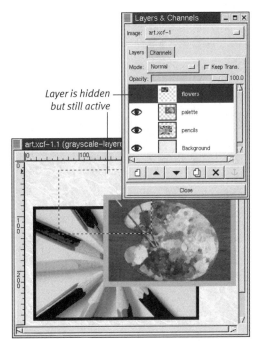

Layer is hidden but still active

Figure 18. When you click the eye icon the layer is hidden. In this example, the flowers layer is hidden, but still active. Since it's active there's a dashed rectangle, indicating where the layer is.

Figure 19. When you click again, the eye icon and the layer in the image window reappear.

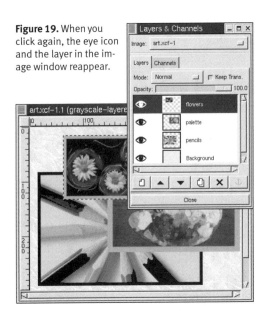

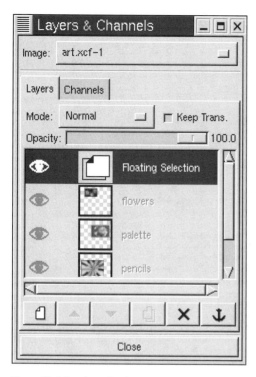

Figure 20. A floating selection appears at the top of the layer window in the Layers & Channels dialog box.

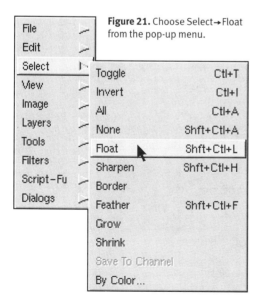

Figure 21. Choose Select→Float from the pop-up menu.

Floating Selections

A floating selection is a selected area that is not attached to any layer. It is displayed in the Layers & Channels dialog box as a "Floating Selection" (**Figure 20**). Any changes or edits made to a floating selection won't affect any other part of the image. Floating selections are very flexible since they can be moved independently of any layer, used to create a new layer, or attached to an existing one. In fact, you can use a floating selection to move part of an image from one layer to another. There are four ways to create a floating selection:

◆ When a selected area is moved, it detaches from its layer and becomes a floating selection. (For details on moving a selection, turn to page 147.)

◆ When text is created using the Text Tool, the text is added to the image as a floating selection. (To find out how to add text to an image, turn to page 208.)

◆ When an item is pasted into an image using the clipboard, it becomes a floating selection. (To learn how to paste an item into an image, turn to page 182.)

◆ When a selected area is set to float using the Float command. (To find out how to do this, see below.)

To float a selected area:

1. Use the selection tool of your choice to select the area you want to float. (For directions on how to do this, turn to Chapter 6, *Making Selections*.)

2. Right-click on the selected area and choose Select→Float from the pop-up menu (**Figure 21**) or press Shift+Ctrl+L on the keyboard. The selected area will float and appear in the Layers & Channels dialog box as a Floating Selection (**Figure 20**).

To anchor a floating selection to a new layer:

1. Open the Layers & Channels dialog box by right clicking on the image and choosing Layers→Layers & Channels from the pop-up menu (**Figure 3**). The Floating Selection will be available in the layer window (**Figure 20**).

2. Click the New Layer button at the bottom left of the dialog 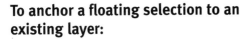 box. The floating selection will be attached to a new layer with the name "Floated Layer" (**Figure 22**). If you wish, you can rename the layer (see page 95 for details about how to do this).

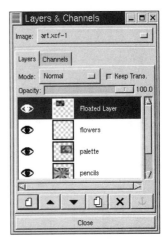

Figure 22. When the floating selection is attached to a layer, the layer is automatically named Floated Layer.

To anchor a floating selection to an existing layer:

1. *Before* you create the floating selection, open the Layers & Channels dialog box by right clicking on the image and choosing Layers→Layers & Channels from the pop-up menu (**Figure 3**).

2. Highlight the layer that you want to add the floating selection to (**Figure 23**).

3. Create the floating selection. The Floating Selection will be available in the layer window (**Figure 24**).

Figure 23. Before you create the floating selection, highlight the layer to which you want to add the selection.

Layers and File Formats

Only the GIMP file format, .xcf, saves multiple layers, channels, and guides. So, if you want to save these things, save your image as a .xcf file. If you save the file to another file format, .tif or .jpg, for instance, all layers will be flattened and individual layer information will be lost.

ANCHOR A FLOATING SELECTION TO A LAYER

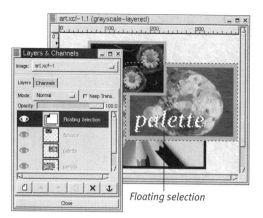

Floating selection

Figure 24. When you create a floating selection, the selection is outlined with a moving, dashed selection boundary. In this example, the text "palette" is the floating selection.

4. To attach the floating selection to a layer:

Click the Anchor Layer button at the bottom right of the dialog box.

or

Right-click on the Floating Selection layer in the layer window and choose Anchor Layer from the pop-up menu (**Figure 25**).

or

Press Ctrl+H on the keyboard.

The floating selection will be attached to the layer that was active before the floating selection was created (**Figure 26**).

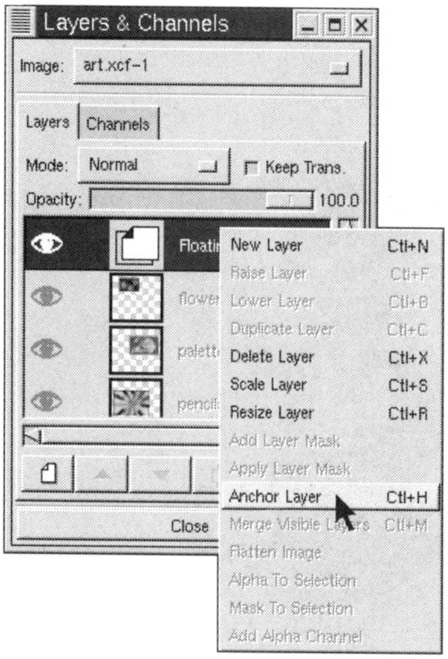

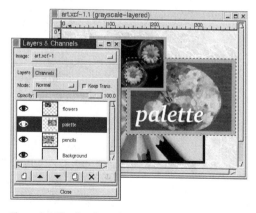

Figure 25. Right-click on the Floating Selection in the layer window and choose Anchor Layer from the pop-up menu.

Figure 26. The floating selection is anchored to the layer you previously selected. In this example, since the palette layer was selected earlier (see Figure 23), the text is anchored to that layer.

Changing the Stacking Order

The layers shown on the Layers tab page in the Layers & Channels dialog box are positioned one on top of the other in a stacking order. The uppermost layer in the layer window is the layer on top in the image window (**Figure 27**). The lowermost layer (usually the background layer) is on the bottom. You can change the way the layers are stacked, moving them up or down the pile. (The background layer always remains on the bottom.)

To move a layer up in the stacking order:

1. Open the Layers & Channels dialog box by right clicking on the image and choosing Layers→Layers & Channels from the pop-up menu (**Figure 3**). The layers will appear in the layer window stacked from top to bottom. Notice how this stacking corresponds to the overlapping layers in the image window (**Figure 27**).

2. Highlight the layer you want to move up in the stacking order (**Figure 27**).

3. Click the Raise Layer button at the bottom left of the dialog box.

   or

   Right-click on the layer's name and choose Raise Layer from the pop-up menu (**Figure 28**).

   or

   Press Ctrl+F on the keyboard.

   The layer will move up the list and move forward in the image window (**Figure 29**).

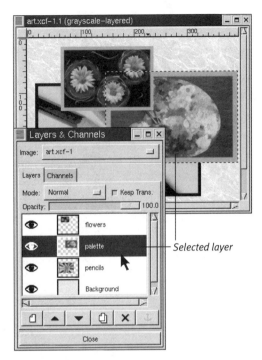

Selected layer

Figure 27. Highlight the layer you want to move in the stacking order. Notice that in this example the palette layer is selected. This layer is behind the flowers layer, but in front of the pencils layer in the stacking order and the image window.

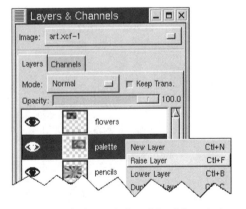

Figure 28. In the layer window, right-click on the layer you want to move up and choose Raise Layer from the pop-up menu.

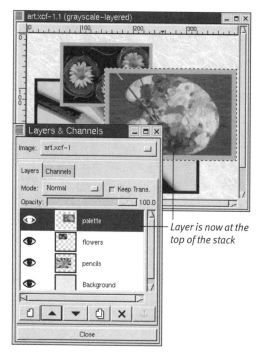

— Layer is now at the top of the stack

Figure 29. The layer moves up the list in the layer window and forward in the image window. In this example, the palette layer has moved to the top of the stack and is now in front of all the layers in the image window.

To move a layer down in the stacking order:

1. Open the Layers & Channels dialog box by right clicking on the image and choosing Layers→Layers & Channels from the pop-up menu (**Figure 3**). The layers will appear in the layer window stacked from top to bottom. Notice how this stacking corresponds to the overlapping layers in the image window (**Figure 27**).

2. Highlight the layer you want to move down in the stacking order (**Figure 27**).

4. Click the Lower Layer button at the bottom center of the dialog box.

   or

   Right-click on the layer's name and choose Lower Layer from the pop-up menu (**Figure 30**).

   or

   Press Ctrl+B on the keyboard.

   The layer will move down the list and move back in the image window (**Figure 31**).

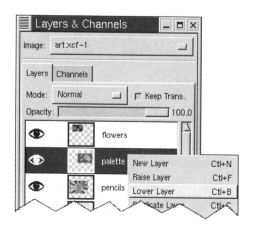

Figure 30. Right-click on the layer you want to move down, then choose Lower Layer from the pop-up menu.

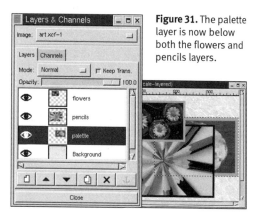

Figure 31. The palette layer is now below both the flowers and pencils layers.

Merging and Flattening Layers

Merging and flattening layers perform essentially the same thing, but with one very important difference. When layers are merged, only the ones that are visible (with the eye icon showing in the Layers & Channels dialog box) are combined together into one layer. When layers are flattened, all layers visible and invisible are combined together into one layer.

To merge all visible layers:

1. Right-click on the image and choose Layers→Merge Visible Layers from the pop-up menu (**Figure 32**).

   or

   In the Layers & Channels dialog box, right-click in the layer window and choose Merge Visible Layers from the pop-up menu (**Figure 33**).

   or

   Press Ctrl+M on the keyboard.

   The Layer Merge Options dialog box will appear (**Figure 34**).

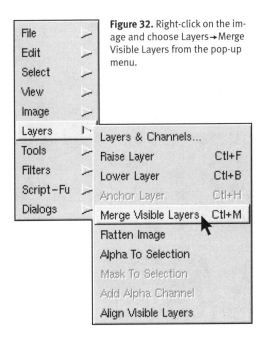

Figure 32. Right-click on the image and choose Layers→Merge Visible Layers from the pop-up menu.

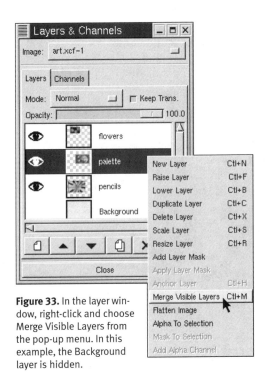

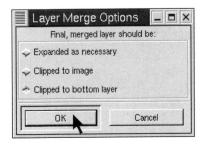

Figure 34. Select the radio button next to the option you would like to choose. In this figure, Clipped to bottom layer has been selected. This means that the merged layers will be cropped to fit the bottommost visible layer (in this example, the pencils layer as shown in Figure 33).

Figure 33. In the layer window, right-click and choose Merge Visible Layers from the pop-up menu. In this example, the Background layer is hidden.

Figure 35. Since Clipped to bottom layer was selected in Figure 34, this example shows how the two upper layers—flowers and palette—have been cropped to fit the bottom, visible layer—pencils.

2. Select the radio button that describes how you want the layers combined into one layer:

   ◆ **Expanded as necessary**— this option sizes the resulting layer to accommodate the merged layers.

   ◆ **Clipped to image**—this option also sizes the resulting layer to accommodate the merged layers. (It has the exact same effect as the option above.)

   ◆ **Clipped to bottom layer**—this option creates a resulting layer that is the same size as the bottom visible layer. If one (or more) of the layers being merged are larger than the bottom layer, the layer(s) are cropped to fit the smaller, bottom layer.

3. Click OK. The Layer Merge Options dialog box will close and the visible layers will combine into one layer. You may be able to see the effect of this in the image if you chose Clipped to bottom layer (**Figure 35**) or just in the Layers & Channels dialog box where the merged layer remains (**Figure 36**).

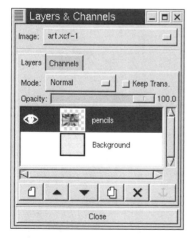

Figure 36. The three visible layers are merged into one visible layer named "pencils." The Background layer was not included in the merge because it is not visible. (Notice that its eye icon is turned off.)

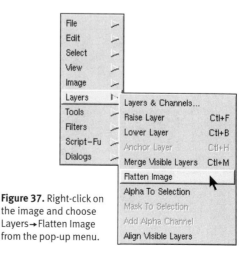

Figure 37. Right-click on the image and choose Layers→Flatten Image from the pop-up menu.

To flatten all layers:

Right-click on the image and choose Layers→Flatten Image from the pop-up menu (**Figure 37**). All layers will flatten down to a single layer and the single layer will be shown in the Layers & Channels dialog box (**Figure 38**).

or

In the Layers & Channels dialog box, right-click in the layer window and choose Flatten Image from the pop-up menu (**Figure 39**). All layers will flatten down to a single layer and the single layer will be shown in the Layers & Channels dialog box (**Figure 38**).

Figure 38. It doesn't matter whether all layers are visible or not. When the Flatten command is used, all layers are combined into one layer.

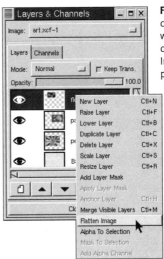

Figure 39. Right-click in the layer window and choose Flatten Image from the pop-up menu.

Summary

In this chapter you learned how to:

- Make a layer active

- Create a new layer or duplicate a layer

- Rename and delete layers

- Scale and resize layers

- Show and hide layers

- Create a floating selection

- Attach a floating selection to a new or existing layer

- Move layers up and down the stacking order

- Merge and flatten layers

PAINTING LINES AND SHAPES

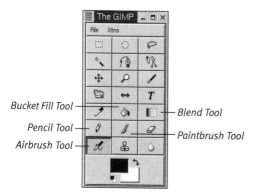

Bucket Fill Tool

Pencil Tool

Airbrush Tool

Blend Tool

Paintbrush Tool

Figure 1. Use the painting tools in the Toolbox to add amazing color effects to your images.

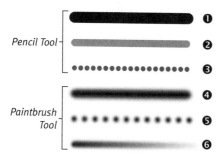

Pencil Tool

Paintbrush Tool

❶
❷
❸
❹
❺
❻

Figure 2. Various strokes made with the Pencil and Paintbrush Tools: ❶ Circle fuzzy (19) brush, 100% opacity; ❷ Circle (15) brush, 35% opacity; ❸ Circle (11) brush, 50% opacity, spacing set to 130; ❹ Circle fuzzy (19) brush, 100% opacity; ❺ Circle fuzzy (17) brush, 100% opacity, spacing set to 150; ❻ Circle fuzzy (17) brush, fade out set to 70. Notice that strokes ❶ and ❹ are made with the same brush but different tools. No matter what brush you select, a Pencil Tool stroke will always have a sharp edge.

*I*n Chapter 4, *Selecting Colors*, you learned how to choose colors using the Color Picker Tool and color palettes. In this chapter, you'll discover how to apply those colors using the Pencil, Paintbrush, Airbrush, Bucket Fill, and Blend Tools (**Figure 1**). In addition to solid colors, you'll find out how to paint with patterns and *gradients*—a graduated blend of two or more colors. Painting with the GIMP is fun and easy, so let's get started!

The Pencil and Paintbrush Tools

The Pencil and Paintbrush Tools work much like a pencil on paper or a brush on canvas. Just press the left mouse button and drag to draw a line. Unlike an ordinary pencil or brush, though, they do have a few fancy features: you can easily draw perfectly straight lines, and change the properties of the line that the tool will draw—the shape, thickness, spacing, and *opacity* (**Figure 2**).

To draw a line with the Pencil or Paintbrush Tool:

1. Use the Layers & Channels dialog box to select the layer on which you would like to draw. (For directions on how to do this, turn to page 92).

2. Choose a foreground color. (For details about how to do this, turn to pages 42–45.)

3. To select the Pencil Tool, click the Pencil Tool button in the Toolbox or press Shift+P on the keyboard. The mouse pointer will change to a tiny pencil.

   or

   To select the Paintbrush Tool, click the Paintbrush Tool button in the Toolbox or press P on the keyboard. The mouse pointer will change to a tiny pencil.

4. In the image window, position the mouse pointer where you would like to start the line.

5. Press the left mouse button and drag. A line will appear as you drag (**Figure 3**).

6. When you are finished drawing, release the left mouse button (**Figure 4**).

✔ Tips

- If you want to keep the line within a specific area, use a selection tool to select that area.

- No matter what kind of brush you select, the Pencil Tool will always draw a line with a clearly defined edge.

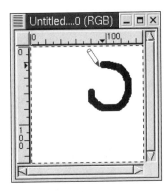

Figure 3. A line appears as you drag the mouse. In this figure the Pencil Tool is used.

Figure 4. You can draw as many lines as you need. A few lines and dots can add some personality.

Figure 5. When you click, a dot appears. In this figure, the Paintbrush Tool is used.

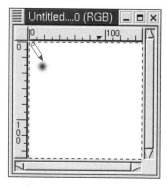

Figure 6. A straight line appears when you click again.

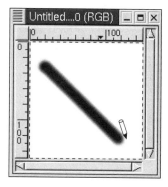

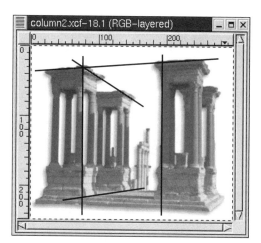

Figure 7. Several straight lines have been added to this image using the Pencil Tool.

To draw a straight line with the Pencil or Paintbrush Tool:

1. Use the Layers & Channels dialog box to select the layer on which you would like to draw. (For directions on how to do this, turn to page 92).

2. Choose a foreground color. (For details about how to do this, turn to pages 42–45.)

3. To select the Pencil Tool, click the Pencil Tool button in the Toolbox or press Shift+P on the keyboard. The mouse pointer will change to a tiny pencil.

   or

   To select the Paintbrush Tool, click the Paintbrush Tool button in the Toolbox or press P on the keyboard. The mouse pointer will change to a tiny pencil.

4. In the image window, position the mouse pointer where you would like the line to start.

5. Click. A dot will appear under the mouse pointer (**Figure 5**).

6. Press and hold down the Shift key.

7. Move the mouse pointer to where you want the line to end and click. A straight line will appear between the two points where you clicked (**Figure 6**).

8. To add another straight line to the one you just drew, continue holding down the Shift key, and then move the mouse pointer to a new position and click. A second line segment will appear attached to the first.

9. Continue adding lines or release the Shift key to draw a new line (**Figure 7**).

PENCIL OR PAINTBRUSH TOOL: DRAW A LINE

Changing Brushes

You can set almost every aspect of the lines you draw—from thickness and shape, to spacing and opacity—by changing brush properties.

To change the brush properties:

1. In the GIMP Toolbox, choose File→Dialogs→Brushes (**Figure 8**).

   or

   Right-click on an image and choose Dialogs→Brushes from the pop-up menu (**Figure 9**).

   or

   Press Shift+Ctrl+B on the keyboard.

   The Brush Selection dialog box will open (**Figure 10**).

2. To select a new line shape, click on a brush in the brush window (**Figure 11**). The brush name and pixel size will appear in the Brush Selection dialog box.

3. To set the opacity of the line, use the Opacity slider bar (**Figure 12**). The higher the setting the more opaque the line will be. A setting of 0 is completely transparent, whereas a setting of 100 is completely opaque.

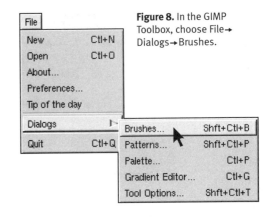

Figure 8. In the GIMP Toolbox, choose File→Dialogs→Brushes.

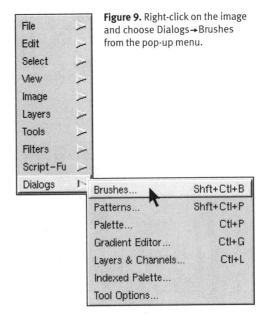

Figure 9. Right-click on the image and choose Dialogs→Brushes from the pop-up menu.

CHANGE BRUSH PROPERTIES

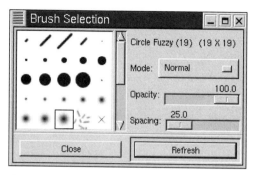

Figure 10. Using the Brush Selection dialog box, you can choose different brush shapes and sizes, and set the opacity and spacing of the brush stroke.

Brush window Selected brush Brush name

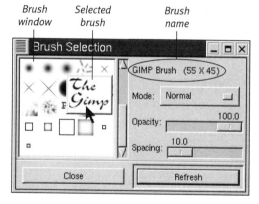

Figure 11. Click on one of the brushes in the brush window to select it. Yes, the selected brush really is composed of the text "The Gimp."

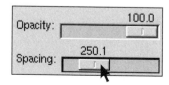

Figure 12. Use the sliders to set the Opacity and Spacing of the stroke.

4. To set how far apart each pencil stroke is, use the Spacing slider bar. The smaller the setting is, the closer together the strokes are. You can create some interesting effects with different settings (**Figure 13**).

5. When you have finished changing the line properties, click Close to close the Brush Selection dialog box.

✔ Tips

■ You can leave the Brush Selection dialog box open to select different types of lines while you are drawing.

■ To return the Brush Selection dialog box to its original default setting, click Refresh.

■ You may have noticed that there's a Mode drop-down list available in the Brush Selection dialog box. This drop-down list lets you set blending modes. To learn more about these modes and the effects they have, turn to pages 170–173.

CHANGE BRUSH PROPERTIES

Figure 13. The heart in this figure was created using Calligraphy Brush #3 and "The Gimp" was added with just a click using the brush shown in Figure 11.

Fade Out with the Paintbrush Tool

One other interesting option available with the Paintbrush Tool is the ability to set the line to gradually fade out.

To set a Paintbrush stroke to fade out:

1. Double-click on the Paintbrush Tool button in the GIMP Toolbox. The Tool Options dialog box will open (**Figure 14**).

2. Use the Fade Out slider to set how long it takes for a brush to fade out. The higher the setting, the longer the brush stroke must be before the line will fade out. A setting of 0, disables the effect.

3. Click Close to close the Tool Options dialog box. You can create some interesting effects using fade out (**Figure 15**).

Figure 14. Use the slider to set the length of a stroke's fade out. Setting Fade Out to 0 disables the effect.

Figure 15. The fiery eyelashes in this image were created using the Paintbrush Tool with a fade out setting of 50.

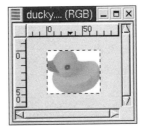

Figure 16. Create or find a small image that will become the new brush.

Where Can I Find More Brushes?

There are many GIMP resources on the Web, and there are several sites where you can find and download brushes. Two of them are:

http://www.gimp.org/brushes1.html
http://www.geocities.com/Tokyo/1474/gimp/brushes.html

To load brushes that you download into the Brush Selection dialog box, copy the brush files to the GIMP directory where brushes are stored. By default, the GIMP installation places brushes in /usr/share/gimp/brushes.

Figure 17. Right-click on the image and choose Image→Grayscale from the pop-up menu.

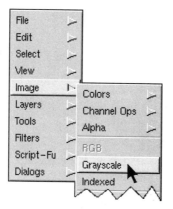

Custom Brushes

You may have already noticed that there are some interesting brushes available in the Brush Selection dialog box (**Figure 10**). Many of these were created by GIMP users and incorporated into the program over time. You, too, can create custom brushes and add them to the Brush Selection dialog box.

To create a custom brush:

1. Create a small image on a white background (**Figure 16**).

2. Right-click on the image and choose Image→Grayscale from the pop-up menu (**Figure 17**). The image will change to grayscale mode.

3. Right-click on the image and choose Image→Colors→Invert from the pop-up menu (**Figure 18**). This will create a negative of the image (**Figure 19**). When the image is saved as a brush, it will change back to its original positive.

4. Right-click on the image and choose File→Save as from the pop-up menu (**Figure 20**). The Save Image dialog box will open (**Figure 21**).

5. Use the Directories list box to move to a personal directory where you can save the file.

6. In the Selection text box, type in the name of the file with a .gbr file extension. This will tell the GIMP that you are creating a brush file.

7. Click OK. The Save As Brush dialog box will open (**Figure 22**).

8. Type in a descriptive name for the brush in the Description text box.

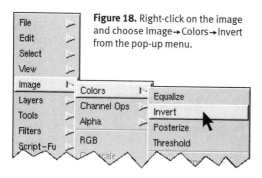

Figure 18. Right-click on the image and choose Image→Colors→Invert from the pop-up menu.

Figure 19. The image inverts, becoming a negative. It will automatically revert to a positive image when saved as a brush.

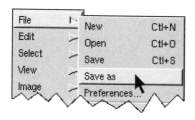

Figure 20. Right-click on the image and choose File→ Save As from the pop-up menu.

(continued)

CREATE A CUSTOM BRUSH

9. Click OK. The Save As Brush and Save Image dialog boxes will close.

10. Use your computer's file manager (or a terminal window) to copy the brush file from the directory where you just saved it to the GIMP directory where brushes are stored. By default, the GIMP installation places brushes in **/usr/share/gimp/brushes**. (You may need to log on as root or su to root to do this.)

11. Return to the GIMP and open the Brush Selection dialog box (**Figure 10**) by choosing File→Dialogs→Brushes from the Toolbox (**Figure 8**) or right clicking on an image an choosing Dialogs→ Brushes from the pop-up menu (**Figure 9**).

12. Click Refresh. Your custom brush will appear in the brush window (**Figure 23**). Try it out! Custom brushes can add interesting effects to images (**Figure 24**).

✔ Tip

■ Custom brushes can be created for many uses. For instance, you can create a brush that stamps an image—a star perhaps— or even your signature (just scan your signature in and create the brush).

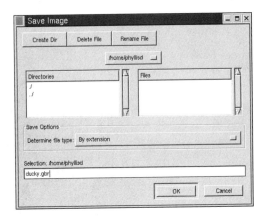

Figure 21. Use the Directories list box to move to a personal directory where you can save the file. Save the file with a .gbr file extension.

Figure 22. Use the Save As Brush dialog box to enter a few descriptive words about the brush.

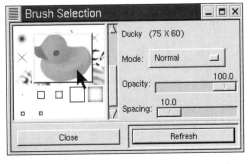

Figure 23. When you click Refresh, the custom brush appears in the brush window.

Figure 24. Creating custom brushes is just ducky!

CREATE A CUSTOM BRUSH

Figure 25. Create the shape you want to outline using the selection tools. In this example, the Bezier Selection Tool was used to create a heart.

Draw Using the Selection Tools

You can also add shapes and lines to an image using the selection tools. All you need to do is create the selection that will become the outline, then apply the Stroke command.

To draw using the selection tools:

1. Use the Layers & Channels dialog box to select the layer on which you would like to draw. (For directions on how to do this, turn to page 92).

2. Choose a foreground color. (For details about how to do this, turn to pages 42–45.)

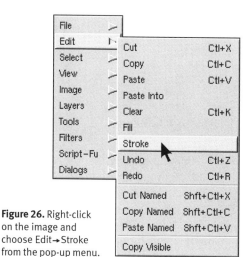

Figure 26. Right-click on the image and choose Edit→Stroke from the pop-up menu.

3. Use the selection tool(s) of your choice to create the shape that you want to outline (**Figure 25**).

4. Use the Brush Selection dialog box to select a brush. (For details about how to do this, turn to page 110.)

5. Right-click in the image window and choose Edit→Stroke from the pop-up menu (**Figure 26**). An outline will appear around the selection (**Figure 27**).

✔ Tips

- To find out how to use the selection tools, take a look at Chapter 6, *Making Selections*.

- You can use several selection tools in conjunction with the Shift and Alt keys to create complex shapes.

Figure 27. When the Stroke command is applied an outline appears. In this example, Calligraphy Brush #1 was used.

The Airbrush Tool

The Airbrush Tool works in a similar fashion to the Pencil and Paintbrush Tools—to draw a line, just click and drag; to draw straight lines, hold down the Shift key while clicking. What's really neat about the Airbrush Tool is that it works like, well, an airbrush. If a simple line is drawn, the Airbrush Tool produces a semi-transparent, soft stroke that looks much like sprayed paint. And, if the Airbrush Tool is held in one place while drawing a line, the area under the tools gets darker, as if more paint is being applied.

Figure 28. Drag the mouse pointer to draw a line.

To draw a line with the Airbrush Tool:

1. Use the Layers & Channels dialog box to select the layer on which you would like to draw. (For directions on how to do this, turn to page 92).

2. Choose a foreground color.

3. Click the Airbrush Tool button in the Toolbox or press A on the keyboard. The mouse pointer will change to a tiny pencil.

4. In the image window, position the mouse pointer where you would like to start the line.

5. Press the left mouse button and drag. An airbrushed line will appear as you drag (**Figure 28**).

6. When you are finished drawing, release the left mouse button.

✔ Tip

■ The shape, size, and opacity of a line created by the Airbrush Tool can be changed using the Brush Selection dialog box. For directions on changing brush properties, turn to page 110.

Setting Airbrush Tool Options

As you may have already guessed, there are two Airbrush Tool options that can be set—Rate and Pressure. Rate sets how fast the "paint" comes out of the tool and Pressure sets how much "paint" is sprayed. The higher settings for both of these options make the Airbrush Tool act more like a real airbrush.

To set these options, double-click on the Airbrush Tool in the Toolbox to open the Tool Options dialog box (**Figure 29**). Use the Rate and Pressure sliders to set the options.

Figure 29. Use the sliders to set the Rate and Pressure options.

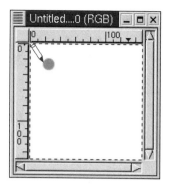

Figure 30. With the Airbrush Tool selected, click where you want the line to start in the image window.

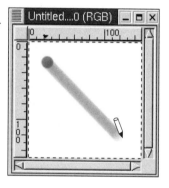

Figure 31. Move the mouse pointer to a new position and click again. A straight line appears between the two points.

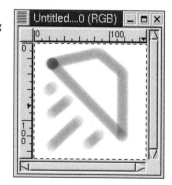

Figure 32. Continue holding down the Shift key to add additional straight lines to the original one.

To draw a straight line with the Airbrush Tool:

1. Use the Layers & Channels dialog box to select the layer on which you would like to draw.

2. Choose a foreground color.

3. Click the Airbrush Tool button in the Toolbox or press A on the keyboard. The mouse pointer will change to a tiny pencil.

4. In the image window, position the mouse pointer where the line will start.

5. Click. A fuzzy dot will appear under the mouse pointer (**Figure 30**).

6. Press and hold down the Shift key.

7. Move the mouse pointer to where you want the line to end and click. A straight line will appear between the two points where you clicked (**Figure 31**).

8. To add another straight line to the one you just drew, continue holding down the Shift key, and then move the mouse pointer to a new position and click. A second line segment will appear attached to the first.

9. Continue adding lines or release the Shift key to draw a new line (**Figure 32**).

✔ Tips

■ If you want the line to be darker just move the mouse slower as you drag.

■ The shape, size, and opacity of a line created by the Airbrush Tool can be changed using the Brush Selection dialog box. For directions on changing brush properties, turn to page 110.

AIRBRUSH TOOL: DRAW A STRAIGHT LINE

The Bucket Fill Tool

The Bucket Fill Tool can be used to fill an area or selection with the current foreground or background colors or a pattern. There are several options you can set before using the Bucket Fill Tool:

◆ **Fill Opacity**—this option sets how transparent the fill will be.

◆ **Fill Threshold**—if you're filling an area that contains different colors, this option sets how far the fill will spread. The higher the setting is, the further out the fill will spread into other color areas.

◆ **Sample Merged**—with this option on, the Bucket Fill Tool will use the blended, *composite* colors from all layers to detect where area boundaries are.

To set Bucket Fill Tool options:

1. Double-click on the Bucket Fill Tool in the Toolbox. The Tool Options dialog box will open (**Figure 33**).

2. Use the Fill Opacity slider to set how opaque the fill will be (**Figure 34**). The higher the setting the more opaque the fill. A setting of 0 is completely transparent (invisible), whereas a setting of 100 is completely opaque.

3. Use the Fill Threshold slider to set how far a fill will spread. The higher the setting is, the further the fill will spread (**Figures 35a–b**).

4. Select the Sample Merged check button to set the tool to detect area boundaries based on the combined colors of all layers (not just one layer).

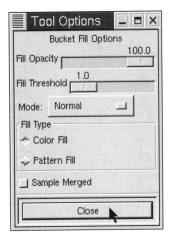

Figure 33. Use the Tool Options dialog box to set Bucket Fill Tool options.

Figure 34. Opacity sets how transparent a fill is. In this figure, the background area was divided into 4 sections and each area was filled using a different opacity setting.

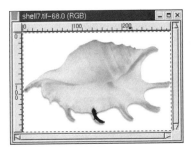

Figure 35a. The Fill Threshold setting determines how far a fill will spread. In this figure, the Fill Threshold was set to 50. Notice how the black fill only covers a tiny portion of the shell.

Figure 35b. In this figure the Fill Threshold was set to 100. Instead of filling only the tiny area at the bottom of the shell, the black fill covers the entire shell in varying degrees.

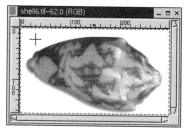

Figure 36. Position the mouse crosshair over the area you want to fill. In this figure, the crosshair is positioned over the white background.

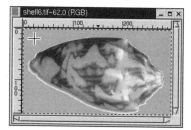

Figure 37. When the mouse is clicked, the area fills with the current background color in the color selector. In this figure, the white area has been replaced with gray.

5. When you are finished setting the options, click Close to close the Tool Options dialog box.

✔ Tip

■ You may have noticed that there's a Mode drop-down list available in the Tool Options dialog box (**Figure 33**). This drop-down list lets you set blending modes. To learn more about these modes and the effects they have, turn to pages 170–173.

To fill an area:

1. Use the Layers & Channels dialog box to select the layer on which you would like to draw on. (For directions on how to do this, turn to page 92).

2. Choose foreground and background colors. (For details about how to do this, turn to pages 42–45.)

3. Use one of the selection tools to select the area you would like to fill (this is optional).

4. Click the Bucket Fill Tool button in the Toolbox or press Shift+B on the keyboard. The mouse pointer will change to a crosshair.

5. Position the mouse crosshair over the area you want to fill (**Figure 36**).

6. Click to fill the area with the foreground color. To fill the area with the background color, press the Shift key and click. The area will fill with color (**Figure 37**).

The Fill Command

Another way to fill an area with the current background color is to use the Fill command. It works just like the Bucket Fill Tool with a maximum fill threshold setting.

To fill an area using the Fill Command:

1. Use the Layers & Channels dialog box to select the layer on which you would like to draw. (For directions on how to do this, turn to page 92).

2. Choose a background color. (For details about how to do this, turn to pages 45–47.)

3. Use one of the selection tools to select the area you would like to fill (this is optional).

4. Right-click on the image and choose Edit→Fill from the pop-up menu (**Figure 38**). The area will fill with the background color.

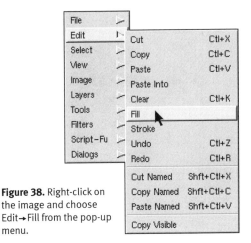

Figure 38. Right-click on the image and choose Edit→Fill from the pop-up menu.

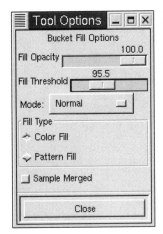

Figure 39. Use the Tool Options dialog box to set the Bucket Fill Tool to fill areas with patterns.

Downloading Patterns from the Web

There are several GIMP Web sites that contain interesting patterns, ready for download. Two of them are:

http:www.gimp.org/patterns.html
http://empyrean.lib.ndsu.nodak.edu/~nem/gimp/tuts/patterns.html

To load patterns that you download into the Pattern Selection dialog box, copy the pattern files to the GIMP directory where patterns are stored. By default, the GIMP installation places patterns in /usr/share/gimp/patterns.

THE FILL COMMAND

Figure 40.
In the Fill Type area, select the Pattern Fill radio button.

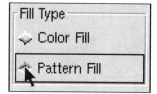

Figure 40. In the Fill Type area, select the Pattern Fill radio button.

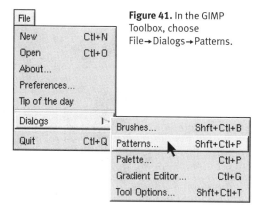

Figure 41. In the GIMP Toolbox, choose File→Dialogs→Patterns.

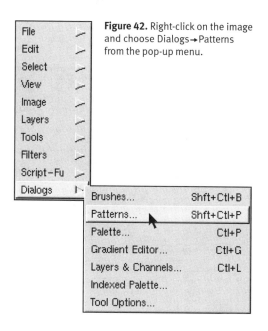

Figure 42. Right-click on the image and choose Dialogs→Patterns from the pop-up menu.

Patterns

When a solid color won't do, try a pattern! More than 50 patterns come with the GIMP. If you don't like what you find, you can download more patterns from the Web or create your own.

To fill an area with a pattern:

1. Use the Layers & Channels dialog box to select the layer on which you would like to draw. (For directions on how to do this, turn to page 92).

2. Double-click on the Bucket Fill Tool in the Toolbox. The Tool Options dialog box will open (**Figure 39**).

3. In the Fill Type area, select the Pattern Fill radio button (**Figure 40**).

4. Click Close. The Tool Options dialog box will close.

5. Use one of the selection tools to select the area you would like to fill (this is optional).

6. Choose File→Dialogs→Patterns from the Toolbox (**Figure 41**).

   or

   Right-click on the image and choose Dialogs→Patterns from the pop-up menu (**Figure 42**).

   or

   Press Shift+Ctrl+P on the keyboard.

   The Pattern Selection dialog box will appear (**Figure 43**).

   (continued)

FILL AN AREA WITH A PATTERN

7. Click a pattern in the pattern window to select it (**Figure 44**).

8. With the Bucket Fill Tool still selected, position the mouse crosshair over the area you want to fill and click. The pattern will fill the area (**Figure 45**).

✔ Tip

■ Just like a solid color fill, you can alter a pattern's opacity and set the Bucket Fill Tool's fill threshold and sample merged options. For details on how to do this, turn to page 118.

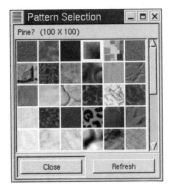

Figure 43. Use the Pattern Selection dialog box to choose a pattern fill.

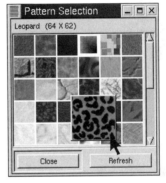

Figure 44. Click a pattern swatch to select it. In this figure, a Leopard pattern is selected.

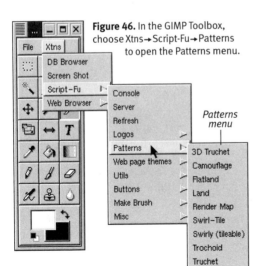

Figure 46. In the GIMP Toolbox, choose Xtns→Script-Fu→Patterns to open the Patterns menu.

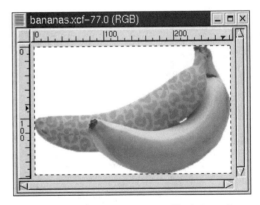

Figure 45. When you click, a pattern fills the area. In this figure, the upper banana was selected using the Bezier Selection Tool. The Leopard fill set to 25% opacity was used.

FILL AN AREA WITH A PATTERN

Figure 47. Use the Script-Fu dialog box to set the pattern's variables.

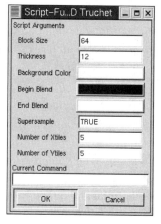

Figure 48. When the script-fu mini-program runs, a pattern appears in a new image window.

Figure 49a. Camouflage pattern script-fu.

Figure 49b. Render Map pattern script-fu.

Figure 49c. Swirly pattern script-fu.

Figure 49d. Trochoid pattern script-fu.

A Quick Way to Make Patterns

There are some amazing tools that come with the GIMP! Open the Xtns→Script-Fu→ Patterns menu on the Toolbox (**Figure 46**) and you will find nine mini-programs (called script-fus) that will quickly create seamless patterns.

To create a pattern:

1. In the GIMP Toolbox, choose Xtns→ Script-Fu→Patterns (**Figure 46**). The Patterns menu will open.

2. Choose one of the mini-programs listed on the Patterns menu. For this example, 3D Truchet is chosen. A Script-Fu dialog box for the mini-program will appear (**Figure 47**).

3. Use the text boxes and drop-down lists to set the effect you would like to create. (To start, don't change anything, just leave the default settings.)

4. Click OK. The mini-program will run. When it is finished, an amazing pattern will appear in a new image window (**Figure 48**). Try out all the pattern mini-programs. It's amazing what you can create with just a few clicks (**Figures 49a–d**)!

✔ Tip

■ All the mini-programs found on the Patterns menu work basically in the same way. Just select one of the items from the Patterns menu, set the various options, and click OK to create a fantastic pattern!

Gradients and the Blend Tool

Another way to add interesting color to an image is to use a gradient. A gradient is a graduated blend of two or more colors created using the Blend Tool. You can create gradients using just the foreground and background colors in the color selector, or use the Gradient Editor to create fantastic blends of color.

To apply a gradient:

1. Use the Layers & Channels dialog box to select the layer on which you would like to draw. (For directions on how to do this, turn to page 92).

2. Choose foreground and background colors. (For details about how to do this, turn to pages 42–45.)

3. Use one of the selection tools to select the area you would like to fill (this is optional).

4. Click the Blend Tool button in the Toolbox or press L on the keyboard to select the tool.

5. Position the mouse crosshair at one side of the area you want to fill with a gradient (**Figure 50**).

6. Press the left mouse button and drag. A line will appear indicating the direction and angle you have dragged the mouse (**Figure 51**).

7. Release the left mouse button. A two color gradient will fill the area (**Figure 52**).

✔ Tip

■ The further you drag the mouse, the smoother the transition will be from the foreground color to the background color.

Figure 50. Position the mouse crosshair where you would like the gradient to start. In this figure, the lower part of the telephone has been selected.

Figure 51. When you press the mouse and drag, a line appears showing where the gradient will appear.

Figure 52. When you release the mouse button, the gradient appears, filling the area.

Figure 53a.
Linear gradient.

Figure 53b.
Bilinear gradient.

Figure 53c.
Radial gradient.

Figure 53d.
Square gradient.

Figure 53e.
Conical (symmetric) gradient.

Figure 53f.
Conical (asymmetric) gradient.

Figure 53g.
Shapeburst (angular) gradient.

Figure 53h.
Shapeburst (spherical) gradient.

Figure 54a.
Sawtooth wave repeat.

Figure 54b.
Triangular wave repeat.

Blend Tool Options

There are numerous options that can be set for this amazing tool:

◆ **Opacity**—this option sets how opaque the gradient fill is.

◆ **Offset**—this option sets where the foreground color starts to blend into the background color. The higher the value is, the sharper the edge is between the color blends.

◆ **Blend**—this drop-down list sets which color starts and finishes the blend.

◆ **Gradient**—there are many gradient types you can choose to change the shape of the gradient blend. Several of them are shown in **Figures 53a–h**.

◆ **Repeat**—this option sets the gradient fill to automatically repeat (**Figures 54a–b**). When creating a gradient, the shorter distance the mouse is dragged, the more repeats there will be.

◆ **Adaptive supersampling**—this option makes a blend look smoother by adding intermediate colors to the transition.

To set Blend Tool options:

1. Double-click on the Blend Tool in the Toolbox. The Tool Options dialog box will open (**Figure 55**).

2. Use the Opacity slider to set how opaque the fill will be. The higher the setting the more opaque the fill. A setting of 0 is completely transparent (invisible), whereas a setting of 100 is completely opaque.

3. Use the Offset slider to set where the foreground color starts to blend into the background color.

(continued)

4. Use the Blend drop-down list (**Figure 56**) to select which color will start the gradient and which will finish it.

5. Use the Gradient drop-down list (**Figure 57**) to set the shape of the gradient blend.

6. Use the Repeat drop-down list (**Figure 58**) to set whether the gradient will repeat.

7. If you wish, select the Adaptive super-sampling check button to make a gradient blend appear smoother.

8. When you have finished selecting options, click Close to close the Tool Options dialog box.

✔ Tip

■ You may have noticed that there's a Mode drop-down list available in the Tool Options dialog box. This drop-down list lets you set blending modes. To learn more about these modes and the effects they have, turn to pages 170–173.

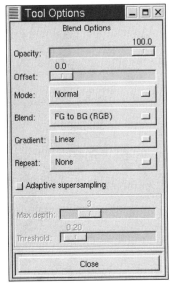

Figure 55. Use the Tool Options dialog box to set Blend Tool options.

Figure 56. Use the Blend drop-down list to set which color starts and finishes the gradient blend.

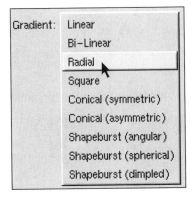

Figure 57. Use the Gradient drop-down list to set the shape of the gradient blend. Many of the available gradients are shown in Figures 53a–h.

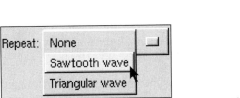

Figure 58. Use the Repeat drop-down list to set the gradient repeat pattern.

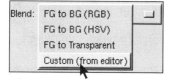

Figure 59. Use the Blend drop-down list to select Custom (from editor).

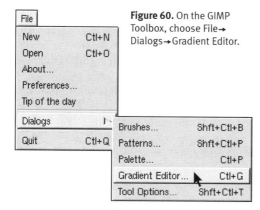

Figure 60. On the GIMP Toolbox, choose File→ Dialogs→Gradient Editor.

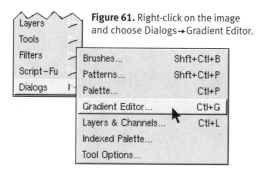

Figure 61. Right-click on the image and choose Dialogs→Gradient Editor.

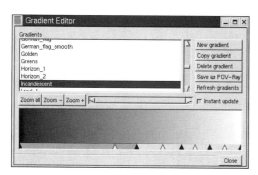

Figure 62. Use the Gradient Editor to choose from some fantastic gradients.

The Gradient Editor

Creating gradient blends with two colors is pretty fancy, but there's more that you can do with the GIMP. Using the Gradient Editor, you can apply gradients with as many colors as you wish. In fact, the GIMP comes with an amazing list of multicolor gradients.

To apply a gradient using the Gradient Editor:

1. Double-click on the Blend Tool in the GIMP Toolbox. The Tool Options dialog box will open (**Figure 55**).

2. Use the Blend drop-down list to select Custom (from editor) (**Figure 59**).

3. Click Close to close the Tool Options dialog box.

4. Choose File→Dialogs→Gradient Editor on the Toolbox (**Figure 60**).

   or

   Right-click on the image and choose Dialogs→Gradient Editor from the pop-up menu (**Figure 61**).

   or

   Press Ctrl+G on the keyboard.

   The Gradient Editor dialog box will appear (**Figure 62**).

   (continued)

5. Use the Gradients list box to select the gradient you want to apply. When you highlight a gradient, it appears in the preview window.

6. With the Blend Tool still selected, position the mouse crosshair where you would like to start the blend.

7. Press the mouse button and drag. A line will appear indicating the direction and angle you have dragged the mouse (**Figure 51**).

8. Release the left mouse button. The gradient you selected in the Gradient Editor will fill the area in your image (**Figures 63**). Gradients can create some interesting effects (**Figure 64a–b**).

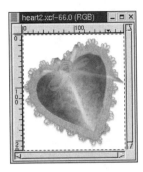

Figure 63. When you release the left mouse button, the gradient you selected appears in the image. In this figure, the center heart was selected using the Bezier Selection Tool. A Rounded edge gradient was applied as a linear gradient at 45% opacity.

Figure 64b. The highlight on this apple was created using a radial setting of Flare_Radial_102 gradient. The gaussian blur and noisify filters were also applied.

Figure 64a. The pipes in this figure were created using a linear setting of the Tube_Red gradient.

Summary

In this chapter you learned how to:

- Use the Pencil and Paintbrush Tools to draw lines

- Change brush properties

- Create custom brushes

- Draw using the selection tools

- Use the Airbrush Tool

- Fill an area using the Bucket Fill Tool and the Fill command

- Apply patterns

- Create patterns using script-fus

- Create gradients using the Blend Tool

- Use the Gradient Editor

THE GRADIENT EDITOR

ADJUSTING COLOR AND TONE

*E*ventually, you will come across an image—be it a photograph, scanned image, or image from another source—that needs to be adjusted. The GIMP offers many color correction tools to enhance and adjust the color and tone of an image. All of these tools work in basically the same way—by determining the existing range of pixel values in an image and replacing them with a new range of values. The main difference between the color correction tools is the amount of control you have over the range of values.

This chapter will take you through using the GIMP's color correction tools, from the most sophisticated ones that give the greatest control—such as *levels*, and *curves*—to those that give the least control—such as *invert*, *threshold*, *normalize*, and *posterize*. The Levels and Curves tools let you make exact adjustments to a layer's highlights, midtones, and shadows using the lightest and darkest pixels in each individual channel. The simpler tools make adjustments using the combined values of all channels.

All of the commands in this chapter can be applied to a selected area of a layer or an entire layer. The more complex tools let you see a preview of an adjustment to let you decide whether the change is what you want.

Original image.

Posterize applied.

Invert applied.

Threshold applied.

Levels

Levels are used to make exact adjustments to a layer's or selection's tonal range by adjusting highlights, midtones, and shadows using a *histogram*. A histogram is a graph that shows the number of pixels at each level of brightness in a layer or selection.

To adjust color and tone using Levels:

1. Use the Layers & Channels dialog box to select a layer. (For details about how to do this, turn to page 92.)

2. If you wish, use the selection tool of your choice to select an area of the image. (For directions on how to use the selection tools, turn to Chapter 6, *Making Selections*.)

3. Right-click on the image and choose Image→Colors→Levels from the pop-up menu (**Figure 1**). The Levels dialog box will appear (**Figure 2**).

4. Make sure the Preview check button is selected.

5. Use the Modify Levels for Channel drop-down list to select which channel will be adjusted (**Figure 3**). (It's best to use Value first. This is the combination of all three channels—Red, Green, and Blue. After correcting the Value, you can move on to individual channels, if need be.)

6. To adjust the shadows, enter a number in the leftmost Input Levels text box or slide the black Input Level triangle to the right (**Figure 4**).

7. To adjust midtones, enter a number in the center Input Levels text box or slide the gray Input Level triangle to the left or right.

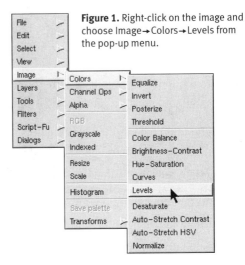

Figure 1. Right-click on the image and choose Image→Colors→Levels from the pop-up menu.

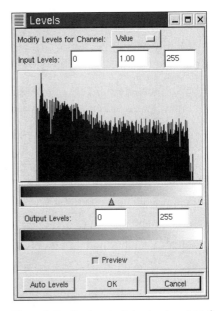

Figure 2. Use the Levels dialog box to adjust the color and tone of an image.

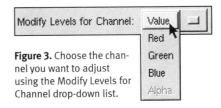

Figure 3. Choose the channel you want to adjust using the Modify Levels for Channel drop-down list.

Shadows   Midtones   Highlights

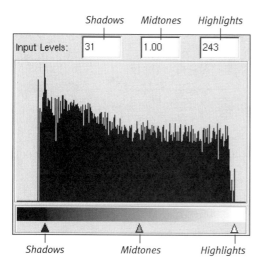

Shadows   Midtones   Highlights

Figure 4. Use the Input Levels text boxes and/or triangles to adjust the shadows, midtones, and highlights in an image.

Shadows   Highlights

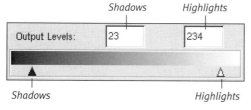

Shadows   Highlights

Figure 5. Use the Output Levels text boxes and/or triangles to adjust shadows and highlights.

8. To adjust highlights, enter a number in the rightmost Input Levels text box or slide the white Input Level triangle to the left.

9. To make the image brighter overall, enter a number in the left Output Levels text box or slide the black Output Level triangle to the right (**Figure 5**).

10. To make the image darker overall, enter a number in the right Output Levels text box or slide the white Output Level triangle to the left.

11. When you are finished adjusting the levels, click OK to close the Levels dialog box. Levels change color and tone in subtle ways (**Figures 6a–b**).

✔ Tips

■ You can also click the Auto Levels button in the Levels dialog box to let the GIMP detect and automatically set new levels.

■ You can adjust the levels of an alpha channel. If your image contains one, you'll be able to select it using the Modify Levels for Channel drop-down list shown in Figure 3.

Figure 6a. The original image before level adjustment. Notice how the entire image has a grayish tone.

Figure 6b. The image after levels adjustment. Shadows and highlights have been changed.

USE LEVELS TO ADJUST COLOR AND TONE

Curves

Curves, like Levels, are also used to adjust the tonal range of a layer or selection. But, instead of using a histogram to make corrections using highlights, midtones, and shadows, the Curves tool lets you make changes using a plotted curve representation of the image's colors.

To adjust color and tone using Curves:

1. Use the Layers & Channels dialog box to select a layer. (For details about how to do this, turn to page 92.)

2. If you wish, use the selection tool of your choice to select an area of the image.

3. Right-click on the image and choose Image→Colors→Curves from the pop-up menu (**Figure 7**). The Curves dialog box will appear (**Figure 8**).

4. Make sure the Preview check button is selected.

5. Use the Modify Curves for Channel drop-down list to select which channel will be adjusted (**Figure 9**). (It's best to use Value first. This is the combination of all three channels—Red, Green, and Blue. After correcting the Value, you can move on to individual channels, if need be.)

6. To adjust the darker tones of the image, position the mouse crosshair over the lower portion of the curve, press the left mouse button and drag the curve up or down (**Figure 10**).

7. To adjust the midtones of the image, position the mouse crosshair over the center portion of the curve, press the left mouse button and drag the curve up or down (**Figure 11**).

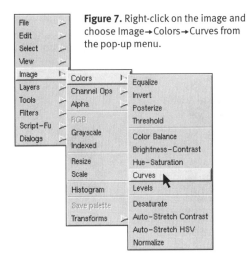

Figure 7. Right-click on the image and choose Image→Colors→Curves from the pop-up menu.

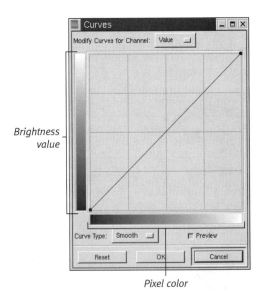

Figure 8. Use the Curves dialog box to adjust the color and tone of an image.

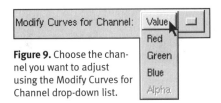

Figure 9. Choose the channel you want to adjust using the Modify Curves for Channel drop-down list.

USE CURVES TO ADJUST COLOR AND TONE

Figure 10. Drag the lower part of the curve up or down to adjust the darker tones in the image.

Dark tone area ——

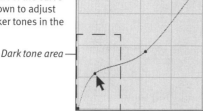

Figure 11. Drag the middle part of the curve up or down to adjust the midtones in the image.

Midtone area ——

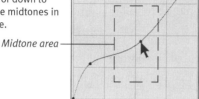

Light tone area

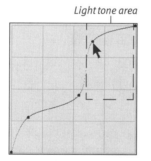

Figure 12. Drag the upper part of the curve up or down to adjust the lighter tones in the image.

8. To adjust the lighter tones of the image, position the mouse crosshair over the upper portion of the curve, press the left mouse button and drag the curve up or down (**Figure 12**).

9. When you are finished adjusting the curves, click OK to close the Curves dialog box. Curves allow you to adjust color and tone in interesting ways (**Figures 13a–b**).

✔ Tips

- The best way to learn how to use Curves is to experiment. Open an image and see how an image changes when the curve is dragged different ways in the Curves dialog box.

- You can adjust the curves of an alpha channel. If your image contains one, you'll be able to select it using the Modify Curves for Channel drop-down list shown in Figure 9.

- If you decide you don't like the changes you have made to the curve in the Curves dialog box, you can start over by clicking the Reset button.

USE CURVES TO ADJUST COLOR AND TONE

Figure 13a. The original image before curves are adjusted.

Figure 13b. The image after curves adjustment. Notice how the lights and darks have been emphasized.

Color Balance

When adjusting individual color elements in an image, it's important to remember that each color adjustment affects the overall color balance of an image. The Color Balance command is used to change the color mixture in an image. This tool uses a generalized color correction, creating subtle changes in color.

To adjust color balance:

1. Use the Layers & Channels dialog box to select a layer. (For details about how to do this, turn to page 92.)

2. If you wish, use the selection tool of your choice to select an area of the image. (For directions on how to use the selection tools, turn to Chapter 6, *Making Selecitons*.)

3. Right-click on the image and choose Image→Colors→Color Balance from the pop-up menu (**Figure 14**). The Color Balance dialog box will appear (**Figure 15**).

4. Make sure the Preview check button is selected.

5. Select the radio button next to the color tone you would like to adjust: Shadows, Midtones, or Highlights (**Figure 16**).

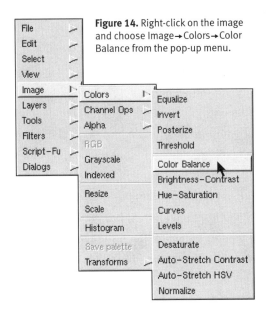

Figure 14. Right-click on the image and choose Image→Colors→Color Balance from the pop-up menu.

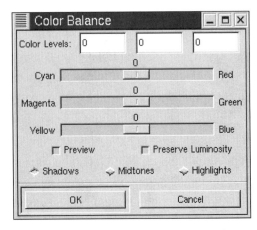

Figure 15. Use the Color Balance dialog box to adjust the color values in an image.

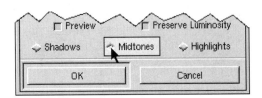

Figure 16. Select the radio button next to the color tone you would like to adjust—Shadow, Midtones, or Highlights.

Complementary colors   *Channel names*

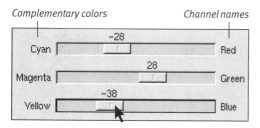

Figure 17. Use the channel sliders to adjust the color balance.

Red   Green   Blue

Figure 18. Enter new color levels in the appropriate channel text boxes.

6. Use the channel slider to adjust the color balance (**Figure 17**). Notice that there is a slider for each channel. The channel name—Red, Green, or Blue—is listed at the right side of the slider. Each channel's complementary color is listed at the left side of the slider.

or

Enter values for each channel in the Color Levels text boxes (**Figure 18**). The left text box corresponds to the Red channel, the center text box corresponds to the Green channel, and the right text box corresponds to the Blue channel. You can enter values from -100 up to 100. Zero (0) represents the current setting of the image.

7. When you are finished adjusting the color balance, click OK. Or click Cancel to close the Color Balance dialog box without applying any changes. Adjusting the color balance can make all the difference (**Figures 19a–b**).

Figure 19a. The original image before color balance adjustment. Notice how the shadows and highlights are very flat.

Figure 19b. The image after color balancing. Highlights and shadows have been emphasized, and midtones have been brightened.

Hue, Lightness, and Saturation

Hue–Saturation changes the color mixture in an image just as the Color Balance command does, but with more dramatic results. Using the Hue-Saturation command, you can adjust the hue, lightness, and saturation of an image's individual color components. This color adjustment tool is based on the HSV color model (for a description of this color model, turn to page 35).

To adjust hue, lightness, and saturation:

1. Use the Layers & Channels dialog box to select a layer. (For details about how to do this, turn to page 92.)

2. If you wish, use the selection tool of your choice to select an area of the image. (For directions on how to use the selection tools, turn to Chapter 6, *Making Selections*.)

3. Right-click on the image and choose Image→Colors→Hue–Saturation from the pop-up menu (**Figure 20**). The Hue–Saturation dialog box will appear (**Figure 21**).

4. Make sure the Preview check button is selected.

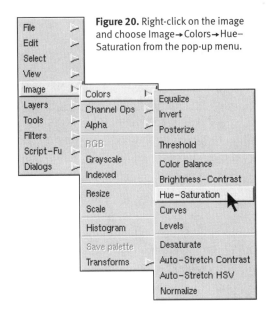

Figure 20. Right-click on the image and choose Image→Colors→Hue–Saturation from the pop-up menu.

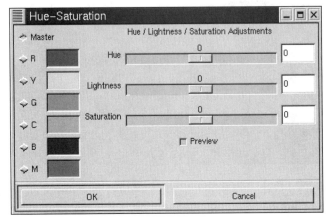

Figure 21. Use the Hue–Saturation dialog box to adjust the hue, lightness, and saturation of an image.

Figure 22. Select the radio button next to the color spectrum you want to adjust.

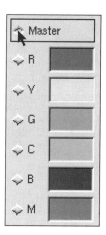

5. Select the radio button next to the part of the color spectrum you want to change—Master (a combination of all the colors), R (red), Y (yellow), G (green), C (cyan), B (blue), or M (magenta) (**Figure 22**). (It's best to start with Master since this is the combination of all the colors. After adjusting the Master, you can move on to individual colors, if need be.)

6. Use the Hue, Lightness, and Saturation sliders to adjust the color tone (**Figure 23**).

   or

   Enter a number in each of the corresponding text boxes at the right of the dialog box (**Figure 23**). You can enter values from -180 to 180. Zero (0) represents the current value of the image.

7. When you are finished adjusting the hue, lightness, and saturation, click OK. Or click Cancel to close the Hue–Saturation dialog box without applying any changes. Adjusting the hue, lightness, and saturation of an image can make all the difference (**Figures 24a–b**).

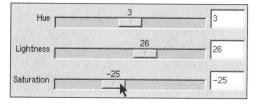

Figure 23. Use the sliders to adjust the Hue, Lightness, and Saturation. You can also enter values in the corresponding text boxes.

Figure 24a. The original image before hue, lightness, and saturation are adjusted. Notice the overall gray cast to the image.

Figure 24b. The image after adjusting hue, lightness, and saturation. The flower color (yellow) has been brightened considerably.

ADJUST HUE, LIGHTNESS, AND SATURATION

Brightness and Contrast

Like Curves and Levels, the Brightness–Contrast command adjusts the highlights, midtones, and shadows in an image, but in a simpler way. Instead of making adjustments channel by channel, Brightness-Contrast makes changes using all the pixel values in an image at the same time.

To adjust brightness and contrast:

1. Use the Layers & Channels dialog box to select a layer.

2. If you wish, use the selection tool of your choice to select an area of the image.

3. Right-click on the image and choose Image→Colors→Brightness–Contrast from the pop-up menu (**Figure 25**). The Brightness–Contrast dialog box will appear (**Figure 26**).

4. Make sure the Preview check button is selected.

5. Use the Brightness and Contrast sliders to adjust the image.

   or

   Enter a number in the corresponding text boxes at the right of the dialog box. You can enter values from -127 to 127. Zero (0) represents the current values of the image. The higher the setting for each slider, the brighter and more contrasted the image will be.

6. When you are finished adjusting the brightness and contrast, click OK. Or click Cancel to close the Brightness–Contrast dialog box without applying any changes. Brightness and contrast can make quite a difference (**Figures 27a–b**).

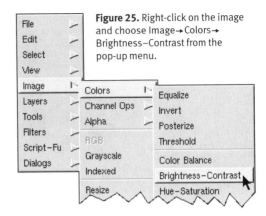

Figure 25. Right-click on the image and choose Image→Colors→Brightness–Contrast from the pop-up menu.

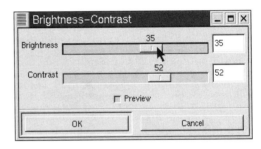

Figure 26. Use the Brightness–Contrast dialog box to adjust the brightness and contrast values of an image.

Figure 27a. The original image before adjusting brightness and contrast.

Figure 27b. The image after brightness and contrast adjustment. Notice how the lights and darks are emphasized.

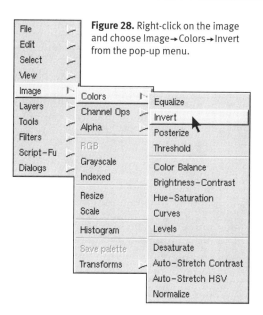

Figure 28. Right-click on the image and choose Image→Colors→Invert from the pop-up menu.

Specialized Adjustments

There are several other commands that also change the brightness values and colors in an image. These include Invert, Equalize, Desaturate, Posterize, Threshold, and three automatic color enhancement commands— Normalize, Auto-stretch Contrast, and Auto-stretch HSV. In many cases, these specialized commands create dramatic effects that can be applied to entire layers or selected areas. By and large, these commands are used to create special effects and enhance the color in an image rather than correct it.

Invert

The Invert command switches pixel color values with opposite color values, making a positive image appear as a negative and a negative image appear as a positive.

To invert a layer or selection:

1. Use the Layers & Channels dialog box to select a layer. (For details about how to do this, turn to page 92.)

2. If you wish, use the selection tool of your choice to select an area of the image. (For directions on how to use the selection tools, turn to Chapter 6, *Making Selections.*)

3. Right-click on the image and choose Image→Colors→Invert from the pop-up menu (**Figure 28**). The colors in the image will invert (**Figures 29a–b**).

Figure 29a. The original image before inversion.

Figure 29b. The image after the Invert command is chosen.

Equalize

The Equalize command finds the brightest and darkest values in an image and averages them out so the darkest value becomes black and the brightest value becomes white. This command can improve dark images or images that don't have enough contrast.

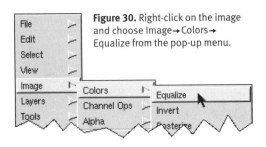

Figure 30. Right-click on the image and choose Image→Colors→ Equalize from the pop-up menu.

To equalize a layer or selection:

1. Use the Layers & Channels dialog box to select a layer. (For details about how to do this, turn to page 92.)

2. If you wish, use the selection tool of your choice to select an area of the image.

3. Right-click on the image and choose Image→Colors→Equalize from the pop-up menu (**Figure 30**). The area or layer will be brightened and contrast will be added (**Figures 31a–b**).

Figure 31a.
The original image before being equalized.

Desaturate

The Desaturate command removes color from the currently selected layer or selection. You can create an attention-getting effect by leaving one object colored while removing all other color from an image.

Figure 31b.
The image after the Equalize command is applied.

To desaturate a layer or selection:

1. Use the Layers & Channels dialog box to select a layer. (For details about how to do this, turn to page 92.)

2. If you wish, use the selection tool of your choice to select an area of the image. (For directions on how to use the selection tools, turn to Chapter 6, *Making Selections.*)

3. Right-click on the image and choose Image→Colors→Desaturate from the pop-up menu (**Figure 32**). The color in the layer will change to grayscale.

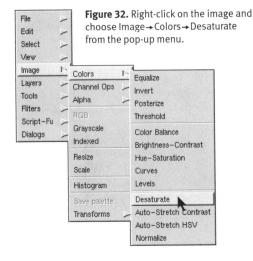

Figure 32. Right-click on the image and choose Image→Colors→Desaturate from the pop-up menu.

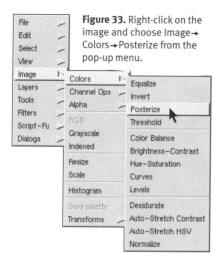

Figure 33. Right-click on the image and choose Image→Colors→Posterize from the pop-up menu.

Figure 34. Enter a number in the Posterize Levels text box. A value between 2 and 10 creates dramatic results.

Figure 35a.
The image before being posterized.

Figure 35b.
The image after the Posterize command, set to 6 levels, is chosen.

Posterize

The Posterize command reduces the number of color levels in the currently selected layer or selected area to a specific number of levels.

To posterize a layer or selection:

1. Use the Layers & Channels dialog box to select the layer you want to posterize. (For details about how to do this, turn to page 92.)

2. If you wish, use the selection tool of your choice to select an area of the image. (For directions on how to use the selection tools, turn to Chapter 6, *Making Selections*.)

3. Right-click on the image and choose Image→Colors→Posterize from the pop-up menu (**Figure 33**). The Posterize dialog box will appear (**Figure 34**).

4. Make sure the Preview check button is selected.

5. Enter the number of levels you would like to use in the Posterize Levels text box.

6. Click OK to apply the posterize effect to the image or click Cancel to close the Posterize dialog box without applying the effect. Applying the Posterize command to an image can create interesting results (**Figures 35a–b**).

✔ Tip

■ For dramatic effects, enter a number between 2 and 10 in the Posterize Levels text box. The default setting is 3.

POSTERIZE A LAYER OR SELECTION

Threshold

The Threshold command changes color or grayscale images to high contrast, black and white images. With this command, you can specify a threshold range. Any pixels lighter than the specified threshold are converted to white. Any pixels darker than the specified threshold are converted to black.

To make a layer or selection high contrast:

1. Use the Layers & Channels dialog box to select a layer. (For details about how to do this, turn to page 92.)

2. If you wish, use the selection tool of your choice to select an area of the image. (For directions on how to use the selection tools, turn to Chapter 6, *Making Selections*.)

3. Right-click on the image and choose Image→Colors→Threshold from the pop up menu (**Figure 36**). The Threshold dialog box will open (**Figure 37**).

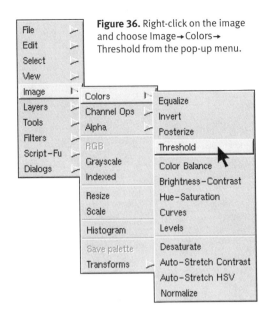

Figure 36. Right-click on the image and choose Image→Colors→Threshold from the pop-up menu.

MAKE A LAYER OR SELECTION HIGH CONTRAST

Histogram brightness window   Range bar

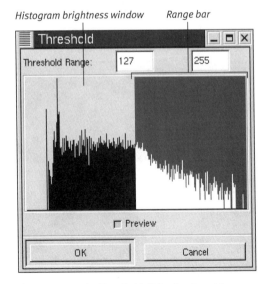

Figure 37. Use the Threshold dialog box to set the number of black and white pixels in an image.

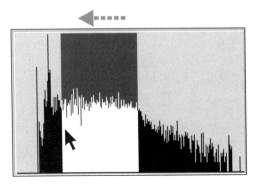

Figure 38. Increase the number of white pixels in the image by clicking in the histogram brightness window and dragging the range bar to the left.

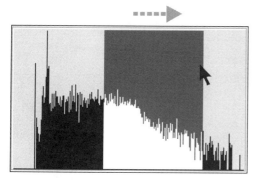

Figure 39. Increase the number of black pixels in the image by clicking in the histogram brightness window and dragging the range bar to the right.

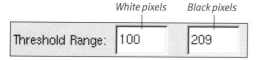

White pixels   *Black pixels*

Threshold Range: 100   209

Figure 40. Enter values in the Threshold Range text boxes to set the number of white and black pixels in the image.

4. Make sure the Preview check button is selected.

5. Click in the histogram brightness window and drag the range bar to the left to increase the number of white pixels (**Figure 38**).

or

Click in the histogram brightness window and drag the range bar to the right to increase the number of black pixels (**Figure 39**).

or

Enter numbers in the Threshold Range text boxes. The left text box sets white pixel value, and the right text box sets black pixel value (**Figure 40**).

A preview of the settings you have chosen will appear in the image window (**Figure 41a–b**).

6. Click OK to apply the threshold effect to the image or click Cancel to close the Threshold dialog box without applying the effect.

Figure 41a. The image before the Threshold command is applied.

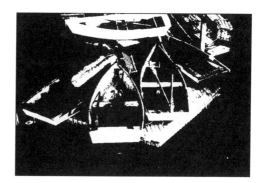

Figure 41b. After the Threshold command is applied, only black and white elements remain.

Automatic Color Enhancements

These three commands—Auto-Stretch Contrast, Auto-Stretch HSV, and Normalize—automatically enhance an image's color using various channels. Auto-stretch Contrast uses RGB channels to find the lowest and highest value of each channel and expand them to cover the full contrast range. Auto-stretch HSV, does the same thing as Auto-stretch Contrast, but using HSV channels instead. Just like Auto-stretch Contrast, Normalize also finds the lowest and highest value using RGB channels. But, Normalize combines the channel values instead of using them individually. (For a discussion about the RGB and HSV color models, turn to pages 34–35. To learn more about channels, take a look at Chapter 13, *Channels and Layer Masks*.)

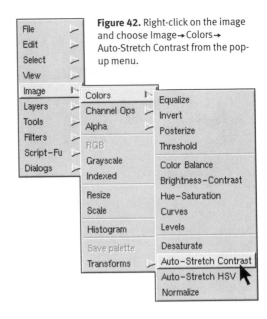

Figure 42. Right-click on the image and choose Image→Colors→ Auto-Stretch Contrast from the pop-up menu.

To apply Auto-stretch Contrast to a layer or selected area:

1. Use the Layers & Channels dialog box to select a layer. (For details about how to do this, turn to page 92.)

2. If you wish, use the selection tool of your choice to select an area of the image. (For directions on how to use the selection tools, turn to Chapter 6, *Making Selections*.)

3. Right-click on the image and choose Image→Colors→Auto-Stretch Contrast from the pop-up menu (**Figure 42**). The command will automatically read the RGB values and enhance the image (**Figure 43a–b**).

✔ Tip

■ Generally, this command will give an image a red cast.

Figure 43a. The original image before Auto-stretch Contrast is applied.

Figure 43b. The image tone is adjusted when Auto-stretch Contrast is chosen. Notice how the lights and darks in the image are emphasized.

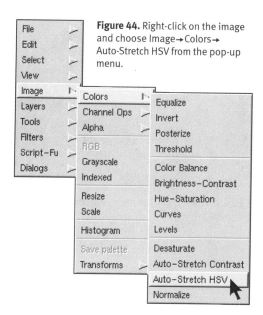

Figure 44. Right-click on the image and choose Image→Colors→ Auto-Stretch HSV from the pop-up menu.

To apply Auto-stretch HSV to a layer or selected area:

1. Use the Layers & Channels dialog box to select a layer. (For details about how to do this, turn to page 92.)

2. If you wish, use the selection tool of your choice to select an area of the image. (For directions on how to use the selection tools, turn to Chapter 6, *Making Selections.*)

3. Right-click on the image and choose Image→Colors→Auto-Stretch HSV from the pop-up menu (**Figure 44**). The command will automatically read the HSV values and enhance the image (**Figure 45a–b**).

✔ Tip

■ Generally, this command will give an image a yellow cast.

Figure 45a. The original image before Auto-stretch HSV is applied.

Figure 45b. After the color and tone of the image are adjusted using the HSV color model, the highlights in this image are more pronounced.

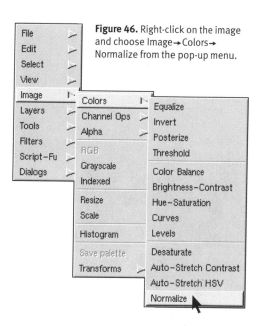

Figure 46. Right-click on the image and choose Image→Colors→ Normalize from the pop-up menu.

To apply Normalize to a layer or selected area:

1. Use the Layers & Channels dialog box to select a layer. (For details about how to do this, turn to page 92.)

2. If you wish, use the selection tool of your choice to select an area of the image. (For directions on how to use the selection tools, turn to Chapter 6, *Making Selections*.)

3. Right-click on the image and choose Image→Colors→Normalize from the pop-up menu (**Figure 46**). The command will automatically read the combined RGB values and enhance the image (**Figure 47a–b**).

✔ Tip

■ Normalize works well for enhancing scanned photos and images.

Figure 47a. The original image before the Normalize command is chosen.

Figure 47b. After choosing Normalize, the image's tone is brightened considerably.

Summary

In this chapter you learned how to:

◆ Use Levels and Curves to adjust the colors and tones of an image

◆ Adjust the color balance of an image

◆ Change hue, lightness, saturation, brightness, and contrast in an image

◆ Invert a layer or selection

◆ Equalize a layer or selection

◆ Desaturate a layer or selection

◆ Posterize a layer or selection

◆ Apply the Threshold command

◆ Use the automatic color enhancement tools

NORMALIZE A LAYER OR SELECTION

TRANSFORM YOUR ART

10

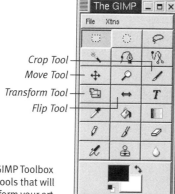

Crop Tool
Move Tool
Transform Tool
Flip Tool

Figure 1. The GIMP Toolbox contains four tools that will help you transform your art.

Figure 2. Select the area you want to move using one of the selection tools.

Figure 3. Drag the selected area to its new position. In this figure, the space left behind by the moved area is automatically filled with the current background color because the image only contains one layer.

A s you may have already noticed, there are four transformation tools available in the GIMP Toolbox (**Figure 1**). The transformation tools alter an image in some way, making it look different. For instance, using these tools you can *flip* an image horizontally or vertically, rotate a portion of an image, or even *crop* the image down to a smaller size. Transformations are fast and easy, so let's get started!

The Move Tool

The Move Tool lets you, well, move things. There are two ways to move things: you can select an area, then immediately move it without using the Move Tool; or select an area, make it float, then move it using the Move Tool.

To move a selected area without using the Move Tool:

1. Select the area you want to move using one of the selection tools (**Figure 2**).

2. Position the mouse pointer over the selection, press the left mouse button and drag. The selected area will move (**Figure 3**).

To move a selected area using the Move Tool:

1. Select the area you want to move using one of the selection tools (**Figure 4**). (For details about using the selection tools, turn to Chapter 6, *Making Selections.*)

2. Click the Move Tool in the GIMP Toolbox to select it or press M on the keyboard. The mouse pointer will change to double-headed arrows.

3. Right-click on the image and choose Select→Float from the pop-up menu (**Figure 5**) or press Shift+Ctrl+L on the keyboard. The selected area will become a floating selection. (To learn more about floating selections, turn to page 99.)

4. Position the mouse pointer over the floating selection, press the left mouse button, and drag the selection to a new position (**Figures 6a–b**).

✔ Tips

■ When the Move Tool is selected, you can *nudge* a floating selection up, down, or sideways, using the arrow keys on the keyboard.

■ To anchor the floating selection back to the layer it came from, move the mouse pointer outside of the selected area. The mouse pointer will change to a downward pointing arrow. Click. The layer will be anchored.

Figure 4. If you wish, select the area that you want to move. In this figure, the body of the fish is selected.

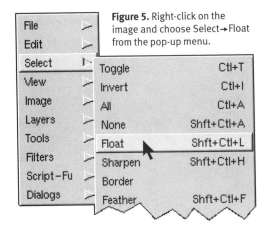

Figure 5. Right-click on the image and choose Select→Float from the pop-up menu.

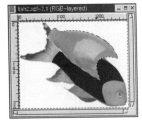

Figure 6a. When a selection is moved on the Background layer, the exposed area is filled with the current background color (in this case black).

Figure 6b. When a selection is moved on a layer, the exposed area is filled with transparency.

Cropping rectangle

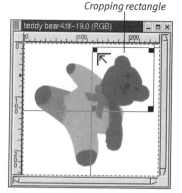

Figure 7. Drag the mouse to create a cropping rectangle. Everything within the cropping rectangle will remain after the image is cropped.

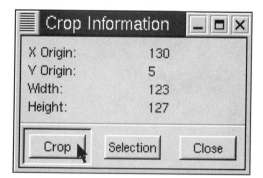

Figure 8. The Crop Information box tells you the width, height, and location of the selected area.

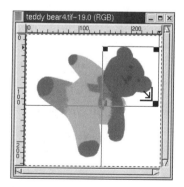

Figure 9. Drag the mouse to resize the cropping rectangle.

The Crop Tool

When an image is cropped, unneeded edges or portions of the image are cut away.

To crop an image:

1. Click the Crop Tool in the Toolbox to select it or press Shift+C on the keyboard. The mouse pointer will change to a crosshair.

2. Position the mouse at the upper-left corner of the area you want to keep.

3. Press the left mouse button and drag diagonally down to the right to select the area you want to keep (**Figure 7**). Horizontal and vertical lines forming a *cropping rectangle* will appear, indicating the area that you have selected. The rectangle will contain four black *handles*—black squares—that let you resize and move the cropping rectangle. Also, a Crop Information dialog box will open (**Figure 8**).

4. If you need to make the cropping rectangle smaller or larger, you can resize it:

   A. Position the mouse crosshair over either the top-left or bottom-right handle. The mouse pointer will change to an arrow pointing into a corner (**Figure 9**).

   B. Press the left mouse button and drag to resize the cropping rectangle.

   C. Release the left mouse button when you are happy with the size and shape of the cropping rectangle.

(continued)

CROP TOOL: CROP AN IMAGE

5. If you need to move the cropping rectangle to a new position:

    A. Position the mouse crosshair over either the bottom-left or top-right handle. The mouse pointer will change to a double-headed arrow that looks like the Move Tool (**Figure 10**).

    B. Press the left mouse button and drag the cropping rectangle to a new position.

    C. Release the left mouse button when you are happy with the position of the cropping rectangle.

6. To crop the image either click Crop in the Crop Information dialog box or position the mouse pointer at the center of the cropping rectangle and click. The edges of the image not included in the cropping rectangle will disappear (**Figure 11**).

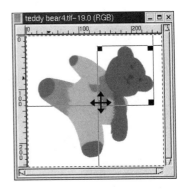

Figure 10. When you position the mouse pointer over the bottom-left or top-right handle, the pointer changes to look like the Move Tool.

Figure 11. After cropping an image, the area inside the cropping rectangle remains.

✔ Tips

- You can also crop a selected area using the Crop Tool. To do this, select the area you want to save using the selection tool of your choice. Next, click the Crop Tool in the Toolbox and click in the center of the selected area. The Crop Information dialog box will appear (**Figure 8**). Click Selection. A cropping rectangle will appear around the selected area. Click Crop. The edges not included in the cropping rectangle will disappear.

- If you decide not to crop an area after selecting it with the Crop Tool, click Close in the Crop Information dialog box and the cropping rectangle will disappear.

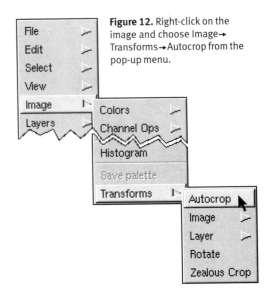

Figure 12. Right-click on the image and choose Image→Transforms→Autocrop from the pop-up menu.

Figure 13a. This is the original image before the Autocrop command is chosen.

Autocrop and Zealous Crop

There are two other ways to crop an image in the GIMP—using the Autocrop or Zealous Crop commands. The Autocrop command removes excess space around an image by detecting pixels that contain no color variation—all white, all black, or all red, for instance—then, cropping in to pixels with color variation. Zealous crop works just like Autocrop, but with one difference, in addition to cropping the edges of an image, it also moves objects together eliminating any extra space between them.

To apply Autocrop to an image:

Right-click on the image and choose Image→ Transforms→Autocrop from the pop-up menu (**Figure 12**). The image will be cropped (**Figures 13a–b**).

To apply Zealous Crop to an image:

Right-click on the image and choose Image→ Transforms→Zealous Crop from the pop-up menu (**Figure 14**). The image will be cropped (**Figure 15**).

Figure 13b.
When Autocrop is chosen, the extra area around the bears is cut away.

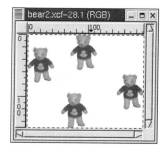

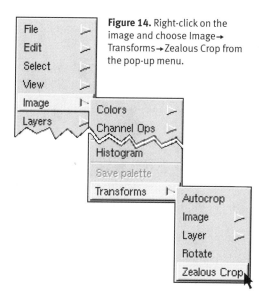

Figure 14. Right-click on the image and choose Image→ Transforms→Zealous Crop from the pop-up menu.

Figure 15. When Zealous Crop is selected, the extra area around the bears and between the bears is removed. Compare this image with the original image in Figure 13a.

The Flip Tool

With the Flip Tool, you can flip a selection or layer vertically or horizontally with just a click of the mouse.

To flip a selection or layer horizontally:

1. Use the Layers & Channels dialog box to select which layer will be flipped (for details about this dialog box, see page 92).

   and/or

   Use one of the selection tools of your choice to select an area. (For directions about using the selection tools, turn to Chapter 6, *Making Selections*.)

2. Double-click on the Flip Tool in the GIMP Toolbox. The Tool Options dialog box will open (**Figure 16**).

3. Select the Horizontal radio button.

4. Click Close to close the Tool Options dialog box.

5. With the Flip Tool selected, click on the layer or selected area. The layer or selection will flip horizontally (**Figures 17a–b**).

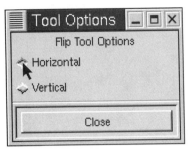

Figure 16. In the Tool Options dialog box, select the Horizontal radio button, then click Close.

Figure 17a. Position the mouse pointer over the layer or area you would like to flip.

Figure 17b. When you click the mouse, the layer or selection flips horizontally.

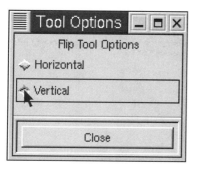

Figure 18. In the Tool Options dialog box, select the Vertical radio button, then click Close.

Figure 19a. When you click the mouse, the image flips vertically. Compare this image with the original shown in Figure 17a.

Figure 19b. This image has been flipped both horizontally and vertically.

To flip a selection or layer vertically:

1. Use the Layers & Channels dialog box to select which layer will be flipped (for details about this dialog box, see page 92).

   and/or

   Use one of the selection tools of your choice to select an area. (For directions about using the selection tools, turn to Chapter 6, *Making Selections*.)

2. Double-click on the Flip Tool in the GIMP Toolbox. The Tool Options dialog box will open (**Figure 18**).

3. Select the Vertical radio button.

4. Click Close to close the Tool Options dialog box.

5. With the Flip Tool selected, click on the layer or selected area. The layer or selection will flip vertically (**Figures 19a–b**).

What's Left after a Transformation?

If you apply a transformation to a layer or selection on a layer, any empty space that remains after the transformation will be replaced by transparency. If a selection on the Background layer is transformed, any empty space will be filled with the currently selected background color.

FLIP TOOL: FLIP AN IMAGE VERTICALLY

The Transform Tool

The Transform Tool is one of those all time great tools. With it you can rotate, scale, *shear*, and add *perspective* to an image.

To rotate a layer or selection using the Transform Tool:

1. Use the Layers & Channels dialog box to select which layer will be rotated.

   and/or

   Use one of the selection tools of your choice to select an area (**Figure 20**).

2. Double-click on the Transform Tool in the GIMP Toolbox. The Tool Options dialog box will open (**Figure 21**).

3. In the Transform area, select the Rotation radio button.

4. Click Close to close the Tool Options dialog box.

5. With the Transform Tool selected, position the mouse pointer over the image or selected area. The mouse pointer will change to swirling arrows.

6. Press the left mouse button and drag to the right or left. A yellow dashed rectangle with squares at the corners will appear and the image will rotate (**Figure 22**). In addition, a Rotation Information dialog box will open, displaying the angle of the layer or selection (**Figure 23**).

7. Release the left mouse button when you are happy with the rotation angle.

✔ Tip

■ To rotate an area in 15° increments, hold down the Ctrl key while rotating.

Figure 20. The bear is selected and ready to rotate.

Figure 21. In the Tool Options dialog box, select the Rotation radio button, then click Close.

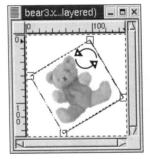

Figure 22. When you press the left mouse button and drag right or left, the layer or area rotates.

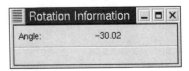

Figure 23. The Rotation Information dialog box displays the angle at which the layer or selection is rotated.

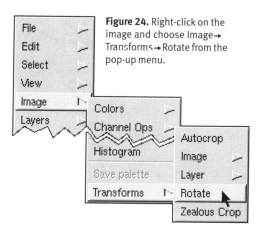

Figure 24. Right-click on the image and choose Image→ Transforms→Rotate from the pop-up menu.

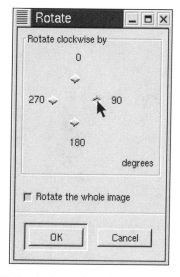

Figure 25. Use the Rotate dialog box to select the angle of rotation.

To rotate a selection or image in exact 90° increments:

1. If you wish, use one of the selection tools to select the area to be rotated (**Figure 20**).

2. Right-click on the image and choose Image→Transforms→Rotate from the pop-up menu (**Figure 24**). The Rotate dialog box will open (**Figure 25**).

3. In the Rotate clockwise by area, select one of the radio buttons to rotate the image or selection either 90, 180, or 270 degrees.

4. If you selected an area using one of the selection tools, make sure the Rotate the whole image check button is unselected. Otherwise, a GIMP Message will appear (**Figure 26**) and the selected area will not be rotated.

5. Click OK. The image or selection will rotate the specified amount (**Figure 27**) and the Rotate dialog box will close.

✔ Tip

- Another way to quickly rotate an image or selection either 90° or 270° is to right-click on the image and choose Image→ Transforms→Image, then choose either Rotate 270 or Rotate 90 from the Image menu.

Figure 27. When you click OK in the Rotate dialog box, the image rotates the specified amount. Compare this image with the original in Figure 20.

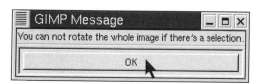

Figure 26. This message appears if an area is selected and the Rotate the whole image check button is selected in the Rotate dialog box as well.

Scaling and Resizing an Image

Scaling and resizing both change the size of an image but with different results. Scaling changes both the size of the image display area and the image itself. Resizing changes the size of the image display area, but doesn't alter the image. (It works the same way for scaling and resizing a layer as discussed on page 96.)

Unfortunately, the GIMP is a bit inconsistent with scaling. When an image is scaled using the Scale command found on the Image menu, it follows the scaling rule as stated above. However, when an image is scaled using the Transform Tool, only the image size changes—the image display area remains the same.

To scale a selected area or layer using the Transform Tool:

1. Use the Layers & Channels dialog box to select which layer will be rotated (for details about this dialog box, see page 92).

   and/or

   Use one of the selection tools of your choice to select an area.

2. Double-click on the Transform Tool in the GIMP Toolbox. The Tool Options dialog box will open (**Figure 28**).

3. In the Transform area, select the Scaling radio button.

4. Click Close to close the Tool Options dialog box.

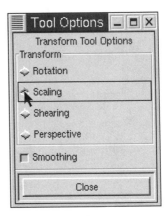

Figure 28. In the Tool Options dialog box, select the Scaling radio button, then click Close.

Figure 29. When you drag the mouse, the image scales to a new size.

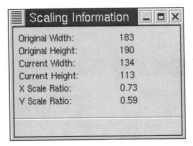

Figure 30. The Scaling Information dialog box displays the original and new width and heights of the image.

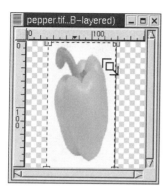

Figure 31. If you hold down the Shift key while dragging, only the width of the selection or layer scales.

Figure 32. If you hold down the Ctrl key while dragging, only the height of the selection or layer scales.

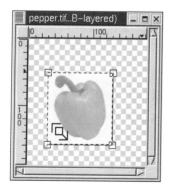

Figure 33. If you hold down both the Shift and Ctrl keys while dragging, the selection or layer scales proportionally.

5. With the Transform Tool selected, position the mouse pointer over the image or selected area. The mouse pointer will change to an arrow connected to a square.

6. Press the left mouse button and drag in any direction (up, down, sideways, or diagonally). A yellow dashed rectangle with squares at the corners will appear and the selection or layer will scale up or down (**Figure 29**). In addition, a Scaling Information dialog box will open, displaying the old and new width and height of the selection or layer (**Figure 30**).

7. When you are pleased with the new size of the scaled selection or layer, release the left mouse button.

✔ Tips

■ To only change the width of a selection or layer, hold down the Shift key while dragging (**Figure 31**).

■ To only change the height of a selection or layer, hold down the Ctrl key while dragging (**Figure 32**).

■ To scale a selection or layer keeping both the width and height proportionally the same, hold down both the Shift and Ctrl keys while dragging (**Figure 33**).

Repeating a Transformation

To repeat the last transformation, right-click on the image and choose Filters→ Repeat last from the pop-up menu or press Atl+F on the keyboard.

TRANSFORM TOOL: SCALE AN IMAGE

To scale an image using the Scale command:

1. Right-click on the image and choose Image→Scale from the pop-up menu (**Figure 34**). The Image Scale dialog box will open (**Figure 35**).

2. Enter new dimensions (in pixels) in the New width and New height text boxes.

   or

   Enter new proportions in the X ratio and Y ratio text boxes, where X is the width and Y is the height.

3. If you want to keep the width and height of the image proportionally the same, make sure the Constrain Ratio check button is selected.

4. Click OK. The image display area and the image itself will scale to the new size (**Figures 36a–b**) and the Image Scale dialog box will close.

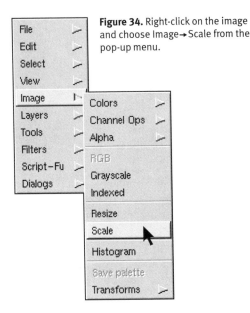

Figure 34. Right-click on the image and choose Image→Scale from the pop-up menu.

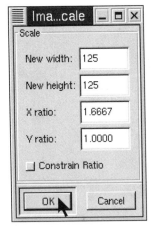

Figure 35. Use the Image Scale dialog box to set the new width and height of the image. If you select the Constrain Ratio check button, the width and height will remain proportionally the same.

Figure 36b. The image scaled using the width and height shown in the Image Scale dialog box in Figure 35. Notice that the width and height are not proportionally the same and that the image has been stretched horizontally.

Figure 36a. This is the original image before it is scaled.

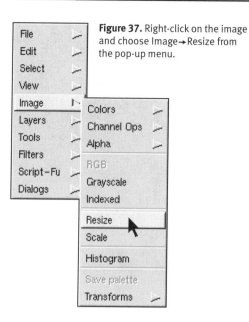

Figure 37. Right-click on the image and choose Image→Resize from the pop-up menu.

To resize an image:

1. Right-click on the image and choose Image→Resize from the pop-up menu (**Figure 37**). The Image Resize dialog box will open (**Figure 38**).

2. Enter new dimensions (in pixels) in the New width and New height text boxes.

   or

   Enter new proportions in the X ratio and Y ratio text boxes, where X is the width and Y is the height.

3. If you want to keep the width and height of the image proportionally the same, make sure the Constrain Ratio check button is selected.

4. If the new size of the image display area will be smaller than it originally was, you can set where the image (which will remain at its original size) will be positioned using the X and Y Offset text boxes or the preview window. Enter pixel amounts in the text boxes or position the mouse pointer over the original image display area rectangle, press the left mouse button, and drag the rectangle to a new position.

5. Click OK. The image display area will resize (**Figure 39**) and the Image Scale dialog box will close.

Figure 38. Use the Image Resize dialog box to set a new width and height for the image. You can also change the image size using the X and Y ratio text boxes.

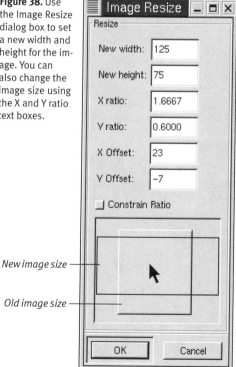

New image size

Old image size

Figure 39. This image has been resized. Notice that the size of the image display area has changed, but the image itself has not. The original image is shown in Figure 36a.

Shearing a Layer or Selection

Shearing moves the vertical planes of an image up or down, or horizontal planes sideways, creating a leaning effect. You can shear a selected area or a layer. (Remember that if your image consists of one layer, the Background, then the entire image will be sheared.)

To shear a layer or selection:

1. Use the Layers & Channels dialog box to select which layer will be sheared.

   and/or

   Use one of the selection tools of your choice to select an area (**Figure 40**).

2. Double-click on the Transform Tool in the GIMP Toolbox. The Tool Options dialog box will open (**Figure 41**).

3. In the Transform area, select the Shearing radio button.

4. Click Close to close the Tool Options dialog box.

5. With the Transform Tool selected, position the mouse pointer over the image or selected area. The mouse pointer will change to a black arrow.

6. Position the mouse pointer over the layer or selection.

7. Press the left mouse button and drag either up, down, left, or right. A dashed rectangle with squares at the corners will appear and the image will shear vertically or horizontally (**Figure 42**). In addition, a Shearing Information dialog box will open, displaying X and Y Shear Magnitude (**Figure 43**). If you drag left or up, the Shear Magnitude values will be positive. If you drag right or down, the values will be negative.

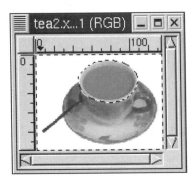

Figure 40. If you wish, you can select the area that will be skewed. In this figure, the tea in the cup is selected.

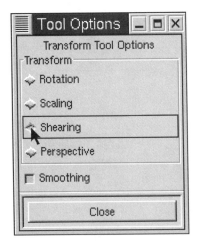

Figure 41. In the Tool Options dialog box, select the Shearing radio button, then click Close.

Figure 42. Drag the mouse to shear the image.

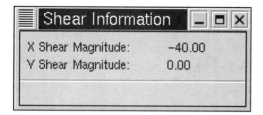

Figure 43. The Shear Information dialog box displays the amount of X and Y shearing.

Figure 44. In the Tool Options dialog box, select the Perspective radio button, then click Close.

Figure 45. When you click on the image, a dashed rectangle with squares at the corners appears.

Adding Perspective

Adding perspective to a layer or selection gives the illusion that the area is receding to a vanishing point. (Remember that if your image consists of one layer, the Background, then perspective will be added to the entire image.)

To add perspective to a layer or selection:

1. Use the Layers & Channels dialog box to select which layer will be sheared (for details about this dialog box, see page 92).

   and/or

   Use one of the selection tools of your choice to select an area.

2. Double-click on the Transform Tool in the GIMP Toolbox. The Tool Options dialog box will open (**Figure 44**).

3. In the Transform area, select the Perspective radio button.

4. Select the Smoothing check button if you want the edges of the image blurred to create a smooth look.

5. Click Close to close the Tool Options dialog box.

(continued)

6. With the Transform Tool selected, position the mouse pointer over the image or selected area.

7. Click. A dashed rectangle with squares at the corners will appear (**Figure 45**).

8. Position the mouse pointer over one of the corner squares, press the left mouse button and drag. The perspective of the image will change (**Figure 46**).

9. Continue dragging the corner squares until the effect you want is achieved (**Figure 47**).

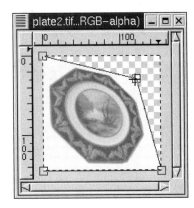

Figure 46. When you drag one of the squares, the perspective of the image changes.

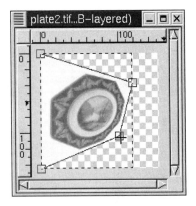

Figure 47. Continue dragging the squares until the perspective of the image is the way you want it.

Summary

In this chapter you learned how to:

◆ Move a selected area

◆ Crop an image

◆ Flip a layer or selection horizontally or vertically

◆ Rotate a layer or selection

◆ Scale an image

◆ Resize an image

◆ Shear a layer or selection

◆ Add perspective

TRANSFORM TOOL: ADD PERSPECTIVE

© Federico Mena Quintero

© Federico Mena Quintero

Federico Mena Quintero has created some wonderful text art using the GIMP. To see more and find out how he created the images you see here, visit his Website at:

http://luthien.nuclecu.unam.mx/~federico/gimp/

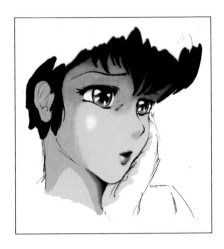

Marco Lamberto sketches his art by hand as shown in the drawings on the left side on these two pages. He then scans the sketches and uses the GIMP to create the special effects shown on the right side. To see more of Marco's art, as well as descriptions of his techniques, go to:

http://www.geocities.com/marcolamberto/slm/

The images on these two pages are ©Marco Lamberto.

Erin Parker's Background ©Nathan Oostendorp

Beginning of Fall 98 ©Nathan Oostendorp

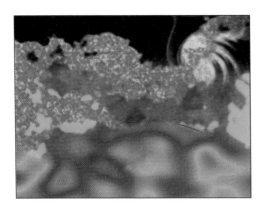

Horizon2 ©Nathan Oostendorp

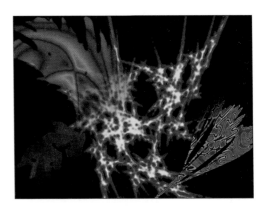

IfsWorship ©Nathan Oostendorp

Nate Oostendorp creates interesting GIMP art using different textures and shapes. To see more of Nate's work, go to:

http://www.oostendorp.net/gimpart/

Space ©Tuomas Kuosmanen

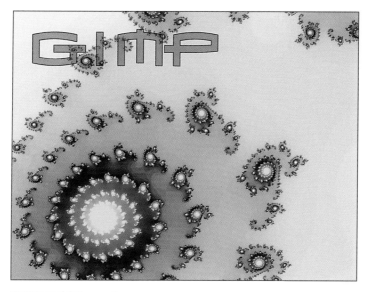

GIMP Fractal ©Tuomas Kuosmanen

Tuomas Kuosmanen creates wall paper (two of which are shown above) and Web graphics using the GIMP. To see more of his art, visit his great Web site at:

http://tigert.gimp.org/

Chaotic Moonlight ©Hirotsuna Mizuno

On The Beach ©Hirotsuna Mizuno

Hirotsuna Mizuno creates colorful, often surreal art. To see more of his work, go to:

http://www.u-aizu.ac.jp/%7es1041150/

Chilly Candles ©Hirotsuna Mizuno

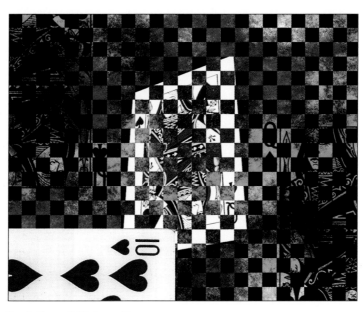

Spade Queen ©Hirotsuna Mizuno

Kayaking the Grand Canyon ©Harold Davis

Evolution Lake ©Harold Davis

The appearance of motion in the top picture was created using the GIMP's Motion Blur filter. To find out how to create this effect, turn to page 238. The lower image was originally a color photograph. The GIMP's Old Photo script-fu was applied to give it the look of an old sepia-tone photograph. For details on creating this effect, see page 256.

LAYER TECHNIQUES

Figure 1. Right-click on the image and choose Layers→ Layers & Channels from the pop-up menu.

In Chapter 7, *A Layer Primer*, you discovered the basics of what layers are and how they work. In this chapter, you'll learn more about layers—locking them together, as well as rotating and aligning layers. In addition, you'll find out about blending modes and how to use them to create special effects.

Locking Layers Together

If you have created an image using several layers, you may want to lock them together. That way, if one of the locked layers is moved, the entire group of layers will move, keeping the image intact.

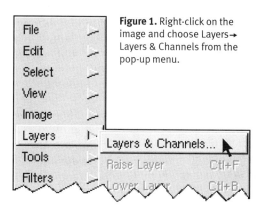

Locked layers

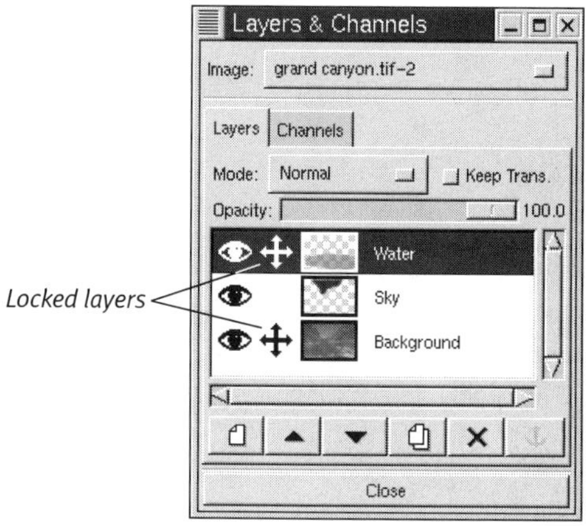

Figure 2. When the double-headed arrows appear, you know that the layers are locked together.

To lock layers together:

1. Right-click on the layered image and choose Layers→Layers & Channels from the pop up menu (**Figure 1**). The Layers & Channels dialog box will open (**Figure 2**).

2. Position the mouse pointer over one of the layers you want to lock together.

3. Click in the area between the eye icon and the layer thumbnail. An icon that looks like the Move Tool will appear (**Figure 2**). All layers displaying the crossed arrow icon will be locked together.

Moving Layers as a Unit

Once layers are locked together, it's easy to move them as one unit with the Move Tool.

To move layers as a unit:

1. Lock the layers together that you want to move as a unit.

2. Select the Move Tool from the GIMP Toolbox.

3. Position the mouse pointer over the image, press the left mouse button, and drag. The layers will move together.

Figure 3. Click the eye icon to hide any layers you don't want aligned. In this figure, all layers are visible.

Types of Alignment

There are so many options in the plug_in_align_layers dialog box (**Figure 5**) that it can become a bit confusing! Below are illustrations that show how horizontal and vertical alignment work together. Not all the possibilities are listed here, but this sampling should give you a pretty good idea of what is possible. In the caption below each illustration, the first word is the Horizontal Base setting and the second word is the Vertical Base setting. For these illustrations, the Horizontal Style and Vertical Style settings were both set to Collect.

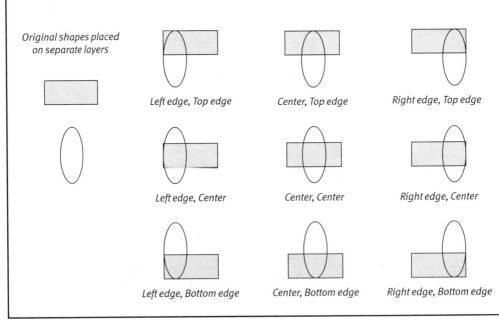

Original shapes placed on separate layers

Left edge, Top edge   Center, Top edge   Right edge, Top edge

Left edge, Center   Center, Center   Right edge, Center

Left edge, Bottom edge   Center, Bottom edge   Right edge, Bottom edge

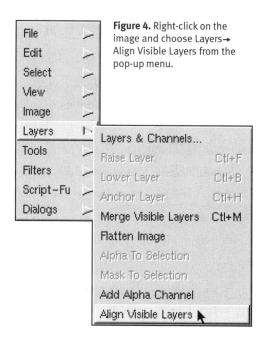

Figure 4. Right-click on the image and choose Layers→ Align Visible Layers from the pop-up menu.

Aligning Layers

The Align Visible Layers command can be used to precisely align all visible (of course!) layers. If you don't want to align a particular layer, just use the Layers & Channels dialog box to hide it (for directions about how to do this, turn to page 98).

To align visible layers:

1. Use the Layers & Channels dialog box to hide the layers you *don't* want aligned (**Figure 3**).

2. Right-click on the image and choose Layers→Align Visible Layers from the pop-up menu (**Figure 4**). The plug_in_align_layers dialog box will open (**Figure 5**).

3. In the Parameter settings area, use the Horizontal style drop-down list to set how the layers will be positioned horizontally in relation to themselves. There are five settings for this option: None, Collect, Fill (left to right), Fill (right to left), or Snap to grid.

4. Use the Horizontal base drop-down list to set the edge to which the layers will line up: Left edge, Center, or Right edge.

5. Use the Vertical style drop-down list to set how the layers will be positioned vertically in relation to themselves. There are five settings for this option: None, Collect, Fill (top to bottom), Fill (bottom to top), Snap to grid.

6. Use the Vertical base drop-down list to set the edge to which the layers will line up: Top edge, Center, or Bottom edge.

(continued)

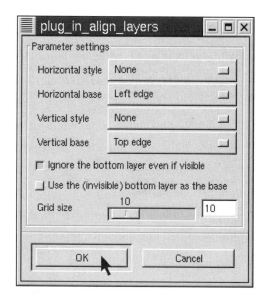

Figure 5. Use the plug_in_align_layers dialog box to set how the visible layers are aligned.

ALIGN VISIBLE LAYERS

165

7. Select the Ignore the bottom layer even if visible check button if you don't want the bottommost layer to move. This is a good idea when the Background layer is selected, because most times you won't want the background moving.

8. Select the Use the (invisible) bottom layer as the base check button if you want the bottommost layer to be aligned. Even if the Background layer is hidden, this option will group the layer with all other visible layers and align them.

9. Use the Grid size slider to set up a grid to which the layers can align (this slider is only relevant if you select Snap to grid from either the Horizontal or Vertical style drop-down lists).

10. Click OK. The plug_in_align_layers dialog box will close and the layers will be aligned (**Figures 6a–b**).

✔ Tips

■ To align layers exactly on top of one another, select Collect from both the Horizontal and Vertical style drop-down lists, and select Center from both the Horizontal and Vertical base drop-down lists.

■ If you decide to use a grid for alignment, you should know that by default the grid is invisible. To view a grid, right-click on the image and choose Filters→Render→ Grid from the pop-up menu (**Figure 7**). A Grid dialog box will open (**Figure 8**). Set the X and Y size to the same Grid size you set using the slider in the plug_in_align_layers dialog box. Click OK in the Grid dialog box. The Grid dialog box will close and a grid will appear on your image.

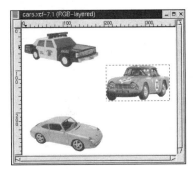

Figure 6a. This image shows the original layout of the three cars. Each car is on its own layer (the layers are displayed in Figure 3).

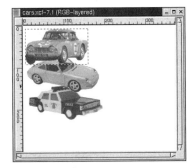

Figure 6b. The three cars after they have been aligned using the plug_in_align_layers dialog box. The cars were aligned using the following settings: Horizontal style, Fill (left to right); Horizontal base, Left edge; Vertical style, Fill (top to bottom); Vertical base, center.

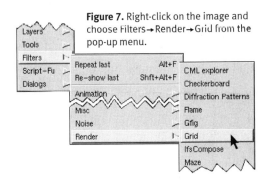

Figure 7. Right-click on the image and choose Filters→Render→Grid from the pop-up menu.

Figure 9. In the Grid dialog box, enter the grid size in the X and Y Size text boxes. Make sure the grid size in this dialog box matches the grid size in the plug_in_align_layers dialog box (shown in Figure 5).

Rotating Layers

There are two ways to rotate layers—you can use the Transform Tool or the Rotate command. While the Transform Tool will rotate a layer to any degree, the Rotate command will only rotate to 90 or 270 degrees. Turn to page 154 for directions on how to rotate a layer using the Transform Tool.

To rotate a layer using the Rotate command:

1. Use the Layers & Channels dialog box to select which layer will be rotated (for directions about how to do this, turn to page 92).

2. Right-click on the image and choose Image→Transforms→Layer. The Layer menu will open (**Figure 9**).

3. Choose either the Rotate 270 or Rotate 90 menu item. The layer will rotate (**Figures 10a–b**).

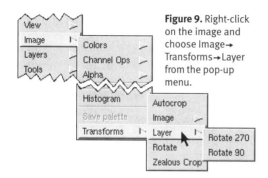

Figure 9. Right-click on the image and choose Image→Transforms→Layer from the pop-up menu.

Figure 10a. This is the original image before rotation.

Figure 10b. This is the same image after Rotate 270 is chosen on the Layer menu.

Transforming Layers

Any of the transformations discussed in Chapter 10, *Transform Your Art*—such as scaling, shearing, and adding perspective—can be applied to individual layers. Chapter 10 starts on page 147.

Erasing Part of a Layer

The Eraser Tool works like the Pencil and Paintbrush Tools—you just click and drag. Instead of adding color though, the Eraser Tool removes it, leaving behind the current background color (if the erasure happens on the Background layer) or transparency (if the erasure is on a transparent layer). In addition, you can select the shape and size of the eraser stroke, its opacity, and spacing using the Brush Selection dialog box (just like the Pencil and Paintbrush Tools).

To erase part of a layer:

1. Use the Layers & Channels dialog box to select which layer will be rotated (for directions about how to do this, turn to page 92).

   and/or

   Use one of the selection tools to restrict the area that will be erased (**Figure 11**).

2. Click the Eraser Tool in the GIMP Toolbox or press Shift+E on the keyboard to select it. The mouse pointer will change to a small pencil.

3. Position the mouse pointer over the area you want to erase.

4. Press the left mouse button and drag. The area that passes under the mouse pointer will be erased (**Figure 12**).

Figure 11. If you wish, you can select an area in order to restrict the erasing. In this image, the rocky area above the kayakers has been selected.

Figure 12. As the mouse is dragged, the area is erased. In this figure the Circle (17) brush was selected, creating the thick, clean erasure.

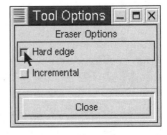

Figure 13. In the Tool Options dialog box, select the Hard edge and/or Incremental check boxes.

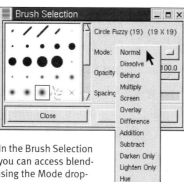

Figure 14a. In the Brush Selection dialog box, you can access blending modes using the Mode drop-down list.

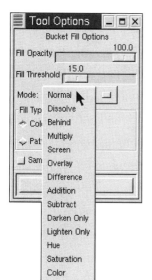

Figure 14b. In the Tool Options dialog box, you can access blending modes using the Mode drop-down list.

Figure 14c. In the Layers & Channels dialog box, you can access blending modes using the Mode drop-down list on the Layers tab page.

✔ Tips

■ To change the shape, size, and opacity of the erasure, change the Brush Selection dialog box settings as described on pages 110–111.

■ You can use the Eraser Tool to erase in straight lines just as you would draw a straight line using the Pencil or Paintbrush Tool. For directions about how to do this, take a look at page 109.

■ When changing the size and shape of an erasure using the Brush Selection dialog box, you may have noticed that there's a Mode drop-down list available in the dialog box. This drop-down list lets you set blending modes. To learn more about these modes, turn to pages 170–173.

Eraser Tool Options

There are two options that you can set to change the effect of the Eraser Tool (**Figure 13**):

◆ **Hard edge** removes any fuzzy edge, no matter which brush is selected.

◆ **Incremental** sets the eraser stroke to become more transparent when strokes cross. This option only works when the brush opacity is set to less than 100% in the Brush Selection dialog box.

To set Eraser Tool Options:

1. Double-click on the Eraser Tool in the GIMP Toolbox. The Tool Options dialog box will open (**Figure 13**).

2. Select the Hard edge and/or Incremental check buttons.

3. Click Close.

Blending Modes

Blending modes work with layer transparency. A blending mode changes the way a layer's pixels blend with the pixels in the layer(s) below it. Some of the blending modes are quite subtle, only changing a few colors or shifting hues, while others produce dramatic effects.

These blending modes are available using the Mode drop-down list in the Brush Selection dialog box (**Figure 14a**), the Tool Options dialog box with either the Bucket Fill or Blend Tool selected (**Figure 14b**), or the Layers & Channels dialog box (**Figure 14c**). (The Tools that use the Brush Selection dialog box to change width and size of strokes are the Pencil, Paintbrush, Airbrush, and Eraser Tools. The blending modes can be set to change the effect various tool strokes have.)

On pages 172–173 are samples of the blending modes. Use the directions below to duplicate how the samples were made using your own image. Try out the blending modes and see what they can do!

To test the blending modes:

1. Open the image you would like to use for the test (**Figure 15**).

2. Right-click on the image and choose Layers→Layers & Channels from the pop-up menu (**Figure 1**). The Layers & Channels dialog box will open (**Figure 2**).

3. Click the New Layer button at the bottom of the Layers & Channels dialog box. The New Layer Options dialog box will appear (**Figure 16**).

4. Make sure the Transparent radio button is selected in the Layer Fill Type area, then click OK. A new layer named "New Layer" will appear selected in the layers window.

Figure 15. Open the image on which you want to test the blending modes.

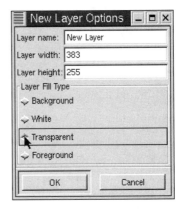

Figure 16. In the New Layer Options dialog box, make sure the Transparent radio button is selected, then click OK.

Figure 17. When the selected area on the new layer is filled with white, the area on the layer underneath is obscured.

Figure 18. After filling the second selected area with black, the new layer contains two filled areas that obscure the layer underneath.

Figure 19. When the Opacity slider is moved to 80%, the layer containing the two filled areas becomes semi-transparent, revealing the obscured areas underneath.

Figure 20. When a blending mode is selected using the Mode drop-down list, the way the filled areas blend with the layer underneath changes. In this figure, Overlay mode is selected.

5. Click the Rectangular Select Tool in the Toolbox.

6. Use the Rectanglar Select Tool to select a rectangular area of the image (see page 64 for directions on how to do this).

7. Select the Bucket Fill Tool.

8. Make sure the foreground color in the color selector is white (turn to page 41 for directions on how to do this).

9. Fill the selected area with white (**Figure 17**). (Notice that a white rectangle appears on the New Layer thumbnail on the Layers tab page of the Layers & Channels dialog box.)

10. Repeat steps 2–9, but use black as the foreground color this time. There will now be two rectangles, one white and one black, on the New Layer positioned over the image (**Figure 18**).

11. On the Layers tab page in the Layers & Channels dialog box, move the Opacity slider to the left to about 80% (this is a good place to start; experiment with this slider as you change modes). The white and black rectangles will become semi-transparent (**Figure 19**).

12. Use the Mode drop-down list to choose a blending mode (**Figure 14c**). Since the New Layer is selected, the blending mode will affect how its pixels—light and dark—blend with the image underneath (**Figure 20**).

✔ Tip

■ If the Keep Trans. check button is selected on the Layers tab page in the Layers & Channels dialog box, the transparent areas of the selected layer (in this case the New Layer) will not change.

TEST THE BLENDING MODES

Blending Mode Examples

The following two pages contain examples of the different blending modes and how they affect an image. In the text describing each mode, the image itself is referred to as the "image layer" and the layer above, using the blending mode, is called the "blending layer." The last four modes described on the next page aren't good examples if they aren't in color, so I've only included descriptions of what they do.

Normal mode. This mode paints each pixel to create a result that is a blend of the image and blending layers.

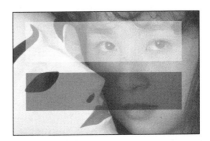

Normal mode, 50% opacity. In this image, the blending layer is set to normal mode with opacity at 50%.

Dissolve mode. This mode creates a stippled texture on the blending layer and becomes more solid with higher opacity settings. This example is set at 50% opacity.

Multiply mode. This mode uses channels to remove the lighter parts of the image layer to create a darker image layer. Multiplying any color with black makes it darker; with white, colors are unchanged.

Screen mode. This mode uses channels and multiplies the inverse of the image layer with the blending layer. The resulting color is always lighter. Screening any color with white makes it lighter; with black, colors are unchanged.

Overlay mode. This mode makes dark areas darker and light areas lighter. Contrast and detail remain in the image layer while the colors are mixed with the blending layer.

Difference mode. This mode uses channels to subtract colors in the image layer from the blending layer or vice versa, depending upon which layer has the higher brightness value.

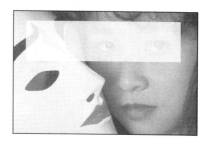

Addition mode. This mode is similar to Screen mode, but instead of multiplying inverse values, it adds the image and blending layers channel values. The resulting color is always lighter.

Subtract mode. This mode subtracts image layer channel values from blending layer values. Subtracting any color with white makes it darker; with black, colors are unchanged.

Darken Only mode. This mode compares image layer and blending layer channel values in order to display the lowest value. Darkening any color with black makes it darker; with white, colors are unchanged.

Lighten Only mode. This mode compares image layer and blending layer channel values in order to display the highest value. Lightening any color with white makes it lighter; with black, colors are unchanged.

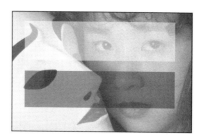

Value mode. This mode uses the image layer to determine hue and saturation values and the blending layer to determine value (brightness). Contrast and detail are retained in the image layer.

Hue mode. In this mode, the blending layer's hue value is applied to the image layer. The saturation and brightness values of the image layer are not changed.

Saturation mode. In this mode, the blending layer's saturation value is applied to the image layer. The image layer's hue and brightness values are not changed.

Color mode. In this mode, the blending layer's hue and saturation values are applied to the image layer. The image layer's brightness value remains unchanged.

Behind mode. This mode is only used for painting transparent areas of the blending layer (it's not available in the Layers & Channels dialog box).

Setting Layer Opacity

When working with a layered image, you may want to create a special effect by making one or more layers semi-transparent. This lets the layers below show through. The lower the opacity setting in the Layers & Channels dialog box, the more transparent an image is.

To set layer opacity:

1. Right-click on the layered image and choose Layers→Layers & Channels from the pop up menu (**Figure 21**). The Layers & Channels dialog box will open (**Figure 22**).

2. Highlight the layer that you want to make transparent.

3. Use the Opacity slider to set the transparency of the layer.

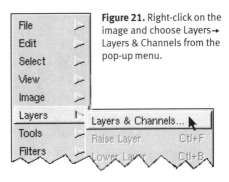

Figure 21. Right-click on the image and choose Layers→ Layers & Channels from the pop-up menu.

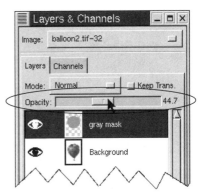

Figure 22. In the Layers & Channels dialog box, use the Opacity slider to set how transparent a layer is. The lower the setting, the more transparent the layer will be.

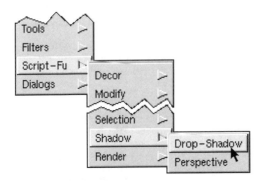

Figure 24. Right-click on the image and choose Script-Fu→Shadow→Drop-Shadow from the pop-up menu.

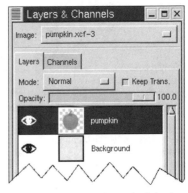

Figure 23. Use the Layers & Channels dialog box to select the layer that will have the drop shadow added to it. In this figure, the pumpkin layer is selected.

Figure 25. Use the Script-Fu Drop-Shadow dialog box to set the offset, size, color, and opacity of the drop shadow. (If this is the first time you are using this feature, try the default settings.)

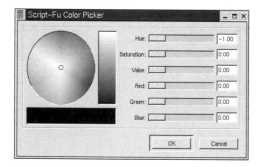

Figure 26. Use the Script-Fu Color Picker dialog box to set the color of the drop shadow.

Quick Layer Effects

There are many special effects you can create using layers and the GIMP. A few quick ones, including Drop Shadow, Perspective (drop shadow), Round Corners, and Alien Glow, are discussed here.

To create a drop shadow:

1. Use the Layers & Channels dialog box to select which layer will have a drop shadow added to it (for directions about how to do this, turn to page 92) (**Figure 23**).

2. Right-click on the image and choose Script-Fu→Shadow→Drop-Shadow from the pop-up menu (**Figure 24**). The Script-Fu Drop-Shadow dialog box will open (**Figure 25**).

3. To set where the drop shadow will appear, enter values in pixels in the X and Y offset text boxes. (X offset moves the shadow horizontally, Y offset moves the shadow vertically, thus positive numbers move the shadow right and down, whereas negative numbers move the shadow left and up, respectively.)

(continued)

CREATE A DROP SHADOW

Figure 27a. This is the original image before the drop shadow is added to the pumpkin layer.

Figure 27b. This is the same image after the drop shadow has been added behind the pumpkin.

4. To set how fuzzy the drop shadow is, enter a value in pixels in the Blur Radius text box. The higher the number, the fuzzier the drop shadow.

5. Click the Color button to open the Script-Fu Color Picker (**Figure 26**).

6. Use the Script-Fu Color Picker to set the color of the drop shadow.

7. In the Opacity text box, enter a percentage value. The lower the number, the more transparent the drop shadow will be.

8. When you have finished setting the various options, click OK. The script-fu mini-program will go to work and create a drop shadow (**Figures 27a–b**). In addition the Script-Fu Drop-Shadow dialog box will close. Notice that a new layer named "Drop-Shadow" appears in the Layers & Channels dialog box when the drop shadow is created (**Figure 28**).

To create a drop shadow with perspective:

1. Use the Layers & Channels dialog box to select which layer will have a perspective shadow added to it (for directions about how to do this, turn to page 92) (**Figure 29**).

2. Right-click on the image and choose Script-Fu→Shadow→Perspective from the pop-up menu (**Figure 30**). The Script-Fu Perspective dialog box will open (**Figure 31**).

3. In the Angle text box enter the perspective (in degrees) of the drop-shadow. (Settings of 0 and 180 degrees won't create a drop shadow.)

Figure 28. When the drop shadow appears behind the pumpkin a new layer, "Drop-Shadow," also appears in the layer window.

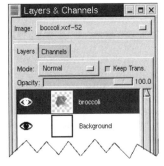

Figure 29. Use the Layers & Channels dialog box to select the layer that will have the perspective shadow added behind it.

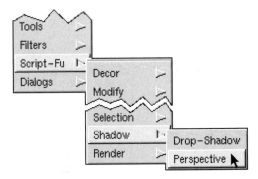

Figure 30. Right-click on the image and choose Script-Fu→Shadow→Perspective from the pop-up menu.

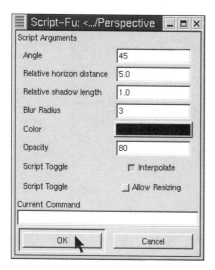

Figure 31. Use the Script-Fu Perspective dialog box to set the angle, size, color, and opacity of the perspective drop shadow. (If this is the first time you are using this effect, try the default settings.)

Figure 32a.
The original image before the perspective drop shadow is added behind the broccoli layer.

Figure 32b.
The same image with the perspective drop shadow added behind the broccoli.

4. To set how long and wide the perspective drop shadow will be, enter values in the Relative horizon distance and Relative shadow length text boxes.

5. To set how fuzzy the drop shadow is, enter a value in pixels in the Blur Radius text box. The higher the number, the fuzzier the drop shadow.

6. Click the Color button to open the Script-Fu Color Picker (**Figure 26**).

7. Use the Script-Fu Color Picker to set the color of the drop shadow.

8. In the Opacity text box, enter a percentage value. The lower the number, the more transparent the drop shadow will be.

9. When you have finished setting the various options, click OK. The script-fu mini-program will go to work and create a drop shadow with perspective (**Figures 32a–b**). In addition the Script-Fu Perspective dialog box will close. Notice that a new layer named "Perspective Shadow" appears in the Layers & Channels dialog box when the drop shadow is created (**Figure 33**).

Figure 33.
When the perspective drop shadow appears behind the broccoli a new layer, "Perspective Shadow," also appears in the layer window.

PERSPECTIVE SHADOW

Rounded Corners and a Drop Shadow

It's easy to add rounded corners with a drop shadow to an image using a script-fu.

To add rounded corners with a drop shadow:

1. Use the Layers & Channels dialog box to select the bottommost layer of the image (for directions about how to do this, turn to page 92) (**Figure 34**).

2. Right-click on the image and choose Script-Fu→Decor→Round Corners from the pop-up menu (**Figure 35**). The Script-Fu Round Corners dialog box will open (**Figure 36**).

3. In the Radius of Edges text box, enter the value (in degrees) for how much the corners will be rounded. The higher the number, the rounder the corners.

4. Select the Add drop-shadow check button.

5. Use the Shadow x and Shadow y text boxes to set how far the drop shadow is offset from the image. (The default setting of 8 for both works pretty well.)

6. To set how fuzzy the drop shadow is, enter a value in pixels in the Blur Radius text box. The higher the number, the fuzzier the drop shadow.

7. If you want the image to have an opaque background filled with the current background color, select the Add background check button. If this check button is unselected, the image will have a transparent background.

8. To set the script-fu to work on a copy of the image and keep the original intact, select the Work on copy check button.

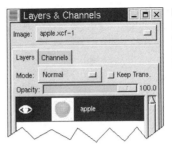

Figure 34. Use the Layers & Channels dialog box to select the bottom layer.

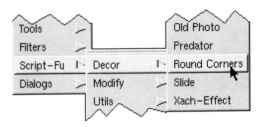

Figure 35. Right-click on the image and choose Script-Fu→Decor→Round Corners from the poop-up menu.

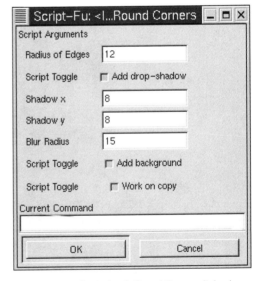

Figure 36. Use the Script-Fu Round Corners dialog box to set the size of the rounded corners, add a drop shadow, set the drop shadow offset and blur, and add a background. (If this is the first time you are using this effect, try the default settings.)

Figure 37. Rounded corners and a drop shadow are added to the image.

Figure 38. When the script-fu is applied to the text, two new layers appear in the Layers & Channels dialog box: Drop-Shadow and Background.

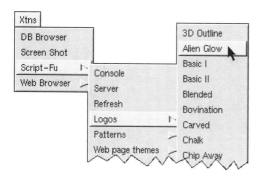

Figure 39. In the GIMP Toolbox, choose Xtns→Script-Fu→Logos→Alien Glow from the pop-up menu.

9. When you have finished setting the various options, click OK. The script-fu mini-program will go to work and add rounded corners and a drop shadow to your image (or a copy of the image) (**Figure 37**). Notice that a new layers named "Drop-Shadow" and "Background" appear in the Layers & Channels dialog box (**Figure 38**).

Adding an Alien Glow

The Alien Glow script-fu is a mini-program that adds a three-dimensional, glowing effect to text using layers. It works just like other script-fu programs in that there is a dialog box that is used to set options.

To add an Alien Glow:

1. In the GIMP Toolbox, choose Xtns→Script-Fu→Logos→Alien Glow (**Figure 39**). The Script-Fu Alien Glow dialog box will appear (**Figure 40**).

2. In the Text String text box, enter the text to which you would like to add a glow.

3. Enter the size of the text in the Font Size (in pixels) text box.

4. Enter a font name that is loaded on your computer in the Font text box. (To find out what's loaded on your computer, take a look at the available font list in the Text Tool dialog box. To open this dialog box, follow steps 2–3 on page 208.)

5. Click the Glow Color button to open the Script-Fu Color Picker (**Figure 26**).

6. Use the Script-Fu Color Picker to set the color of the drop-shadow.

(continued)

7. When you have finished setting the various options, click OK. The script-fu mini-program will go to work and create a new image containing the text with an alien glow (**Figure 41**). In addition the Script-Fu Alien Glow dialog box will close. Notice that a layer named "Alien Glow" and a layer named using the text entered in the Text String text box appear in the Layers & Channels dialog box when the alien glow is created (**Figure 42**).

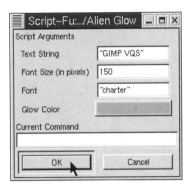

Figure 40. Use the Script-Fu Alien Glow dialog box to enter the text that will be used as well as its size and font, and the color of the glow itself. (If this is the first time you are using this effect, try the default settings.)

✔ Tip

■ To see more effects created by script-fu mini-programs found on the Logos menu, turn to pages 227–230.

Figure 42. The Alien Glow script-fu creates a new image with three layers: one named after the text itself—in this case GIMP VQS—Alien Glow, and Background.

Figure 41. The glowing text does look a bit alien, especially when seen in color!

ADD AN ALIEN GLOW

Summary

In this chapter you learned how to:

- ◆ Lock layers together
- ◆ Move layers as a unit
- ◆ Align layers
- ◆ Rotate layers
- ◆ Erase part of a layer
- ◆ Set Eraser Tool options
- ◆ Use blending modes
- ◆ Create quick layer effects

CREATING COMPOSITE IMAGES

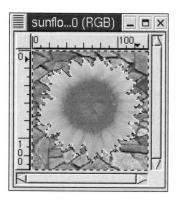

Figure 1. Use a selection tool to select an area of the image. In this figure, the sunflower has been selected using the Fuzzy Selection Tool.

*C*omposite images are made by combining elements from different images or photographs. Using the layer techniques you have learned, you can place these different elements, one of top of the other, and manipulate them any way you want using opacity and blending modes.

But how does one put a composite image together? By using familiar commands, such as copy, cut, and paste. In addition, portions of images can be *cloned*, and then blurred or sharpened to create a uniform look.

To copy a selection:

1. Use the selection tool of your choice to select an area of the image (for details about how to do this, turn to Chapter 6, *Making Selections*) (**Figure 1**).

2. Right-click on the image and choose Edit→Copy from the pop-up menu (**Figure 2**) or press Ctrl+C on the keyboard. The selected area will be copied to the clipboard, ready for you to paste into another layer or image.

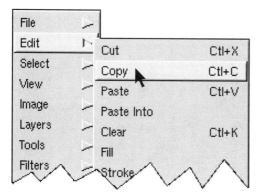

Figure 2. Right-click on the image and choose Edit→ Copy from the pop-up menu.

To cut a selection:

1. Use the selection tool of your choice to select an area of the image (**Figure 1**).

2. Right-click on the image and choose Edit→Cut from the pop-up menu (**Figure 3**) or press Ctrl+X on the keyboard. The selected area will disappear from the image (**Figure 4**) and be saved in the clipboard, ready for you to paste into another layer or image.

To paste a selection:

1. Open the image you want to paste the selection into or create a new image (**Figure 5**).

2. Cut or copy a selected area.

3. Right-click on the image window you want to paste the selection into and choose Edit→Paste from the pop-up menu (**Figure 6**) or press Ctrl+V on the keyboard. The cut or copied area will be pasted into the image window as a floating selection (**Figure 7**).

4. You can then anchor the floating selection to the active layer or put it on a new layer of its own (see page 100 for details).

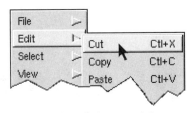

Figure 3. Right-click on the image and choose Edit→Cut from the pop-up menu.

Figure 4. The selected area disappears from the image window.

Figure 5. If you wish, you can create a new image.

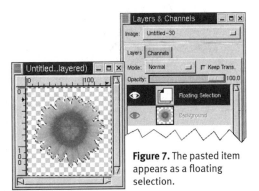

Figure 7. The pasted item appears as a floating selection.

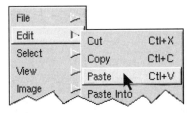

Figure 6. Right-click on the image window where you want to paste the selection and choose Edit→Paste from the pop-up menu.

Figure 8. Open the image you want to paste the selection into.

Figure 9. Select the area you want to paste the cut or copied item into. In this figure, the left lens of the glasses has been selected using the Bezier Selection Tool.

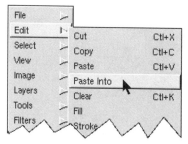

Figure 10. Right-click on the image window with the selected area and choose Edit→Paste Into from the pop-up menu.

Pasting into a Selected Area

The GIMP offers more than one way to paste a selection into an image. As well as using the simple paste command described on page 182, you can also use the Paste Into command. Paste Into lets you paste a selection from the clipboard into a selected area of an image.

To paste into a selected area:

1. Open the image you want to paste the selection into or create a new image (**Figure 8**).

2. Cut or copy a selected area.

3. Using the selection tool of your choice, select the area that you want to paste the cut or copied item into (**Figure 9**).

4. Right-click on the image and choose Edit→Paste Into from the pop-up menu (**Figure 10**). The cut or copied item will appear in the selected area (**Figure 11**).

✔ Tip

■ If the cut or copied selection is larger than the selected area you are going to paste into, the cut or copied selection will automatically be cropped to fit the smaller area.

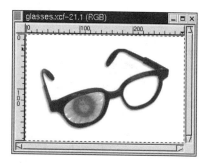

Figure 11. The cut or copied item appears in the selected area.

Cutting, Copying, and Pasting More than One Selection

If you need to paste several cut or copied selections many times, then the Paste Named command is for you. It works in conjunction with the Copy Named and Cut Named commands. First, using the Copy Named or Cut Named commands, you create selections saved to the clipboard with names. Then you use the Paste Named command to choose the named selection and paste it into an image.

Figure 12. Select the area using a selection tool. In this figure, the balloon was selected using the Bezier Selection Tool.

To copy a selection using Copy Named:

1. Use the selection tool of your choice to select an area (for details about how to do this, turn to Chapter 6, *Making Selections*) (**Figure 12**).

2. Right-click on the image and choose Edit→Copy Named from the pop-up menu (**Figure 13**) or press Shift+Ctrl+C on the keyboard. The Copy Named dialog box will open (**Figure 14**).

3. Enter a name for the selected area in the text box, then click OK. The selected area will be copied and saved in the clipboard with the name you gave it, ready for you to paste into another layer or image using the Paste Named command.

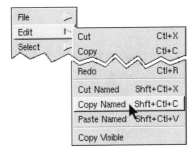

Figure 13. Right-click on the image and choose Edit→Copy Named from the pop-up menu.

Figure 14. Enter a name for the copied selection, then click OK.

Figure 16. Enter a name for the cut selection, then click OK.

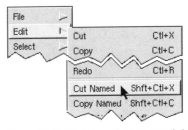

Figure 15. Right-click on the image and choose Edit→Cut Named from the pop-up menu.

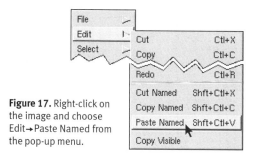

Figure 17. Right-click on the image and choose Edit→Paste Named from the pop-up menu.

Figure 18. Highlight one of the named selections, then click Paste.

Figure 19. The named selection appears in the image window as a floating selection.

To cut a selection using Cut Named:

1. Use the selection tool of your choice to select an area (for details about how to do this, turn to Chapter 6, *Making Selections*).

2. Right-click on the image and choose Edit→Cut Named from the pop-up menu (**Figure 15**) or press Shift+Ctrl+X on the keyboard. The Cut Named dialog box will appear (**Figure 16**).

3. Enter a name for the selected area in the text box, then click OK. The selected area will disappear from the image and be saved in the clipboard with the name you gave it, ready for you to paste into another layer or image using the Paste Named command.

To paste a selection using Paste Named:

1. Right-click on the image you want to paste a selection into and choose Edit→Paste Named from the pop-up menu (**Figure 17**) or press Shift+Ctrl+V on the keyboard. The Paste Named Buffer dialog box will open (**Figure 18**).

2. In the Select a buffer to paste window, choose the named selection you want to paste.

3. Click Paste. The Paste Named Buffer dialog box will close and the selection you chose will be pasted into the image as a floating selection (**Figure 19**).

✔ Tip

■   To delete a named selection in the Paste Named Buffer dialog box, highlight the selection, then click Delete.

Creating Clones

The Clone Tool works like the Paintbrush Tool, letting you stroke color into an image. But instead of painting in solid colors, the Clone Tool paints using part of an image or pattern. The Clone Tool is great for retouching photographs. Instead of trying to fix a damaged area from scratch, and attempting to match color and texture, you can just clone the exact colors and textures from a similar area of the photo.

To clone an area in an image:

1. Double-click the Clone Tool in the GIMP Toolbox. The Tool Options dialog box will open (**Figure 20**).

2. Select the Image Source radio button, then click Close.

3. Use the Brush Selection dialog box to select a brush, blending mode, and opacity (**Figure 21**). (For details about how to do this turn to page 110; blending modes are discussed on pages 170–173.)

4. Use the Layer & Channels dialog box to select the layer containing the area you want to clone. (To find out how to do this, turn to page 92.)

5. With the Clone Tool still selected, position the mouse pointer over the area of the *source image* that you want to clone (**Figures 22a–b**).

6. Press and hold down the Ctrl key, and then click.

7. Release the Ctrl key, move the mouse pointer to the *destination image,* and position the pointer where you want to paint the clone (this can be in the same or another image window) (**Figure 23**).

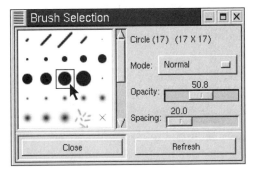

Figure 20.
In the Tool Options dialog box, select the Image Source radio button, then click Close.

Figure 21. Use the Brush Selection dialog box to select a brush, blending mode, and opacity.

Figures 22a–b. Position the mouse pointer over the area you want to clone. In this example, both of these smiling faces will be cloned.

CLONE TOOL: CLONE AN AREA IN AN IMAGE

Figure 23. Position the mouse pointer over the area of the destination image where you want the clone to appear.

8. Press the left mouse button and drag. As you drag, a crosshair will appear where you clicked, indicating the area that you are cloning, and the clone will appear under the mouse pointer (**Figure 24**). Cloning can produce some smiling results (**Figure 25**).

✔ Tip

■ If you select the area of the source image that will be cloned, you can feather the selection. This will remove the visible seam between the clone and the destination image. The faces in Figures 24 and 25 have been feathered by 5 pixels. To find out how to feather a selection, turn to page 82.

Figure 24. As you drag the mouse pointer back and forth, the clone appears. In this figure the Circle (17) brush was selected and set to an opacity of 50%.

Figure 25. After cloning in the second image, the flowers definitely look very happy.

CLONE TOOL: PAINT A PATTERN

To paint a pattern:

1. Double-click the Clone Tool in the GIMP Toolbox. The Tool Options dialog box will open (**Figure 26**).

2. Select the Pattern Source radio button, then click Close.

3. Use the Brush Selection dialog box to select a brush, blending mode, and opacity (**Figure 21**). (For details about how to do this turn to page 110; blending modes are discussed on pages 170–173.)

4. Use the Pattern Selection dialog box to select a pattern (**Figure 27**). (Use steps 6–7 on pages 121–122 to find out how to do this.)

5. Use the Layer & Channels dialog box to select the layer you want to paint the pattern onto. (To find out how to do this, turn to page 92.)

6. If you wish, use any of the selection tools to select an area where you would like the pattern to appear. This will restrict the painting to that area.

7. Click the Clone Tool in the GIMP Toolbox to select it or press C on the keyboard.

8. Position the mouse pointer over the area where you want to paint the pattern (**Figure 28**). The mouse pointer will change to a tiny pencil.

9. Press the left mouse button and drag back and forth. The pattern will appear in the image window (**Figure 29**).

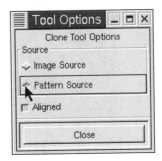

Figure 26. In the Tool Options dialog box, select the Pattern Source radio button, then click Close.

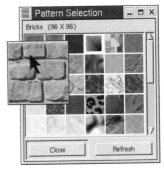

Figure 27. Use the Pattern Selection dialog box to choose a pattern.

Figure 28. Position the mouse pointer over the area where you want to paint the pattern.

Figure 29. As the mouse is dragged back and forth, the pattern appears.

Figure 30. In the Tool Options dialog box, select the Blur radio button, then click Close.

The Convolver Tool

The Convolver Tool is used to blur or sharpen areas of an image. This can be handy when you are trying to blend cloned or pasted areas into an image. Another way to blur or sharpen an image (or area of an image) is to use the Blur or Sharpen filters. Examples of these filters are shown on pages 239 and 242, respectively.

To blur an area:

1. Double-click on the Convolver Tool in the GIMP Toolbox. The Tool Options dialog box will open (**Figure 30**).

2. Select the Blur radio button, then click Close.

Figure 31. If you wish, you can use a selection tool to select an area. In this figure, the leftmost balloon is selected.

3. Use the Brush Selection dialog box to select a brush. (For details about how to do this, turn to page 110; blending modes are discussed on pages 170–173.)

4. If you wish, use one of the selection tools to select the area that you want to blur (**Figure 31**). This will restrict the blurring to that area.

5. With the Convolver Tool still selected, position the mouse pointer over the area you want to blur.

Figure 32. As the mouse is dragged back and forth, the area under the pointer becomes blurred.

6. Press the left mouse button and drag back and forth over the area. As you drag, it will become blurred (**Figure 32**).

✔ Tip

■ Like the Airbrush Tool, you can set the Convolver Tool to blur more or less by setting the Pressure slider in the Tool Options dialog box. The higher the setting, the more blurring will appear as you drag.

To sharpen an area:

1. Double-click on the Convolver Tool in the GIMP Toolbox. The Tool Options dialog box will open (**Figure 33**).

2. Select the Sharpen radio button, then click Close.

3. Use the Brush Selection dialog box to select a brush. (For details about how to do this turn to page 110; blending modes are discussed on pages 170–173.)

4. If you wish, use one of the selection tools to select the area that you want to sharpen (**Figure 31**). This will restrict the sharpening to that area.

5. With the Convolver Tool still selected, position the mouse pointer over the area you want to sharpen.

6. Press the left mouse button and drag back and forth over the area. As you drag, it will become sharper (**Figure 34**).

Figure 33. In the Tool Options dialog box, select the Sharpen radio button, then click Close.

Figure 34. As the mouse is dragged back and forth, the area under the pointer becomes sharper.

Summary

In this chapter you learned how to:

◆ Cut, copy, and paste a selection

◆ Paste into a selected area

◆ Create named selections saved to the clipboard

◆ Paste named selections

◆ Clone an area

◆ Paint a pattern

◆ Blur and sharpen an image

CONVOLVER TOOL: SHARPEN AN AREA

CHANNELS AND LAYER MASKS $\Big|$ 13

*E*very image you create in the GIMP contains *channels.* These channels store an image's color information. The number of channels in an image depends upon the color mode in which the image is set. For instance, an image set in RGB mode has three default channels—a Red channel that stores red information, a Green channel that stores green information, and a Blue channel that stores blue information. If an image has more than one layer, each layer has its own set of channels.

Alpha channels are grayscale channels that you can add to an image. They are used to store selections. Alpha channel selections are used to protect specific areas of an image from editing while changes, such as recoloring, filters, and other effects, are applied to the rest of the (unmasked, i.e., unselected) image.

Layer masks in the GIMP work in much the same way a Halloween mask works on one's face. A Halloween mask covers the face, concealing it; but any cutouts—for eyes or mouth, for instance—leave those areas visible. Layer masks are placed on top of an image and "cutouts" are added, making those areas visible.

Layer masks control how different areas of an image are revealed. You can use layer masks as test areas for applying special effects without permanently changing an image. If you like the effects and want to make them permanent, you can then apply a mask to an image. Layer masks can be saved with a layered image in the GIMP's native .xcf file format.

Channels

Each channel is a grayscale image that stores specific color information. Channels are available on the Channels tab page of the Layers & Channels dialog box (**Figure 1**). The individual color channels—Red, Green, and Blue—are listed first, then come any alpha channels that have been added. A thumbnail showing a channel's contents appears to the left of the channel name. Using the Channels tab page, you can select, show, and hide channels. In addition, you can add alpha channels and arrange their order.

To select a channel:

1. Right-click on the image and choose Layers→Layers & Channels from the pop-up menu (**Figure 2**). The Layers & Channels dialog box will open with the Layers tab page in front (**Figure 3**).

2. Click the Channels tab to bring that tab page to the front (**Figure 1**).

3. Click the name of the channel you want to select. The channel will become highlighted (**Figure 4**). You can now make changes to the active channel (for instance, you could adjust the levels or curves of the channel, or add special effects such as applying a filter).

✔ Tips

■ You can select more than one channel at a time just by clicking on the channels you want to select.

■ The contents of an alpha channel can be edited just like any layer. You can cut, copy, and paste selections to and from alpha channels, as well as adjust color and tone, and add special effects such as applying filters.

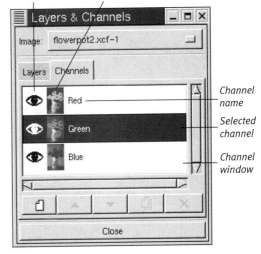

Eye icon indicates visible channel   *Channel thumbnail*

Channel name

Selected channel

Channel window

Figure 1. Use the Channels tab page of the Layers & Channels dialog box to select, hide, and view channels, and add alpha channels.

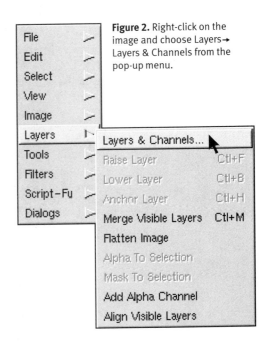

Figure 2. Right-click on the image and choose Layers→ Layers & Channels from the pop-up menu.

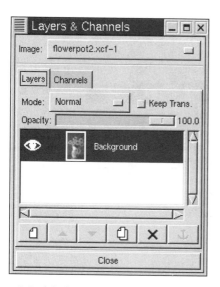

Figure 3. By default, the Layers & Channels dialog box opens with the Layers tab page in front.

To show/hide a channel:

On the Channels tab page, click the eye icon in the channel window to hide the channel (**Figure 5**). To view the channel, click in the eye icon area again.

Hiding Channels

When a channel is hidden, only the visible channels are shown in the image. Below are examples of what an image looks like when only one channel is visible.

Original image   *Red channel*

Green channel   *Blue channel*

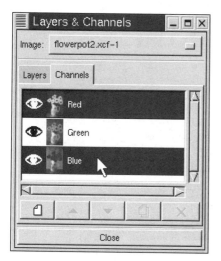

Figure 4. Click the name of the channel to select it. As you can see in this figure, two channels are selected, Red and Blue.

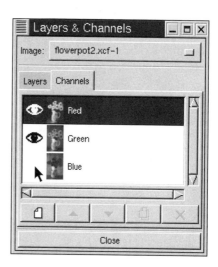

Figure 5. Click the eye icon to hide the channel. In this figure the Blue channel is hidden.

Alpha Channels

Alpha channels store selections that are used to protect areas of image from editing. These selections can be activated at anytime. When working with an alpha channel, its thumbnail on the Channels tab page appears as black and white. The black area represents the protected area of the image that cannot be edited. The white area represents the part of the image that can be changed.

Using the Layers & Channels dialog box, it's easy to add alpha channels, duplicate channels, change channel order, and delete channels.

To add an alpha channel using the Layers & Channels dialog box:

1. Right-click on the image and choose Layers→Layers & Channels from the pop-up menu (**Figure 2**). The Layers & Channels dialog box will open with the Layers tab page in front (**Figure 3**).

2. Click the Channels tab to bring that tab page to the front (**Figure 6**).

3. Click the New Channel button near the bottom left of the Channel tab page.

   or

   Right-click in the channel window and choose New Channel from the pop-up menu (**Figure 7**).

   or

   Press Ctrl+N on the keyboard.

   The New Channel Options dialog box will appear (**Figure 8**).

4. Enter a name for the new channel in the Channel name text box.

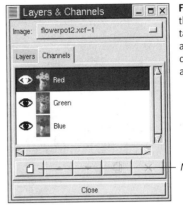

Figure 6. Use the Channels tab page to add alpha channels to an image.

New Channel

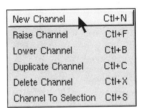

Figure 7. Right-click in the channel window and choose New Channel from the pop-up menu.

Figure 8. Use the New Channel Options dialog box to enter a name and opacity.

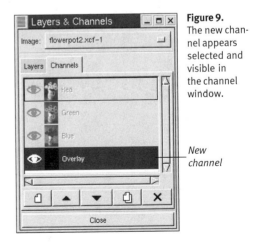

Figure 9. The new channel appears selected and visible in the channel window.

New channel

Figure 10. Select the channel that you want to duplicate.

5. Set transparency using the Fill Opacity slider. (The transparency has no effect on the mask itself. It only lets you see what's behind the dark parts of the mask. 50% opacity is the default and works well.)

6. Click OK. The New Channel Options dialog box will close and the new channel will appear in the channel window on the Channels tab page (**Figure 9**).

✔ Tips

■ If you create a complex selection, you save it as an alpha channel. To find out how to do this, turn to page 86.

■ You can also add an alpha channel to an image by right-clicking on the image and choosing Layers→Add Alpha Channel from the pop-up menu.

To duplicate an alpha channel:

1. On the Channels tab page of the Layers & Channels dialog box, select the channel that you want to duplicate (**Figure 10**). (You can only duplicate alpha channels.)

Figure 11. Right-click in the channel window and choose Duplicate Channel from the pop-up menu.

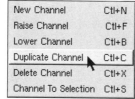

New Channel	Ctl+N
Raise Channel	Ctl+F
Lower Channel	Ctl+B
Duplicate Channel	Ctl+C
Delete Channel	Ctl+X
Channel To Selection	Ctl+S

2. Click the Duplicate Channel button at the bottom right of the Channels tab page.

or

Right-click in the channel window and choose Duplicate Channel from the pop-up menu (**Figure 11**).

or

Press Ctrl+C on the keyboard.

A duplicate of the selected channel will appear in the channel window (**Figure 12**).

Figure 12. The duplicate channel appears selected in the channel window.

Duplicate channel

DUPLICATE AN ALPHA CHANNEL

To change alpha channel order:

1. On the Channels tab page of the Layers & Channels dialog box, select the channel that you want to move up or down (**Figure 13**). (You can only move *alpha* channels. If your image contains Red, Green, and Blue channels, for instance, you can't change their order.)

2. Click either the Raise Channel or Lower Channel button.

   or

   Right-click in the channel window and choose either Raise Channel or Lower Channel from the pop-up menu (**Figure 14**).

   The channel will move either up or down in the channel window (**Figure 15**).

To rename an alpha channel:

1. On the Channels tab page, double-click on the alpha channel's name (**Figure 16**). The Edit Channel Attributes dialog box will appear (**Figure 17**).

2. Enter a new name in the Channel name text box.

3. Click OK. The Edit Channel Attributes dialog box will close and the channel name will change (**Figure 18**).

Figure 13. In the channel window, select the channel that you want to move up or down.

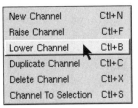

Figure 14. Right-click on the channel window and choose Raise Channel or Lower Channel from the pop-up menu.

Figure 15. The channel moves up or down in the channel window.

Figure 16. Double-click the channel name that you want to change.

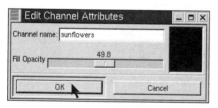

Figure 17. Enter a new name in the Channel name text box, then click OK.

Figure 18. The channel's name changes in the channel window.

To delete an alpha channel:

1. On the Channels tab page of the Layers & Channels dialog box, select the channel that you want to delete (**Figure 13**). (You can only delete *alpha* channels. If your image contains Red, Green, and Blue channels, you won't be able to delete them.)

2. Click the Delete Channel button at the bottom right of the Channels tab page.

    or

    Right-click in the channel window and choose Delete Channel from the pop-up menu (**Figure 19**).

    or

    Press Ctrl+X on the keyboard.

    The channel will disappear from the channel window. (If you discover that you didn't want to delete the alpha channel, you can undo your action by pressing Ctrl+Z on the keyboard.)

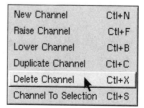

Figure 19. Right-click on the channel you want to delete and choose Delete Channel from the pop-up menu.

How to Use an Alpha Channel

Now that you know how to create alpha channels, it's time to find out what magic you can do with them.

First off, you know that the black area of an alpha channel represents the isolated area of the image that cannot be edited. Conversely, the white area represents the part of the image that can be changed. These black and white areas can be edited and reshaped, changing the uneditable and editable areas.

Second, you can activate an alpha channel as a selection, using it to edit the unselected areas of an image.

Figure 20. In the channel window, select the channel that you want to edit. Make sure that it's visible.

To reshape an alpha channel:

1. On the Channels tab page in the Layers & Channels dialog box, select the alpha channel that you want to edit (**Figure 20**).

2. Make sure the alpha channel is visible.

3. If you find it hard to see the alpha channel, hide the image's layers by clicking the eye icons on the Layers tab page in the Layers & Channels dialog box.

4. Select either the Pencil or Paintbrush Tool from the GIMP Toolbox.

5. Set the foreground color to either black or white—black if you want to add to the protected area, white if you want to add to the editable area. (Turn to page 42 to find out how to set the foreground color.)

6. Use the Brush Selection dialog box to select a brush. (For directions on how to do this, turn to page 110.)

7. Position the mouse pointer over the area you want to edit, press the left mouse button, and start painting (**Figure 21**). The shape of the black and white areas will change as you paint (**Figure 22**).

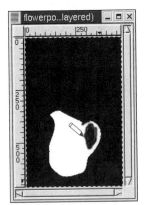

Figure 21. Position the mouse pointer and start painting.

Figure 22. The shape of the black and white areas change as you paint.

RESHAPE AN ALPHA CHANNEL

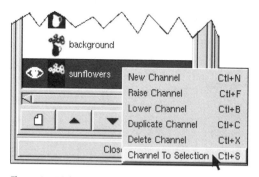

Figure 23. Right-click on the alpha channel you want to use and choose Channel To Selection from the pop-up menu.

Figure 24. The white areas of the alpha channel become selected, making them available for editing. In this figure, only the flower's petals are available for editing.

Figure 25. Select the layer that you want to edit.

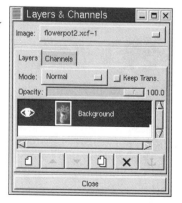

To use an alpha channel to edit unselected areas:

1. On the Channels tab page in the Layers & Channels dialog box, right click on the alpha channel that you want to convert to a selection and choose Channel To Selection from the pop-up menu (**Figure 23**) or press Ctrl+S on the keyboard. The white areas of the alpha channel will be selected, making them available for editing (**Figure 24**).

2. Use the Layers tab page in the Layers & Channels dialog box to select a layer that will contain the editing (this could be an existing or new layer) (**Figure 25**).

3. Edit the selected areas as you please. (You can use any of the painting tools to add color or add a special effect by applying a filter).

4. When you are finished editing the selected area, use the Channels tab page to hide the layer mask. Only the area that was selected has been changed (**Figure 26**).

Figure 26. When the alpha channel is hidden, changes become apparent. In this figure, the three alpha channels shown in Figure 20 were used one at a time. First, the Threshold command was applied to the sunflowers channel. Next, the Embossed filter was applied to the pitcher channel. Finally, the Alien Map filter was applied to the background channel and its levels were adjusted.

Layer Masks

A layer mask controls how different areas of a layer are revealed. In a layer mask, white is opaque, black is transparent, and gray is semi-transparent. Layer masks work as test areas, letting you try out different effects without making permanent changes. If you create an effect you like, you can then apply the mask to the layer and make it permanent. If you don't like it, you can remove the layer mask.

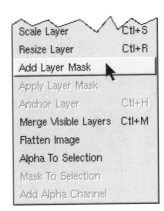

Figure 27. Right-click on the layer and choose Add Layer Mask from the pop-up menu.

To add a mask to a layer:

1. On the Layers tab page in the Layers & Channels dialog box, right-click on the layer that you want to add the mask to, then choose Add Layer Mask from the pop-up menu (**Figure 27**). The Add Mask Options dialog box will open (**Figure 28**).

2. In the Initialize Layer Mask To area select one of the following radio buttons:

    ◆ **White (Full Opacity)** creates an opaque layer mask. (This is the default and a good selection for the first time mask user.)

    ◆ **Black (Full Transparency)** creates a completely transparent layer mask.

    ◆ **Layer's Alpha Channel** creates a layer mask using the values found in the layer's alpha channel.

3. Click OK. The Add Mask Options dialog box will close and the layer mask will appear to the right of the layer's thumbnail on the Layers tab page (**Figure 29**).

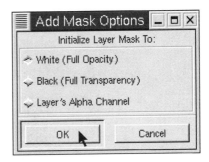

Figure 28. Select a radio button, then click OK.

✔ Tip

■ A layer mask can be added to the Background layer only after an alpha channel has been added.

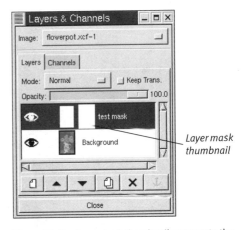

Layer mask thumbnail

Figure 29. The layer mask thumbnail appears to the right of the layer thumbnail.

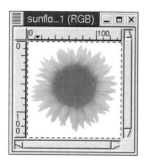

Figure 30. Open a test image.

Trying Out a Layer Mask

If this is the first time you are using a layer mask, follow the directions below to get a sense of what a layer mask can do.

To try a layer mask:

1. Open a test image (**Figure 30**).

2. Using the Layers & Channels dialog box, create a new layer with a white layer fill type. (Turn to page 93 for directions.) The image will disappear under the solid white layer.

3. Add a White (Full Opacity) layer mask (**Figure 31**). (Take a look at page 200 for directions about how to do this.)

4. Set the foreground color to black. (Turn to page 42 for directions.)

5. Select either the Pencil or Paintbrush Tool from the GIMP Toolbox.

6. Use the Brush Selection dialog box to select a brush. (For directions on how to do this turn to page 110.)

7. Make sure the layer mask is selected.

8. Position the mouse pointer over the layer mask, press the left mouse button and drag. As you paint, the image under the layer mask will be revealed (**Figure 32**).

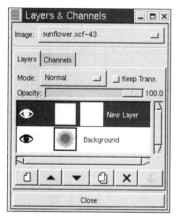

Figure 31. Add a new layer with a white fill, then add a full opacity, white mask to that new layer.

Figure 32. As you paint with black, the image is revealed through the layer mask.

To edit a layer mask:

1. On the Layers tab page in the Layers & Channels dialog box, click the layer mask thumbnail to make it active.

2. Select any painting or editing tool.

3. If you selected a painting tool, use the Brush Selection dialog box to select a brush.

4. To hide the layer, paint the mask with black (the result of painting black onto a layer mask is shown in **Figure 33**).

and/or

To reveal the layer, paint the mask with white (the result of painting white onto a layer mask is shown in **Figure 34**).

and/or

To make the layer semi-transparent, paint the mask with gray (the result of painting gray onto a layer mask is shown in **Figure 35**). (The darker the gray, the more transparent the layer mask will be.)

✔ Tips

■ To edit the layer instead of the layer mask, click the layer's thumbnail on the Layers tab page.

■ Try editing a layer mask by adding a gradient with the Blend Tool. Turn to page 205 for directions.

To view/hide the effects of a layer mask:

Hold down the Ctrl key on the keyboard and click the layer mask thumbnail on the Layers tab page in the Layers & Channels dialog box. When the layer mask effects are hidden, a red outline will appear around the layer mask thumbnail and the layer mask's effects will disappear from the image.

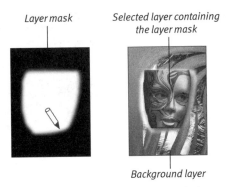

Figure 33. Paint the mask with black to hide the layer. Notice that only the portion of the layer mask that is white still shows the layer underneath.

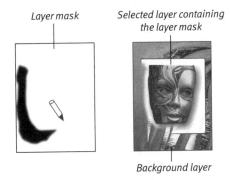

Figure 34. Paint the mask with white to reveal the layer. Notice that the portion of the layer mask that is still black hides the layer underneath.

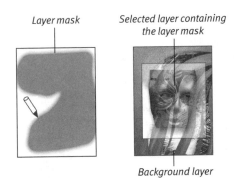

Figure 35. Paint the mask with gray to make the layer semi-transparent. Notice that the portion of the layer mask that is still white leaves the layer underneath completely visible.

EDIT A LAYER MASK; VIEW/HIDE A LAYER MASK

Figure 36. Right-click on the layer mask thumbnail and choose Apply Layer Mask from the pop-up menu.

Applying and Discarding Layer Mask Effects

Once you finish using a layer mask, you may decide that you want to *apply* it to the image, making it a permanent part of the image, or *discard* it, removing it completely.

To apply a layer mask:

1. On the Layers tab page in the Layers & Channels dialog box, right-click on the layer mask thumbnail, and choose Apply Layer Mask from the pop-up menu (**Figure 36**). The Layer Mask Options dialog box will open (**Figure 37**).

2. Click Apply. The Layer Mask Options dialog box will close and the layer mask will become a permanent part of the layer (**Figure 38**). In addition, the layer mask thumbnail will disappear from the layer window.

Figure 37. Use the Layer Mask Options dialog box to either apply the layer mask or discard it.

To discard a layer mask:

1. On the Layers tab page in the Layers & Channels dialog box, right-click on the layer mask thumbnail, and choose Apply Layer Mask from the pop-up menu (**Figure 36**). The Layer Mask Options dialog box will open (**Figure 37**).

2. Click Discard. The Layer Mask Options dialog box will close and the layer mask will disappear from the layer window.

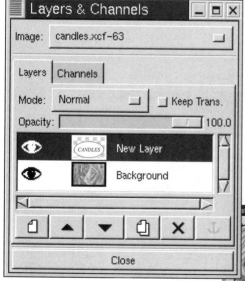

Figure 38. When the layer mask is applied to the layer, the layer mask thumbnail disappears from the layer window. The contents of the layer mask are attached permanently to the layer.

Creating Two Interesting Masks

The number of ways you can use a layer mask is only limited by your imagination. Two interesting ways to use a layer mask include creating a layer mask using a text cutout and using a gradient.

To create a layer mask using a text cutout:

1. Open the image to which you want to add the layer mask text cutout (**Figure 39**).

2. Using the Layers & Channels dialog box, create a new white layer on top of any existing layers. The image will be hidden by the new white layer. (For directions on how to do this, turn to page 93.)

3. Add a white layer mask to the new layer. (See page 200 for directions on how to do this.) The Layers tab page of the Layers & Channels dialog box will now contain the original layers, and the new layer and layer mask (**Figure 40**).

4. Make sure the new layer mask is selected.

5. Set black as the foreground color. (Turn to page 42 to find out how to do this.)

6. Select the Text Tool in the GIMP Toolbox.

7. Position the mouse pointer over the area where you would like the text to appear and click. The Text Tool dialog box will open (**Figure 41**).

8. Use the Text Tool dialog box to select a font and font size. In addition type the text you want to create in the large text box at the bottom of the dialog box. (To learn more about adding text to images, see Chapter 14, *Working with Text*.)

CREATE A LAYER MASK WITH A TEXT CUTOUT

Figure 39. Open the image to which you want to add the layer mask text cutout.

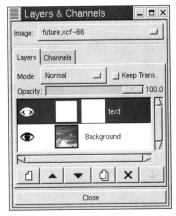

Figure 40. Add a white, full opacity layer mask to the new layer. In this figure, the new layer is named "text."

Choose a font   Enter text size here

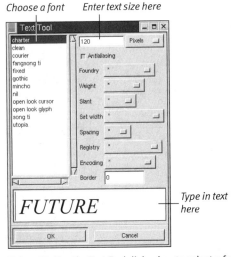

Type in text here

Figure 41. Use the Text Tool dialog box to select a font, enter the text size, and type in the text.

Figure 42. Selected text appears on the layer mask. Notice how it creates the cutout, revealing the layer below. After adding the text to the layer mask, you can move it to the right position.

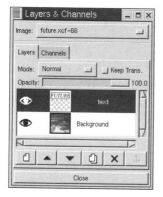

Figure 43a. When the cutout text layer mask is applied to the layer, the layer mask thumbnail disappears and the text cutout becomes a permanent part of the layer.

Figure 43b.
The finished image displaying the layer with the text cutout.

9. Click OK. The Text Tool dialog box will close and the text will appear, selected on the image, creating a text layer mask cutout (**Figure 42**). In addition, the text will appear on the Layers tab page as a floating selection.

10. To move the selected text, position the mouse pointer over the text, press the left mouse button and drag.

11. To anchor the selected text to the layer mask, right-click on the layer window and choose Anchor Layer from the pop-up menu. The text will anchor to the layer mask (**Figures 43a–b**).

To create a gradient layer mask:

1. Open the image you want to add the text layer mask to (**Figure 39**).

2. Using the Layers & Channels dialog box, create a new white layer on top of any existing layers. The image will be hidden by the new white layer. (For directions on how to do this turn to page 93.)

3. Add a white layer mask to the new layer. (See page 200 for directions on how to do this.) The Layers tab page of the Layers & Channels dialog box will now contain the original layers, and the new layer and layer mask (**Figure 40**).

4. Make sure the new layer mask is selected.

5. If you wish, use a selection tool to select an area to restrict the gradient area.

6. Use the color selector to set the foreground and background colors back to the default black and white. (Turn to page 46 for directions.)

(continued)

7. Select the Blend Tool in the GIMP Toolbox.

8. Position the mouse pointer at one side of the image, press the left mouse button, and drag. A line will appear, indicating the direction of the drag (**Figure 44**).

9. Release the left mouse button. The gradient will appear on the layer mask, creating a fade out effect on the image (**Figure 45**).

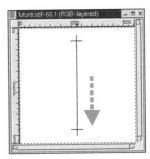

Figure 44. As you drag the Blend Tool, a line appears indicating the direction of the drag.

If You Make a Mistake, Don't Panic!

If you edit an image in a way you didn't mean to or apply a layer mask when you meant to discard it, don't worry! You can always undo it. Just press Ctrl+Z on the keyboard.

Figure 45. When you release the left mouse button, the gradient appears on the layer mask, creating a fade out effect.

Summary

In this chapter you learned how to:

◆ Select a channel

◆ Show/hide a channel

◆ Add and duplicate an alpha channel

◆ Change alpha channel order

◆ Rename an alpha channel

◆ Delete an alpha channel

◆ Use an alpha channel

◆ Add and edit a layer mask

◆ Show/hide the effects of a layer mask

◆ Apply and discard a layer mask

◆ Add text to a layer mask creating a cutout

◆ Apply a gradient to a layer mask to create a fade out effect

CREATE A GRADIENT LAYER MASK

WORKING WITH TEXT

*T*ext is created in the GIMP using the Text Tool in the GIMP Toolbox. It appears selected in the image window on the active layer. The text's *attributes*—font, size, style, and the text itself—are all entered before the text appears in the image window. After the text is created, it can be moved, recolored, filled with a pattern or gradient, or manipulated using filters. You should know, though, that once text is created, none of the text attributes (font, size, style, or the text itself) can be changed—you'll have to create new text.

In this chapter, you'll find out how to create text and discover the difference between Type 1 and TrueType fonts. Then, you'll learn how to add fonts so the GIMP can use them. From there, you'll rotate and transform text, move a text layer, fill text with a pattern, and create fading text. Finally, you'll find out how to add layer effects to semi-transparent text, add a sparkle effect, and create amazing text effects using script-fu mini-programs.

Put Text on Its Own Layer

When working with text in an image, it's always a good idea to create the text on its own layer. That way, you can manipulate it without affecting other image elements. And, if you don't like the text after working with it, you can easily delete it.

Another pointer: since text isn't editable after it's created, there's no way to find out what font it is if you want to create more that's exactly the same. One way to get around this is to enter the font name and size as the layer name. For instance, you could name a layer, "Times, 50 point, bold, italic."

Creating Text

Adding text to an image is easy using the Text Tool. You should know that once text is added to an image, though, the text can't be edited.

To create text:

1. If you want to add the text to an existing layer, use the Layers & Channels dialog box to select that layer. (See page 92 for directions about how to do this.) If you're going to put the text on a new layer, skip this step and move to step 2.

2. Select the Text Tool in the GIMP Toolbox. The mouse pointer will change to an I-beam.

3. Position the mouse I-beam where you want the text to appear, then click. The Text Tool dialog box will appear (**Figure 1**).

4. In the large text box at the bottom of the dialog box, type in the text you want to add to the image.

5. Use the Font list box to select a font. The text that you entered in the large text box will change to that font.

6. Use the Font Size text box to enter the size of the text. By default, the measurement is set to pixels. To change the measurement to points, use the drop-down list to the right of the font size text box (**Figure 2**).

7. Make sure the Antialiasing check button is selected. This will smooth the edges of the text. (If this check button is unselected, the text edge will be quite jagged; turn to page 62 and take a look at Figure 4 to see what antialiased text looks like.)

Available fonts   *Font size*   *Size measurement*

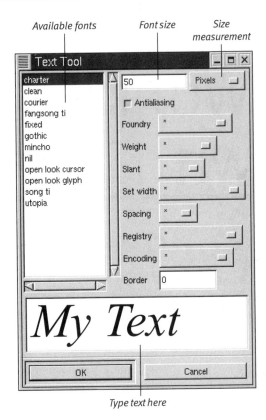

Type text here

Figure 1. Use the Text Tool dialog box to enter the text and select text attributes such as font, size, and style.

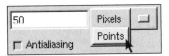

Figure 2. Use the drop-down list to the right of the Font Size text box to set the measurement system.

CREATE TEXT

Figure 3. Use the Weight drop-down list to set whether the text is extra bold (black), bold, or regular (medium).

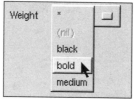

8. Use the Weight drop-down list to set whether the text is black (extra bold), bold, or medium (regular) (**Figure 3**). Different options will be available depending upon the font you selected.

9. Use the Slant drop-down list to set whether the text is normal (r) or italic (i) (**Figure 4**). Different options will be available depending upon the font you selected.

Figure 4. Use the Slant drop-down list to set whether the text is italicized (i) or regular (r).

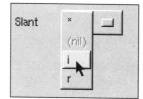

10. Use the Set width drop-down list to set whether the spacing is normal or condensed. Some fonts offer narrower (condensed) versions. Different options will be available depending upon the font you selected.

11. If you want to add extra space around the text, enter a number (in pixels) in the Border text box. This is handy if you want to move letters around and need extra space.

Figure 5. The text appears as a floating selection in the image window.

12. Click OK. The text will appear as a floating selection in the image window (**Figure 5**). You can now move it to a new position, if need be, then anchor it to the layer you selected in step 1, or anchor it to a new layer by clicking the New Layer button in the Layers & Channels dialog box. (For more about floating selections and anchoring them, turn to pages 99–100.)

CREATE TEXT

What Are Points?

Text is usually measured in points in most word processing, page layout, and graphic image manipulation programs. Unlike pixels, which change size depending upon the resolution of your monitor (see page 25 for a sidebar about pixels), a point is a fixed value. 72 point text is 1" (2.54 cm) high; 18 point text is ¼" (6 mm) high. The text in this sentence is set in 10 point type.

Where Have All the Fonts Gone?

The GIMP ships with about 12 fonts. This certainly isn't enough fonts, considering all the incredible fonts that are available. It's possible to install new Type 1 and TrueType fonts and get the GIMP to recognize them, though the process is a bit involved. The following instructions are for those of you running the GIMP on Linux. Have heart, stick to the steps, and you can load in as many fonts as you like.

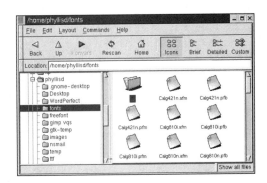

Figure 6. Use File Manager to copy your Type 1 fonts to a directory of your choice.

To install Type 1 fonts:

1. Using File Manager, copy your Type 1 fonts to a directory of your choice (**Figure 6**). In this example, the directory is `/home/phyllisd/fonts`.

2. Use a browser to go to `ftp://sunsite.unc.edu/pub/Linux/X11/xutils/` (**Figure 7**).

3. Scroll down the list until you find the `typelinst-0.6.1.tar.gz` link.

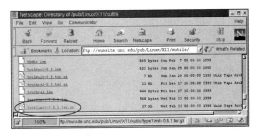

Figure 7. Use a browser to go to `ftp://sunsite.unc.edu/pub/Linux/X11/xutils/`. Scroll down until you find the `typelinst-0.6.1.tar.gz` link.

Type 1 and TrueType Fonts—What's the Difference?

PostScript Type 1 and TrueType are technical standards used to create fonts. Both font standards are resolution independent, meaning that they can be *scaled* to virtually any size and retain their shape. (Fonts that aren't scalable, such as bitmap fonts, will look jagged when their size is changed.)

The difference between Type 1 and TrueType fonts is in the mathematics used to describe the curves of the letters and the size of the font files.

Most high-end output devices, such as Linotronic and Varityper imagesetters, typically use PostScript Type 1 fonts since they can be sent directly to the output device. TrueType fonts can be downloaded as bitmaps, but this can slow down printing.

If you want to learn more about the differences between Type 1 and TrueType fonts, take a look at Thomas W. Phinney's excellent article at:

`http://www.truetype.demon.co.uk/articles/ttvst1.htm`

Figure 8.
Use the Save As dialog box to select the download directory, then click OK.

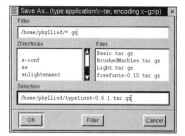

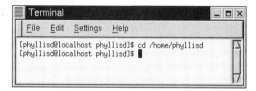

Figure 9. Use the Terminal window to change to the directory where you saved the downloaded file.

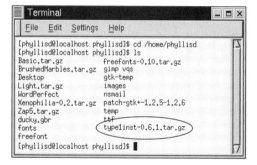

Figure 10. Type ls to view the contents of the directory. You should see the typelinst-0.6.1.tar.gz file.

Figure 11. Unpack the compressed file by typing zcat typelinst-0.6.1.tar.gz | tar -x, then pressing Enter on the keyboard. A new subdirectory, typelinst-0.6.1 appears, containing the unpacked files.

4. Click the link to download the file to your computer. The Save As dialog box will open (**Figure 8**).

5. Use the Directories list box in the Save As dialog box to move to the directory where the downloaded file will be saved. In this example, the file is saved to /home/phyllisd.

6. Click OK. The file will download to the directory you selected.

7. Close the browser window. The next thing you will need to do is unpack the downloaded file since it's compressed.

8. Open a Terminal window (**Figure 9**). (For directions on how to do this, turn to page 23, step 1.)

9. Use the Terminal window to change to the directory where you saved the downloaded file. In this example, cd /home/phyllisd is entered.

10. Type ls at the command prompt, then press Enter on the keyboard to see the contents of the directory (**Figure 10**). You should see the typelinst-0.6.1.tar.gz file.

11. At the command prompt, type zcat typelinst-0.6.1.tar.gz | tar -x then press Enter to unpack the file. The file contents (several compressed files) will be unpacked and stored in its own subdirectory in the current directory called typelinst-0.6.1 (**Figure 11**).

12. Use the Terminal window to change to the new subdirectory where the unpacked files have been saved. In this example the subdirectory is located at /home/phyllisd/typelinst-0.6.1.

(continued)

13. Type ls at the command prompt, then press Enter on the keyboard to see the contents of the new subdirectory (**Figure 12**). The two files that you will use are called typelinst and t1embed. The next thing you will need to do is copy these two files to a directory listed on the path.

Figure 12. Type ls to view the contents of the typelinst-0.6.1 subdirectory.

14. Type su root at the command prompt, press Enter on the keyboard, and then enter the root password. (You need to be root in order to copy the files to the necessary directory.)

15. Type echo $PATH at the command prompt, then press Enter on the keyboard. (You need to type it exactly as it's shown here with the lower and uppercase letters.) The terminal window will display your path (**Figure 13**).

Figure 13. Type echo PATH$ to see the directories on your path.

16. Copy the two files in the new subdirectory to a directory listed on your path (**Figure 14**). In this example, the two files are copied to the /usr/bin directory listed first on the path. In order to do this, the following two commands are typed at the command prompt in the terminal window:

Figure 14. Copy the two files, typelinst and t1embed to a directory on your path.

cp /home/phyllisd/typelinst-0.6.1/typelinst /usr/bin
(press Enter on the keyboard)

cp /home/phyllisd/typelinst-0.6.1/t1embed /usr/bin
(press Enter on the keyboard)

A Free Source for Type 1 Fonts

If you want to add to your Type1 font collection, a free download of 79 Type 1 fonts is available at ftp://metalab.unc.edu/pub/Linux/X11/fonts/. Scroll down the Web page until you find freefonts-0.10.tar.gz. Click the link to download the compressed file.

Figure 15. Enter typelinst, then press Enter on the keyboard to create necessary font files.

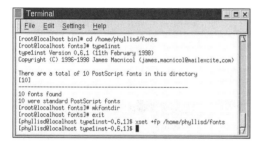

Figure 16. Use the xset +fp command to tell the X font server where the Type 1 fonts are.

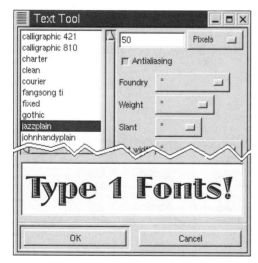

Figure 17. After restarting the GIMP, use the Text Tool to view your new fonts.

17. Use the terminal window to move to the directory where the Type1 fonts that you copied in step 1 are stored. In this example, the directory is named /home/phyllisd/fonts.

18. Enter typelinst at the command prompt, then press Enter on the keyboard. The typelinst program will create and save necessary font files (fonts.dir and fonts.scale) in the directory (**Figure 15**).

19. Type mkfontdir at the command prompt, then press Enter on the keyboard. The mkfontdir program will create a list of the fonts and save it in the directory.

20. Type exit at the command prompt, then press Enter on the keyboard. This will log you off as root and return you to your regular log in.

21. Type xset +fp YourFontDirectory at the command prompt, then press Enter on the keyboard (**Figure 16**). Substitute the full path of the directory where your fonts are stored for YourFontDirectory. In this example, xset +fp /home/phyllisd/fonts is typed. The X font server now knows about the fonts and where to find them. Launch the GIMP and use the Text Tool to see your new fonts (**Figure 17**).

✔ Tips

■ If you log off or shut down your computer, you'll need to perform steps 17–21 again to access the Type 1 fonts.

■ Special thanks to James Macnicol for creating the typelinst program!

To install TrueType fonts:

1. Use a browser to go to `ftp://metalab.unc.edu/pub/Linux/X11/fonts/` (**Figure 18**).

2. Scroll down to the bottom of the Web page where you'll find the `xfstt-1.0.tar.gz` link.

3. Click the link to download the file to your computer. The Save As dialog box will open (**Figure 8**).

4. Use the Directories list box in the Save As dialog box to move to the directory where the downloaded file will be saved. In this example, the file is saved to `/home/phyllisd`.

5. Click OK. The file will download to the directory you selected.

6. Close the browser window. The next thing you will need to do is unpack the downloaded file since it's compressed.

7. Open a Terminal window (**Figure 19**). (For directions on how to do this, turn to page 23, step 1.).

8. Use the Terminal window to change to the directory where you saved the downloaded file. In this example, `cd /home/phyllisd` is entered.

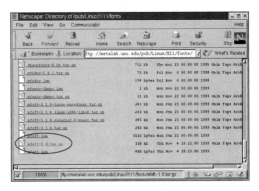

Figure 18. Use a browser to go to `ftp://metalab.unc.edu/pub/Linux/X11/fonts/`, then scroll to the bottom of the Web page where you'll find `xfstt-1.0.tar.gz`.

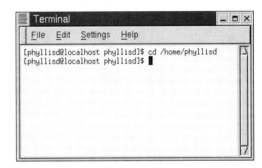

Figure 19. Use the Terminal window to change to the directory where you saved the downloaded file.

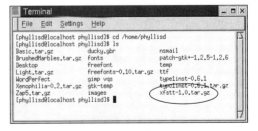

Figure 20. Type `ls` to view the contents of the directory. `xfstt-1.0.tar.gz` should be listed.

Figure 21. Unpack the compressed file by typing zcat xfstt-1.0.tar.gz | tar -x then pressing Enter on the keyboard. A new subdirectory, xfstt-1.0 will automatically be created and contain the unpacked files.

Figure 22. After changing to the new subdirectory where the unpacked files have been saved, type make; make install then press Enter on the keyboard. The files in the directory will compile, creating a program that will load TrueType fonts.

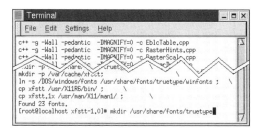

Figure 23. Type mkdir /usr/share/fonts/truetype to create the directory where you will store your TrueType fonts.

9. Type ls at the command prompt, then press Enter on the keyboard to see the contents of the directory (**Figure 20**). You should see the xfstt-1.0.tar.gz file.

10. Type zcat xfstt-1.0.tar.gz | tar -x at the command prompt, then press Enter on the keyboard to unpack the file (**Figure 21**). The file contents (several compressed files) will be unpacked and stored in its own subdirectory in the current directory called xfstt-1.0.

11. Use the Terminal window to change to the new subdirectory where the unpacked files have been saved. In this example the subdirectory is located at /home/phyllisd/xfstt-1.0.

12. Type su root at the command prompt, press Enter on the keyboard, and then enter the root password. (You need to be root in order to perform the next few steps.)

13. Type make; make install at the command prompt, then press Enter on the keyboard (**Figure 22**). The files in the xfstt-1.0 subdirectory will compile and become a program that you can use to load TrueType fonts into Linux.

14. Type mkdir /usr/share/fonts/truetype at the command prompt, then press Enter on the keyboard (**Figure 23**). This will create a directory for storing the TrueType fonts.

15. Copy your TrueType fonts to the directory you just created (/usr/share/fonts/truetype).

(continued)

INSTALL TRUETYPE FONTS

16. Type xfstt --sync at the command prompt, then press Enter on the keyboard (**Figure 24**).

17. Type xfstt & at the command prompt, then press Enter on the keyboard.

18. Type xset fp+ unix/:7101 at the command prompt, then press Enter on the keyboard.

19. Type exit at the command prompt, then press Enter on the keyboard. This will log you off as root and and return you to your regular log in. Congratulations! You made it! Launch the GIMP and use the Text Tool to see your new TrueType fonts (**Figure 25**).

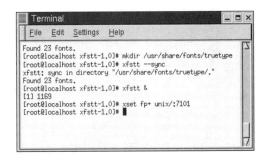

Figure 24. Type xfstt --sync and press Enter on the keyboard. This makes the xfstt program locate the TrueType fonts.

✔ Tips

■ If you want to add new TrueType fonts to your computer, copy them into the /usr/share/fonts/truetype directory, open a terminal window and type xfstt --sync at the command prompt, then press Enter on the keyboard.

■ There is a way to set the xfstt program to run automatically when you boot your computer (which makes the TrueType fonts available), but it's dicey. I'm not including it here because I tried it and it totally crashed my computer (ugh!). I spent the better part of a morning getting my computer up and running again.

■ If you add new fonts to the TrueType font directory, you'll need to let the GIMP know they're there. Just open a terminal window and type xfstt --sync at the command prompt, then press Enter on the keyboard.

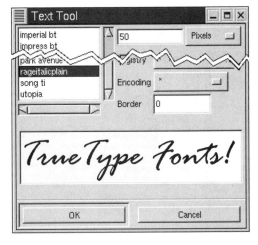

Figure 25. After restarting the GIMP, use the Text Tool to view your new fonts.

Downloading TrueType Fonts

There are thousands of free TrueType fonts ready for download from the Web. Check out Type Euphoria at:

http://fonts.linuxpower.org/

Figure 26. Use a selection tool to select the text that you want to transform.

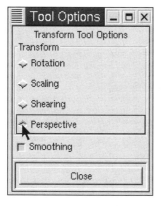

Figure 27. Use the Tool Options dialog box to select the type of transformation.

Figure 28. Drag the mouse to transform the text. In this example, perspective has been added to the text.

Transforming Text

Rotating, scaling, shearing, adding perspective, flipping, and moving text is easy whether it's on its own layer or part of a layer containing an image.

To rotate, scale, shear, or add perspective to text:

1. Use one of the selection tools to select the text you want to rotate (**Figure 26**).

   or

   Use the Layers & Channels dialog box to select a text layer for rotation.

2. Double-click on the Transform Tool in the GIMP Toolbox. The Tool Options dialog box will open (**Figure 27**).

3. In the Transform area, select the radio button next to one of the options—Rotation, Scaling, Shearing, or Perspective.

4. Select the Smoothing check button if you want the edges of the text blurred to create a smoother look.

5. Click Close. The Tool Options dialog box will close.

6. With the Transform Tool selected, position the mouse pointer over the selected text or layer.

7. Press the left mouse button and drag. The selected text or layer will rotate, scale, shear, or add perspective, depending upon the option you selected (**Figure 28**).

✔ Tip

■ To find out more about the Transform Tool and what it can do, turn to pages 154–162.

To flip text vertically or horizontally:

1. Use one of the selection tools to select the text you want to flip (**Figure 29**).

   or

   Use the Layers & Channels dialog box to select a text layer for flipping.

2. Double-click on the Flip Tool in the GIMP Toolbox. The Tool Options dialog box will open (**Figure 30**).

3. Select either the Horizontal or Vertical radio button.

4. Click Close. The Tool Options dialog box will close.

5. With the Flip Tool selected, click on the selected text or layer. The selection or layer will flip horizontally or vertically, depending upon the option you selected (**Figure 31**). You can create interesting results using several transformations (**Figure 32**).

✔ Tip

■ To find out more about the Flip Tool, turn to pages 152–153.

Figure 29. Use one of the selection tools to select the text you want to flip.

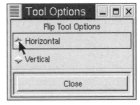

Figure 30. Select either the Horizontal or Vertical radio button, then click Close.

Figure 32. You can create interesting text effects using several transformations.

Figure 31. Depending upon the option you selected, the text will flip horizontally or vertically.

Figure 33. Use the Text Tool to create text.

To move a text layer:

1. Use the Text Tool to create some text (**Figure 33**). It will appear in the image window as a floating selection.

2. In the Layers & Channels dialog box, click New Layer to anchor the text to its own layer.

3. Select the Move Tool from the GIMP Toolbox. The mouse pointer will change to double-headed arrows.

Figure 34. Use the Move Tool to move the text layer.

4. Position the mouse pointer over the selected text layer, then press the left mouse button and drag the text to its new position (**Figure 34**).

✔ Tip

■ To find out how to move text that has been selected, turn to page 148.

To find out how to move text that has been selected, turn to page 148.

MOVE A TEXT LAYER

It's Easy to Add an Outline to Text

If you want to create text that is outlined, here's what you need to do:

1. Create the text using the Text Tool. It will appear in the image window as a floating selection.

2. Use the Brush Selection dialog box to select the Circle (01) brush. (The bigger the brush, the thicker the outline.)

3. Set the foreground color to the color you want to use to outline the text.

4. Right-click on the floating, selected text and choose Edit→Stroke from the pop-up menu. An outline will appear around the text.

Filling Text with a Pattern

It's easy to fill selected text with a pattern in the GIMP. All you need to use is the Pattern Selection dialog box and the Bucket Fill Tool.

Figure 35. Create the text that you want to fill with a pattern. It appears in the image window as a floating selection.

To fill text with a pattern:

1. Use the Text Tool to create the text you want to fill with a pattern (**Figure 35**). The text will appear in the image window as a floating selection.

2. Double-click the Bucket Fill Tool in the GIMP Toolbox. The Tool Options dialog box will open (**Figure 36**).

3. In the Fill Type area, select the Pattern Fill radio button.

4. Click Close to close the Tool Options dialog box.

5. Right-click on the image and choose Dialogs→Patterns from the pop-up menu (**Figure 37**) or press Shift+Ctrl+P on the keyboard. The Pattern Selection dialog box will open (**Figure 38**).

6. Click a pattern in the pattern window to select it.

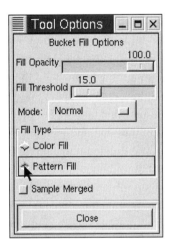

Figure 36.
In the Tool Options dialog box, select the Pattern Fill radio button, then click Close.

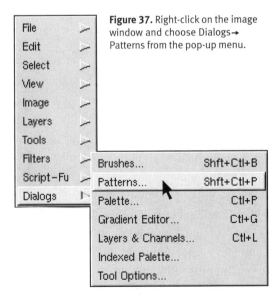

Figure 37. Right-click on the image window and choose Dialogs→ Patterns from the pop-up menu.

FILL TEXT WITH A PATTERN

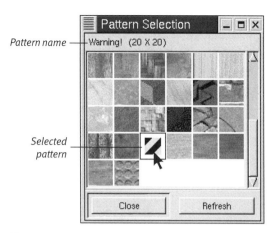

Pattern name

Selected pattern

Figure 38. Use the Pattern Selection dialog box to select a pattern.

7. With the Bucket Fill Tool still selected, position the mouse cursor over one of the selected letters and click. The pattern will fill the letter (**Figure 39**). Continue filling the other letters with the same or a different pattern (**Figure 40**).

✔ Tip

■ Remember that fills in letters work just the same as they do in other objects in the GIMP. You can set fill opacity and blending modes using the Tool Options dialog box. For details about fill opacity, turn to page 110; for information about blending modes, turn to pages 170–173.

Figure 39. When you click, the pattern fills the letter.

Figure 40. Continue filling the rest of the letters with the same or a different pattern.

FILL TEXT WITH A PATTERN

Transformations and Filters

Any of the transformations discussed in Chapter 10, *Transform Your Art*, or filters discussed in Chapter 15, *Using Filters*, can be applied to text. If you want to experiment, just put the text on its own layer and try something out!

Fading Text

Using the Blend Tool and a layer mask, it's easy to quickly create text that fades out.

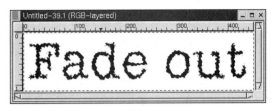

Figure 41. Use the Text Tool to create the text you want to fade out, then anchor it to its own layer.

To create fading text:

1. Use the Text Tool to create some text. It will appear in the image window as a floating selection (**Figure 41**).

2. In the Layers & Channels dialog box, click New Layer to anchor the text to its own layer.

3. Right-click on the new text layer and choose Add Layer Mask from the pop-up menu (**Figure 42**). The Add Mask Options dialog box will open (**Figure 43**).

4. Select the Black (Full Transparency) radio button.

5. Click OK. The Add Mask Options dialog box will close and a layer mask thumbnail will appear next to the layer thumbnail in the Layers & Channels dialog box.

6. Select the Blend Tool in the GIMP Toolbox.

7. Make sure the foreground and background colors are set to the default (black and white, respectively) in the color selector. (Turn to page 46 for directions.)

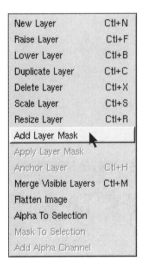

Figure 42. Right-click on the new layer and choose Add Layer Mask from the pop-up menu.

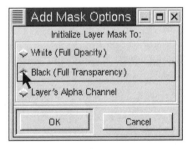

Figure 43. In the Add Mask Options dialog box, select the Black (Full Transparency) radio button, then click OK.

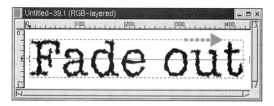

Figure 44. Drag the mouse left to right or top to bottom (or any way you need to drag it). As you drag a line appears indicating the direction of the drag.

Figure 45. When you release the mouse button, the layer mask goes to work and the text appears to fade out.

8. Position the mouse pointer at one side of the layer mask, then press the left mouse button and drag across the image window from top to bottom or left to right. A line will appear indicating the direction of the drag (**Figure 44**).

9. Release the mouse button. When you release the mouse button, the fading text will appear (**Figure 45**).

✔ Tips

- Remember that you can set opacity, blending mode, fill, gradient, and repeat options for the Blend Tool using the Tool Options dialog box. To find out more about these options, turn to page 125.

- To find out more about layer masks, turn to page 200.

Figure 46. Open the image to which you want to add the semi-transparent text.

Figure 47. The text appears as a floating selection in the image window.

Adding Special Effects to Text

There are so many special effects one can add to text that it's mind boggling! In this section you'll find two of the many possibilities. Try mixing different filters, blending modes, and gradients. For some interesting ideas, take a look at http://www.xach.com/GIMP/dates/.

To add semi-transparent, shadowed, and highlighted text to an image:

1. Open the image to which you want to add the effect (**Figure 46**).

2. Select white as the foreground color (see page 42 for directions).

3. Use the Text Tool to create the text you want to add to the image. The text will appear as a floating selection in the image window (**Figure 47**).

4. Right-click on the image window and choose Script-Fu→Decor→Xach-Effect from the pop-up menu (**Figure 48**). The Script-Fu Xach-Effect dialog box will open (**Figure 49**).

5. In the highlight X and Y offset boxes, enter the value (in pixels) that you would like the highlight moved over (offset) from the original.

6. Use the Highlight Color, Opacity, and Drop Shadow Color buttons to open the Script-Fu Color Picker dialog box (**Figure 50**) to select colors for these items.

7. In the Drop shadow Opacity text box, enter a percentage value. The lower the number, the more transparent the drop-shadow will be.

8. To set how fuzzy the drop shadow is, enter a value in pixels in the Drop shadow Blur Radius text box. The higher the number, the fuzzier the drop shadow.

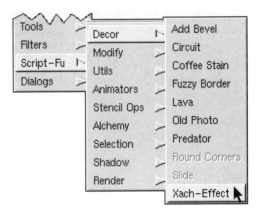

Figure 48. Right-click on the image and choose Script-Fu→Decor→Xach-Effect from the pop-up menu.

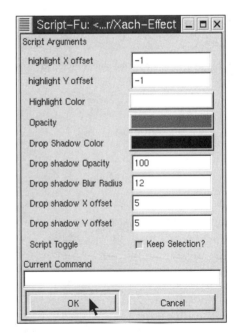

Figure 49. Use the Script-Fu Xach-Effect dialog box to set highlight and drop shadow offset, highlight and drop shadow color and opacity, and drop shadow blur radius. (If this is your first time using the Xach-Effect script-fu, try the default settings—they work pretty well.)

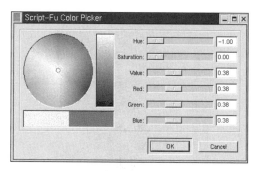

Figure 50. Use the Script-Fu Color Picker dialog box to set the highlight, opacity, and drop shadow colors.

Figure 51. When you click OK, the script-fu goes to work and adds a highlight and shadow to the text.

Figure 52. Lower the opacity setting in the Layers & Channels dialog box to make the text semi-transparent. In this example, the opacity is set to 5%.

9. In the Drop shadow X and Y offset text boxes, enter the value (in pixels) that you would like the drop shadow moved over (offset) up or down from the original.

10. Click OK. The Xach-Effect script-fu will go to work and add a highlight and shadow to the white text (**Figure 51**).

11. Open the Layers & Channels dialog box and use the Opacity slider to make the text semi-transparent (**Figure 52**).

12. When the transparency of the text is the way you want it, anchor the text by clicking the Anchor Layer button at the bottom right of the Layers & Channels dialog box.

To add sparkle to your text:

1. Create the text you want to add sparkles to and anchor it to a layer. In this example 150 point text is created.

2. Use the Layers & Channels dialog box to add a transparent layer on top of the text layer.

3. Set white as the foreground color (turn to page 42 for details on how to do this).

4. Use the Brush Selection dialog box to choose a brush. For this example the Circle (03) brush is selected. (Very small brushes are best, anything too large turns into a giant blob with arms.)

5. Select the Pencil Tool in the GIMP Toolbox. The mouse pointer will change to a small pencil.

6. With the new transparent layer selected, position the mouse pointer over an area of the text where you want to add a sparkle.

(continued)

7. Click. A white circle the size of the brush you selected will appear on the transparent layer.

8. Repeat steps 6–7, adding more white circles where you want sparkles to appear (**Figure 53**).

9. Right-click on the image and choose Filters→Light Effects→Sparkle from the pop-up menu (**Figure 54**). The Sparkle dialog box will open (**Figure 55**).

10. Use the various sliders to set the sparkle parameter settings (you'll need to experiment to get it just right). For this example, Luminosity Threshold is set to .006, Flare Intensity is set to .20, Spike Length is set to 40.4, Spike Points is set to 7, and Spike Angle is set to 12.3.

11. Click OK. The Sparkle filter will go to work and change the small circles on the transparent layer into sparkly stars (**Figure 56**).

Figure 53. Use the Pencil Tool to paint small white dots where you would like the sparkles to appear. In this figure there are four dots, one on the statue's torch, and one each at the top of the letters i, r, and y.

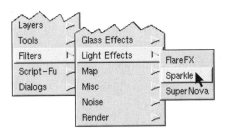

Figure 54. Right-click on the image and choose Filters→Light Effects→Sparkle from the pop-up menu.

Figure 56. When you click OK, the Sparkle filter goes to work and finally (after a bit of a wait, depending upon your computer's speed) creates the sparkles.

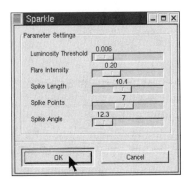

Figure 55. Use the Sparkle dialog box to set the luminosity threshold, flare intensity, and spike length, number of points, and angle.

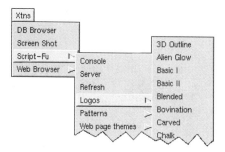

Figure 57. There are many text effect script-fus available on the Logos menu.

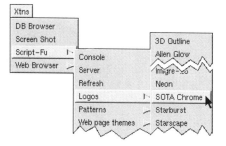

Figure 58. In the GIMP Toolbox choose Xtns→Script-Fu→Logos→SOTA Chrome.

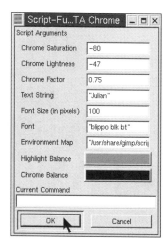

Figure 59. Use the Script-Fu SOTA Chrome dialog box to enter the text, font and font size, and highlight and chrome balance colors. (If this is your first time using this script-fu, try the default settings—they work well.)

Creating Quick Text Effects

Many amazing script-fus come with the GIMP that create text with a myriad of effects. They're all located on the Xtns→Script-Fu→Logos menu found in the GIMP Toolbox (**Figure 57**). These script-fus are all mini-programs that work in basically the same way: select one of the menu items and a script-fu dialog box for that item appears. Set the available options, click OK, and watch the magic happen! Below are directions for how to use two of the script-fus.

To create text with the appearance of chrome:

1. In the GIMP Toolbox, choose Xtns→Script-Fu→Logos→SOTA Chrome (**Figure 58**). The Script-Fu SOTA Chrome dialog box will open (**Figure 59**).

2. In the Text String text box, type in the text that you want to create. The text must be surrounded by quotes or the script-fu won't work (the quotes won't appear in the finished text). In this example, "Julian" is entered.

3. In the Font Size (in pixels) text box, enter the size of the text.

4. In the Font text box, type in a font name that is loaded on your computer. The font name must be surrounded by quotes or the script-fu won't work. Even though a default font name appears in the Font text box, that font isn't necessarily loaded on your computer. (To find out the names of the fonts, select the Text Tool from the GIMP Toolbox and click in an image window. The Text Tool dialog box will open displaying the available fonts (**Figure 1**).)

(continued)

5. Click the Highlight Balance color button. The Script-Fu Color Picker dialog box will open (**Figure 60**).

6. Use the Script-Fu Color Picker dialog box to set the highlight balance color, then click OK to close the dialog box.

7. Click the Chrome Balance color button. The Script-Fu Color Picker dialog box will open.

8. Use the Script-Fu Color Picker dialog box to set the chrome balance color, then click OK to close the dialog box.

9. When you've finished setting options in the Script-Fu SOTA Chrome dialog box, click OK. The dialog box will close and the script-fu will go to work. In a few seconds a new image window will appear, containing the chrome text (**Figure 61**). Take a look at the layers window in the Layers & Channels dialog box to get an idea of how the effect is created (**Figure 62**).

To create textured text:

1. In the GIMP Toolbox, choose Xtns→ Script-Fu→Logos→Textured (**Figure 63**). The Script-Fu Textured dialog box will open (**Figure 64**).

2. In the Text Pattern text box, enter a pattern name in quotes. (To find out the pattern names, choose File→Dialogs→ Patterns in the GIMP Toolbox, then click on a pattern in the Pattern Selection dialog box (**Figure 38**). The pattern name will appear at the top of the dialog box.)

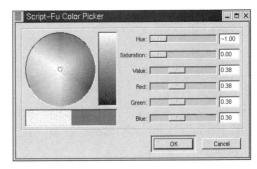

Figure 60. Use the Script-Fu Color Picker dialog box to set the highlight and chrome balance colors.

Figure 61. When you click OK, the script-fu goes to work and creates amazing text with a chrome look.

Figure 62. Take a look at the Layers tab page in the Layers & Channels dialog box to find out how the effect is created.

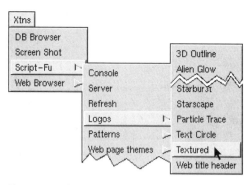

Figure 63. In the GIMP Toolbox, choose Xtns→Script-Fu→Logos→Textured.

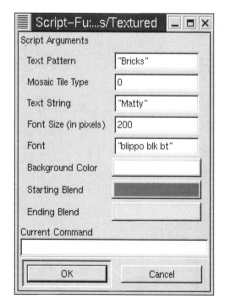

Figure 64. Use the Script-Fu Textured dialog box to set the text pattern, enter the text, set the font and font size, and set the background color and starting and ending blend colors.

3. In the Mosaic Tile Type text box, enter 0 for a background mosaic made up of square tiles, 1 for hexagonal tiles, or 2 for octagonal and square tiles.

4. In the Text String text box, type in the text that you want to create. The text must be surrounded by quotes or the script-fu won't work (the quotes won't appear in the finished text). In this example, "Matty" is entered.

5. In the Font Size (in pixels) text box, enter the size of the text.

6. In the Font text box, type in a font name that is loaded on your computer. The font name must be surrounded by quotes or the script-fu won't work. Even though a default font name appears in the Font text box, that font isn't necessarily loaded on your computer. (To find out the names of the fonts, select the Text Tool from the GIMP Toolbox and click in an image window. The Text Tool dialog box will open displaying the available fonts (**Figure 1**).)

7. Click the Background Color, Starting Blend, and Ending Blend buttons to pick those colors. In each case, the Script-Fu Color Picker dialog box will open (**Figure 60**).

(continued)

8. Use the Script-Fu Color Picker dialog box to choose each color, then click OK to close the dialog box.

9. When you've finished setting options in the Script-Fu Textured dialog box, click OK. The dialog box will close and the Textured script-fu will go to work. In a few seconds, a new image window will open, containing the textured text (**Figure 65**). Take a look at the Layers tab page in the Layers & Channels dialog box to get an idea of how the effect is created (**Figure 66**).

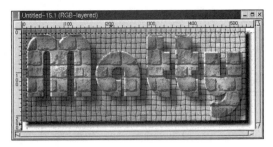

Figure 65. When you click OK, the script-fu goes to work and creates some amazing textured text.

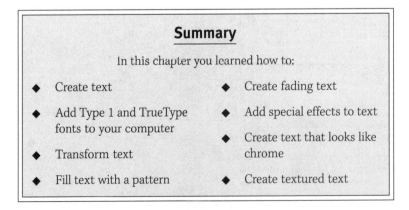

Figure 66. Take a look at the Layers tab page in the Layers & Channels dialog box to find out how the effect is created.

Summary

In this chapter you learned how to:

- Create text
- Add Type 1 and TrueType fonts to your computer
- Transform text
- Fill text with a pattern
- Create fading text
- Add special effects to text
- Create text that looks like chrome
- Create textured text

USING FILTERS

Among the many tools and features that the GIMP has to offer, filters are (in my mind) possibly the coolest of all. Filters can quickly add subtle effects or the most amazing distortions. For instance, you can apply artistic effects that make an image look like it's been painted with oils or created with mosaic tiles. You can use the Blur or Sharpen filters to subtly retouch an image. Apply distortion filters to make an image look like it's been engraved or embossed. Any number of filter effects can be combined using layers, layer masks, and alpha channels.

The Way Filters Work

Filters can be applied to an entire layer or a selection on a layer. If you are using a selection, you can create a smoother transition between the filtered and non-filtered area by feathering the selection before applying the filter. (To find out how to feather a selection, turn to page 82.)

All of the filters work in basically the same way: you select the filter's menu item and a dialog box opens, then you set the options, click OK, and the filter goes to work. Starting on page 239 is a guide to many of the GIMP filters, showing what they can do.

Play It Again, Sam...

If you need to apply a filter more than once to the same selection or different images, right-click on the image and choose Filters→Repeat last from the pop-up menu or press Alt+F on the keyboard. To view the last filter dialog box that you used, right-click on the image and choose Filters→Re-show last from the pop-up menu or press Shift+Alt+F on the keyboard.

Using Filters

There are so many effects you can create using filters! This section will take you, step-by-step, through applying several filters and techniques that you can use to create interesting filter effects. That should give you a good idea of how filters work (since they all work in basically the same way). The next section, which starts on page 239, is a guide to many of the GIMP filters, showing how each one affects an image.

Figure 1. Use the Layers & Channels dialog box to select the layer. In this example, the Background layer containing the flower image is selected.

To make a layer or selection look like it's an oil painting:

1. Use the Layers & Channels dialog box to select the layer that you want to make look like an oil painting (**Figure 1**).

   and/or

   Use a selection tool of your choice to select an area that you want to make look like an oil painting.

2. Right-click on the image and choose Filters→Artistic→Oilify from the pop-up menu (**Figure 2**). The Oilify dialog box will appear (**Figure 3**).

3. Use the Mask Size slider to set the size of the "paintbrush" used to create the oil painting. The higher the setting, the larger the brush.

4. Select the Use intensity algorithm check button if you want the filter to enhance the image's colors.

5. Click OK. The Oilify dialog box will close and the filter will be applied to the layer or selection, making it look like an oil painting (**Figure 4**).

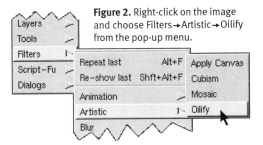

Figure 2. Right-click on the image and choose Filters→Artistic→Oilify from the pop-up menu.

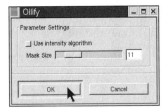

Figure 3. Use the Oilify dialog box to set the Mask Size slider, then click OK.

Figure 4. When the Oilify filter is applied, the image takes on the appearance of an oil painting.

Figure 5. Use the Layers & Channels dialog box to select the layer. In this example, the Background layer containing the flower image is selected.

To make a layer or selection look like it's on a page with a curling corner:

1. Use the Layers & Channels dialog box to select the layer that you want to look as though it's on a curling page (**Figure 5**).

   and/or

   Use a selection tool of your choice to select an area that you want to look as though it's on a curling page.

2. Right-click on the image and choose Filters→Distorts→Pagecurl from the pop-up menu (**Figure 6**). The Pagecurl effect dialog box will open (**Figure 7**).

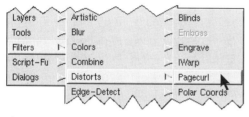

Figure 6. Right-click on the image and choose Filters→Distorts→Pagecurl from the pop-up menu.

3. In the Curl location area, select a radio button to set the page curl at the upper left or right, or lower left or right of the image.

4. In the Curl orientation area, set whether the curl will appear horizontally or vertically.

5. Select the Shade under curl check button to add a shadow.

6. Select the Use current Gradient instead of FG/BG-Color check button to use the currently selected gradient to color the page curl instead of the currently selected foreground and background colors. (Turn to page 127 to find out how to set the current gradient.)

7. Use the Curl opacity slider to set the transparency of the page curl. The lower the setting, the more transparent the page curl will be.

8. Click OK. The Pagecurl effect dialog box will close and the filter will be applied to the layer or selection, making it look like it's on a curling page (**Figure 8**).

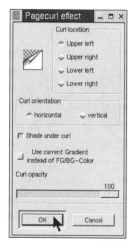

Figure 7. Use the Pagecurl effect dialog box to set the curl's location, orientation, and opacity.

Figure 8. When the Pagecurl filter is applied, the image appears to be on a page that's curling.

Making a Border Wavy

Using the selection tools, it's easy to apply a filter to the edge of an image to give it a rippled, wavy, or whirling border.

To make an image's border wavy:

1. Use the Rectangular Select Tool to select the center portion of the image (**Figure 9**).

2. Right-click on the image and choose Select→Invert from the pop-up menu (**Figure 10**) or press Ctrl+I on the keyboard. The selected area will invert, meaning that the active selection area now encompasses the image border (**Figure 11**).

3. Right-click on the image and choose Select→Feather from the pop-up menu (**Figure 12**). The Feather Selection dialog box will open (**Figure 13**).

4. Enter 10 in the Feather selection by text box, then click OK to close the dialog box.

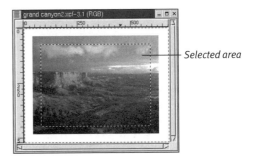

Selected area

Figure 9. Use the Rectangular Select Tool to select the center portion of the image.

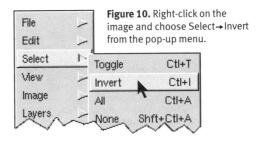

Figure 10. Right-click on the image and choose Select→Invert from the pop-up menu.

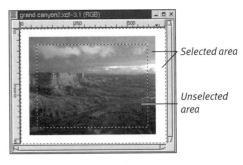

Selected area

Unselected area

Figure 11. After the Invert command is applied the outer edge and border around the image are selected.

Figure 13. In the Feather Selection dialog box, enter a value of 10, then click OK.

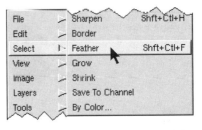

Figure 12. Right-click on the image and choose Select→Feather from the pop-up menu.

MAKE A BORDER WAVY

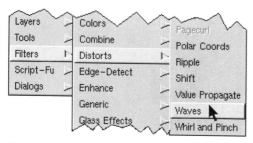

Figure 14. Right-click on the image and choose Filters→Distorts→Waves from the pop-up menu.

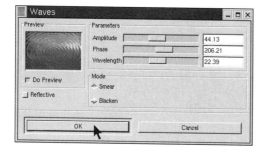

Figure 15. Use the Waves dialog box to set Amplitude, Phase, and Wavelength, then click OK.

Figure 16. When the Waves filter is applied, a wavy edge appears around the image.

5. Right-click on the image and choose Filters→Distorts→Waves from the pop-up menu (**Figure 14**). The Waves dialog box will open (**Figure 15**).

6. In the Parameters area, use the sliders to set the Amplitude (wave height), Phase (wave position), and Wavelength (wave thickness).

7. In the Mode area, select the Smear radio button.

8. Click OK. The Waves dialog box will close and the filter effect will be applied to the border of the image (**Figure 16**).

✔ Tips

- This effect works really well if there's a white border area around the image.

- In Figure 15, you may have noticed that there's a Blacken option in the Mode area. If you select this option, it will add black waves at the edge of the image instead of using colors from the image itself.

- Try other distortion filters such as Ripple and Whirl and Pinch to add interesting effects to image borders (**Figures 17a–b**).

Figure 17a. The Ripple filter creates an interesting edge.

Figure 17b. The Whirl and Pinch filter creates a rotated pinched edge.

Layer Masks and Filters

Using layer masks, you can apply semi-transparent textures to images with filters.

As you probably remember, black areas of a layer mask are transparent, white areas are opaque, and gray areas are semi-transparent. When you apply a filter to a layer mask, the black, white, and gray that the filter creates translates to an interesting texture. (To find out about layer masks and how to use them, turn to pages 200–206.)

To use a layer mask to apply a texture:

1. Create a new image with a white background.

2. Copy and paste a picture or object into the new image (**Figure 18**). The pasted item will appear in the Layers & Channels dialog box as a floating selection (**Figure 19**).

3. In the Layers & Channels dialog box, click the New Layer button. This will place the pasted item onto its own, transparent layer.

Figure 18. Paste an object into a new image window.

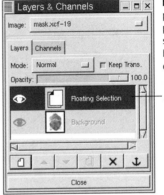

Figure 19. The pasted object appears as a floating selection in the Layers & Channels dialog box.

Pasted object

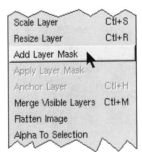

Figure 20. Right-click on the new layer and choose Add Layer Mask from the pop-up menu.

I Can't Access Any Filters!

If you open a filter menu and discover that the filter menu items are all grayed out and unavailable, chances are your image is set in indexed color mode. To use a filter, you'll need to convert the image to RGB mode (turn to page 36–38 for details on color conversion).

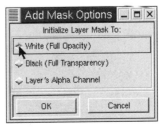

Figure 21. Select the White (Full Opacity) radio button, then click OK.

Figure 22. The layer mask thumbnail appears to the right of the layer thumbnail.

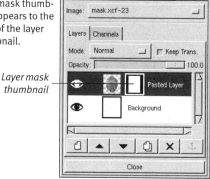

Layer mask thumbnail

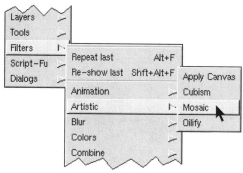

Figure 23. Right-click on the image and choose a filter from the Filters→Artistic menu. In this example, the Mosaic filter is selected.

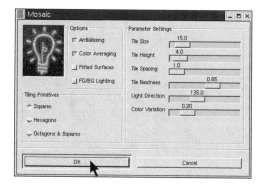

Figure 24. Use the Mosaic dialog box to set tile options, light direction, color variation, and tile shape. In this example, square tiles are selected.

4. In the Layers & Channels dialog box, right-click on the new transparent layer and choose Add Layer Mask from the pop-up menu (**Figure 20**). The Add Mask Options dialog box will appear (**Figure 21**).

5. Select the White (Full Opacity) radio button, then click OK. The Add Mask Options dialog box will close and a layer mask thumbnail will appear selected to the right of the layer thumbnail in the Layers & Channels dialog box (**Figure 22**).

6. With the layer mask thumbnail selected, right-click on the image and choose a filter from the Filters menu on the pop-up menu (**Figure 23**). Depending upon your selection, the dialog box for that filter will open (**Figure 24**). Some filters that work well with this technique are Apply Canvas and Mosaic found on the Artistic sub-menu, Noisify found on the Noise sub-menu, and Checkerboard and Maze found on the Render sub-menu.

7. Use the dialog box for the filter you selected to set the filter's options, then click OK. The filter's dialog box will close and the filter will be applied to the layer mask, resulting in an interesting texture (**Figure 25**).

Figure 25. When a filter is applied to the layer mask, an interesting texture appears on the image. In this example, the Mosaic filter creates a crackled effect.

USE A LAYER MASK TO APPLY TEXTURE

237

Giving an Image the Appearance of Motion

Using the Motion Blur filter, you can give an image the appearance of motion. All you need to do is select the part of the image that will stay "still" while the rest of the image will be blurred, giving the impression of motion.

Figure 26. Select the area that will remain still. In this figure, the kayaker, kayak, and paddle have been selected.

To give an image the appearance of motion:

1. Use the selection tool of your choice to select the area of an image that will remain still (**Figure 26**).

2. Right-click on the Image and choose Select→Feather from the pop-up menu (**Figure 12**). The Feather Selection dialog box will open (**Figure 13**).

3. Enter a value of 10 in the text box, then click OK to close the dialog box.

4. Copy the selected area and paste it into the image. The pasted item will appear as a floating selection.

5. In the Layers & Channels dialog box, click the New Layer button to anchor the floating selection to a new transparent layer.

6. Use the Layers & Channels dialog box to make the original layer active.

7. Right-click on the image and choose Filters→Blur→Motion Blur from the pop-up menu (**Figure 27**). The Motion blur dialog box will appear (**Figure 28**).

8. Set the options using the various sliders and radio buttons. For this example, Length is set to 63, the Blur type is Linear, and the Angle is set to 207.

9. Click OK. The Motion blur dialog box will close and the image will appear to move (**Figure 29**).

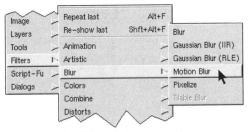

Figure 27. Right-click on the image and choose Filters→Blur→Motion Blur from the pop-up menu.

Figure 28. Use the Motion blur dialog box to set blur length, type, and angle.

Figure 29. When the Motion Blur filter is applied to the original layer, the pasted image appears to be moving.

Artistic Filters

Original image

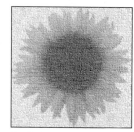

Apply Canvas

Cubism

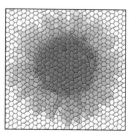

Mosaic

Oilify

Blur Filters

Blur

Gaussian Blur (IIR)

Gaussian Blur (RLE)

Motion Blur

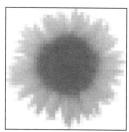

Pixelize

Tileable Blur

ARTISTIC FILTERS; BLUR FILTERS

Colors Filters

Original image

Alien Map

Color Exchange

Colorify

Gradient Map

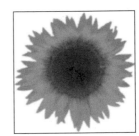

Hot

Max RGB

Scatter HSV

Value Invert

Combine Filters

Depth Merge

Film

Distorts Filters

Original image

Blinds

Emboss

Engrave

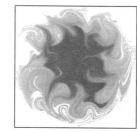

IWarp

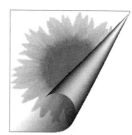

Pagecurl

Polar Coords

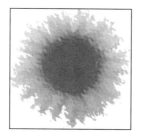

Ripple

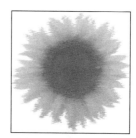

Shift

Value Propagate

Waves

Whirl and Pinch

DISTORTS FILTERS

Edge-Detect Filters

Original image

Edge

Laplace

Sobel

Enhance Filters

Deinterlace

Despeckle

Destripe

NL Filter

Sharpen

Glass Effects Filters

Original image

Apply Lens

Glass Tile

Light Effects Filters

Flare FX

Sparkle

Super Nova

Misc Filter

Video

GLASS AND LIGHT EFFECTS, AND MISC FILTERS

Map Filters

Original image

Bump Map

Displace

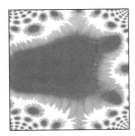

Fractal Trace

Illusion

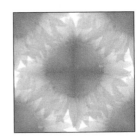

Make Seamless

Map Object

Paper Tile

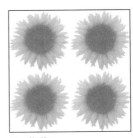

Small Tiles

Noise Filters

Noisify

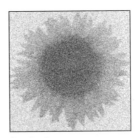

Randomize

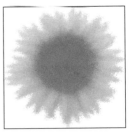

Spread

Render Filters

The Render filters make or *render* solid patterns or backgrounds of some type. The examples below show the Render filters at work on the Background layer that is behind the sunflower.

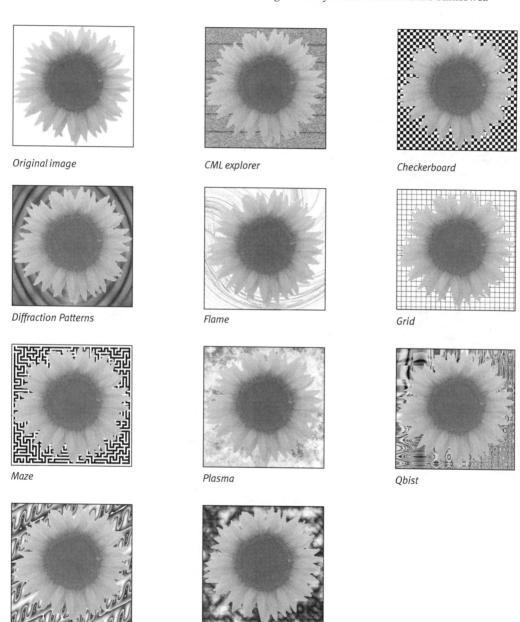

Original image

CML explorer

Checkerboard

Diffraction Patterns

Flame

Grid

Maze

Plasma

Qbist

Sinus

Solid Noise

Some Filter Combinations

Figures 30–33 below show some interesting filter combinations that have been applied to images. Each description contains a listing of the filters used, the filter settings, and any other pertinent information.

Figure 30. In this image, the Oilify filter was applied twice with a Mask Size setting of 11. Then, the Sharpen filter was applied with a sharpness setting of 62.

Figure 31. In this image, the Oilify filter was applied with a Mask Size setting of 17, then the Ripple filter was applied with a Period setting of 20 and an Amplitude setting of 3.

Figure 32. In this image, the section behind the bus was selected and an Abstract 2 gradient was stroked to give the appearance of a motion trail. The wheels and side panel of the bus were then selected and the Motion Blur filter was applied. Finally, the area around the wheels was selected and the Noisify filter was applied to create the grainy road.

Figure 33. The butterfly in this image was pasted onto two layers. With the bottommost butterfly layer selected, the Sharpen filter was applied with a sharpness setting of 65, then the Glass Tile filter was applied with the Tile Width and Height sliders set to 36. The upper butterfly layer was then selected and the Sharpen filter was applied with a Sharpness setting of 36, the Posterize command was applied with a setting of 2 levels, and the layer opacity was set to 50%.

Summary

In this chapter you learned how to:

- Repeat a filter
- Make an image look like an oil painting
- Make an image look like it's on a curling page
- Make an image's border wavy
- Use a layer mask to apply a texture
- Give an image the appearance of motion

PLUG-INS
AND SCRIPT-FUS

Plug-ins and script-fus are two very powerful programming features that add amazing functionality to the GIMP.

Plug-ins are little programs that let the user add extra features to the GIMP. In fact, much of the GIMP— except the core features—consists of plug-ins that have been integrated into the GIMP program. Since the GIMP is a *modular* program, it's easy to enhance the GIMP directly through the use of plug-ins without having to recompile or reinstall the entire program. There are many GIMP users and developers who have written plug-ins and contributed them to the GIMP community on the Web. You have already seen and used many plug-ins when working with filters in Chapter 15, *Using Filters*.

Script-fus are essentially the macros of the GIMP. If you are familiar with macros (or scripting languages) from word processing programs, you know that you can record a macro that will replay various actions or repetitive tasks. The GIMP's script-fus are mini-programs that one can write to automate special effects containing many steps. Creating a script-fu is well beyond the scope of this book, but you can use (and enjoy!) the plethora of script-fus included with the GIMP. In fact, you already worked with some script-fus in Chapter 14, *Working with Text* (see pages 227–230).

This chapter will show you where to find the special plug-ins and script-fus included with the GIMP, and basic instructions on how to use them.

Which Plug-ins and Script-fus are Installed?

It's easy to find out which plug-ins are available in your version of the GIMP using DB Browser. DB Browser is itself a plug-in that contains a database of all installed extensions, script-fus, and plug-ins. You've already seen and used many of the special GIMP plug-ins when working with filters in Chapter 15. These plug-ins are available on the Filters→ Render menu. Take a look at page 245 to can see some of the great effects they create.

Figure 1. In the GIMP Toolbox, choose Xtns→DB Browser.

To view installed plug-ins and script-fus:

1. In the GIMP Toolbox, choose Xtns→DB Brower (**Figure 1**). The DB Browser window will open (**Figure 2**).

2. Use the scroll bars to view the list of installed extensions, script-fus, and plug-ins at the left side of the dialog box.

3. To find out who wrote a particular item, select it. The author's name and a brief description of what the item does will appear on the right side of the DB Browser window.

Figure 2. Use the DB Browser to view the installed extensions, script-fus, and plug-ins.

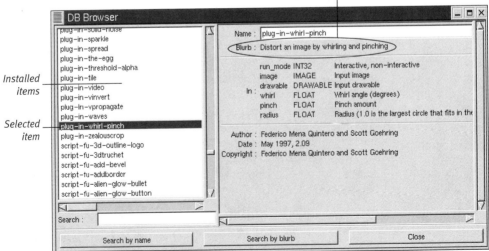

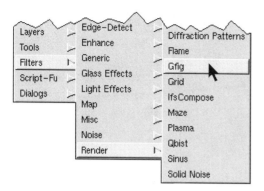

Figure 3. Right-click on the image window and choose Filters→Render→Gfig from the pop-up menu.

Two Special Plug-ins

There are many special graphics plug-ins that come with the GIMP, but we'll discuss just two of them here: Gfig and IfsCompose. Gfig is a self-contained drawing program that works with the GIMP to let you create geometric patterns and shapes. IfsCompose lets you create repetitive, complex geometric shapes and patterns, such as snowflakes and fern leaves.

To create a geometric shape with Gfig:

1. Open an image or create a new one.

2. Use the Layers & Channels dialog box to select the layer where you want the geometric shape to appear. (For details on selecting a layer, turn to page 92.)

Figure 4. Use the Gfig plug-in to draw geometric shapes.

(continued)

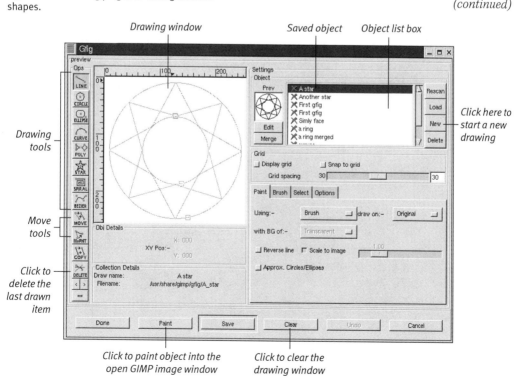

Drawing window   Saved object   Object list box

Drawing tools

Move tools

Click to delete the last drawn item

Click here to start a new drawing

Click to paint object into the open GIMP image window

Click to clear the drawing window

CREATE A GEOMETRIC SHAPE WITH GFIG

3. Right-click on the image and choose Filters→Render→Gfig from the pop-up menu (**Figure 3**). The large Gfig dialog box will open (**Figure 4**). (There are a lot of features available in this dialog box, so it may look a bit confusing at first!)

4. Click the New button at the upper right of the dialog box to start a new drawing (**Figure 4**). The Edit Gfig entry name dialog box will open (**Figure 5**).

5. Type a name for your drawing in the text box, then click OK. The Edit Gfig entry name dialog box will close, the name of your drawing will appear in the Object list box (**Figure 6**), and the drawing window will clear, ready for you to start drawing.

6. Click one of the drawing tool buttons at the left of the Gfig dialog box to select the shape of the item you want to draw. You can select from Line, Circle, Ellipse, Curve, Poly, Star, Spiral, or Bezier. (To set how many sides, points, or turns the Poly, Star, or Spiral Tools will draw, double-click on the tool button. A dialog box will open letting you set the number (**Figure 7**).)

7. In the GFig dialog box, position the mouse pointer in the drawing window over the area where you want to draw the item.

8. Press the left mouse button and drag. The shape will appear in the drawing window (**Figure 8**).

9. Continue adding lines and shapes until your drawing is complete (**Figure 9**). (If you add a line or shape you don't like, click the Delete button at the lower left of the GFig dialog box. The item will disappear.)

Figure 5. Type in a name for the new design, then click OK to close the dialog box.

Figure 6. The name of the new drawing appears in the Object list box.

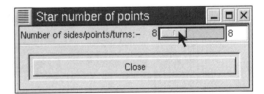

Figure 7. Use the dialog box to set the number of sides/points/turns for the Poly, Star, or Spiral Tool.

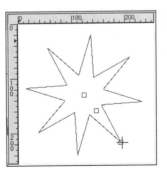

Figure 8. Press the left mouse button and drag to draw a shape.

Figure 9. Continue drawing until the shape is the way you want it to look.

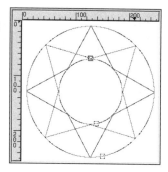

10. To reshape any of the items you have created in the drawing window:

   A. Select either the Move or MvPNT tools at the left of the GFig dialog box (**Figure 2**).

   B. Position the mouse crosshair over the item you want to move.

   C. Press the left mouse button and drag the item to its new position.

11. To paint the shape you have created in Gfig into the GIMP image window you opened or created in step 1:

   A. Select a foreground color in the GIMP toolbox. (To find out how to do this, turn to page 42.)

Figure 10a. The geometric shape appears in the image window.

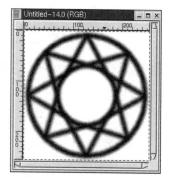

   B. Use the GIMP's Brush Selection dialog brush to select a brush. (To find out how to use the Brush Selection dialog box, turn to page 110.)

   C. Click Paint at the bottom left of the Gfig dialog box. The drawing you created using Gfig will appear in the image window (**Figure 10a**). Apply some filters for an interesting effect (**Figure 10b**).

12. You can continue drawing with Gfig and subsequently add more shapes and designs to the GIMP image window using different brushes and foreground colors.

or

If you're done drawing, click the Done button at the bottom left of the Gfig dialog box to close it (**Figure 2**).

Figure 10b. Applying a filter can make all the difference. The Mosaic filter has been applied to the drawing shown in Figure 10a.

✔ Tip

■ These directions are just a brief overview of what you can do with Gfig. Experiment with it to see what you can create.

CREATE A GEOMETRIC SHAPE WITH GFIG

To create a geometric pattern with IfsCompose:

1. Open an image or create a new one.

2. Use the Layers & Channels dialog box to select the layer where you want the geometric shape to appear. (For details on selecting a layer, turn to page 92.)

3. Select a foreground color in the GIMP toolbox. (To find out how to do this, turn to page 42.)

4. Right-click on the image and choose Filters→Render→IfsCompose from the pop-up menu (**Figure 11**). The large IfsCompose dialog box will open (**Figure 12**).

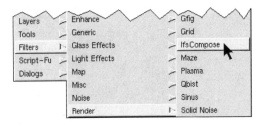

Figure 11. Right-click on the image window and choose Filters→Render→IfsCompose from the pop-up menu.

Figure 12. Use the IfsCompose plug-in to create fractal-based geometric patterns.

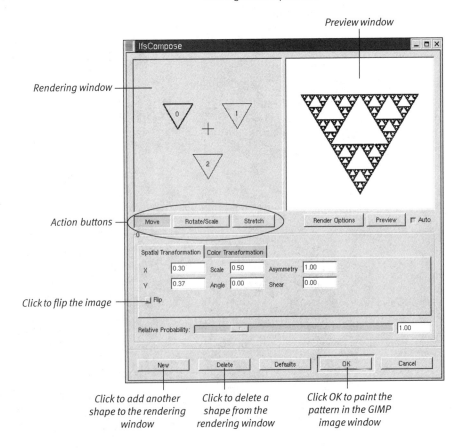

Preview window

Rendering window

Action buttons

Click to flip the image

Click to add another shape to the rendering window

Click to delete a shape from the rendering window

Click OK to paint the pattern in the GIMP image window

Figure 13. The geometric pattern you are creating appears in the preview window.

Figure 14. The geometric pattern appears in the image window.

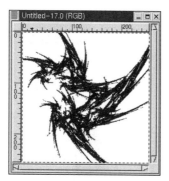

5. Select an action button—Move, Rotate/Scale, Stretch—to set what you want to do.

6. Position the mouse pointer in the rendering window over one of the triangles.

7. Press the left mouse button and drag only a little bit (small movements can create big results with this program—it's very sensitive). The change you have made will appear in the preview window (**Figure 13**).

8. To add another triangle to the rendering window, click the New button at the bottom left of the IfsCompose dialog box.

9. When you are finished creating the geometric pattern, click OK to close the IfsCompose dialog box and paint the geometric pattern in the image window you opened or created in step 1 (**Figure 14**).

✔ Tips

- These directions are just a brief overview of what you can create using IfsCompose. Try experimenting to see what you come up with.

- You can use the Color Transformation tab page in the IfsCompose dialog box to set more complicated color schemes then just using the foreground color selected in step 3.

Playing with Plug-ins

Many of the GIMP's plug-ins are filters that are discussed in Chapter 15, *Using Filters*. Check out pages 239–245 to see these plug-in filters in action.

Finding and Installing More Plug-ins

There are many, many plug-ins available for the GIMP (more are being written all the time!). To see an extensive list of available plug-ins go to `http://registry.gimp.org/`. To compile and install plug-ins, follow the instructions found at:

`http://www.isg.de/people/marc/gimp/prb/gimp.prb.0.03-3.html`

Incredible Script-fus

There are so many wonderful script-fus that come with the GIMP that you'd need several hours to try every one! There are two places where script-fus are found in the GIMP. The script-fus that create new images from scratch are available on the Xtns menu in the GIMP Toolbox (**Figure 15**). The script-fus that alter and enhance an existing image are accessed by right clicking on the image and choosing one from the Script-Fu menu on the pop-up menu that appears (**Figure 16**).

This section will cover just a few of these amazing script-fus. Many script-fus and the effects they create are displayed in the Script-fu gallery at the end of this chapter, starting on page 258. Several script-fus are discussed and explained elsewhere in this book:

◆ Pattern-creating script-fus are discussed in Chapter 8, *Painting Lines and Shapes*, on page 123.

◆ Shadow script-fus are explained in Chapter 11, *Layer Techniques*, on pages 175–180.

◆ The Xach-Effect, a special highlighting and shadowing effect, is discussed in Chapter 14, *Working with Text*, on pages 224–225.

◆ Logos script-fus that create amazing text effects are also discussed in Chapter 14, *Working with Text*, on pages 227–230.

◆ Script-fus that create Web page elements are explained in Chapter 17, *Creating Images for the Web*, on page 268.

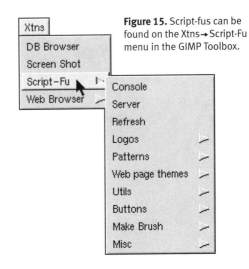

Figure 15. Script-fus can be found on the Xtns→Script-Fu menu in the GIMP Toolbox.

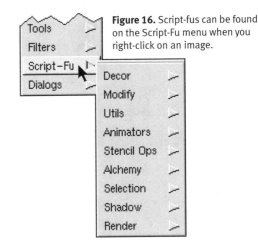

Figure 16. Script-fus can be found on the Script-Fu menu when you right-click on an image.

I Want to Write My Own Script-fu!

If you're interested in finding out more about script-fus and how they work (maybe even write your own!), take a look at *Mike Terry's Black Belt School of ScriptFu* at:

http://cad.ntu-kpi.kiev.ua/~demch/netlib/graph/script-fu-tutorial/

Figure 17. Open the image that's going to be coffee stained.

To add coffee stains to an image:

1. Open the image you want to add coffee stains to (**Figure 17**).

2. Right-click on the image and choose Script-Fu→Decor→Coffee Stain from the pop-up menu (**Figure 18**). The Script-Fu Coffee Stain dialog box will open (**Figure 19**).

3. Enter the number of stains you would like to add to the image in the Stains text box.

4. Click OK. The Script-Fu Coffee Stain dialog box will close and the script-fu will go to work. When it's finished, coffee stains will be added to the image (**Figure 20**). If you take a look at the Layers & Channels dialog box, you will notice that each stain is added on its own layer (**Figure 21**).

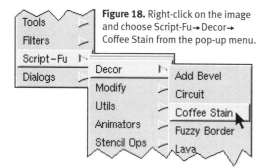

Figure 18. Right-click on the image and choose Script-Fu→Decor→Coffee Stain from the pop-up menu.

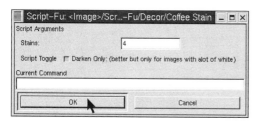

Figure 19. Enter the number of coffee stains in the Stains text box, then click OK.

Figure 20. Coffee stains appear in the image.

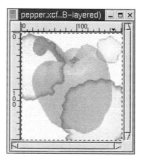

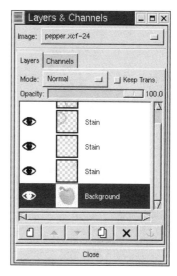

Figure 21. Each coffee stain appears on its own layer in the Layers & Channels dialog box.

ADD COFFEE STAINS TO AN IMAGE

To make an image look like it's an old photograph:

1. Open the image you want to age (**Figure 22**).

2. Right-click on the image and choose Script-Fu→Decor→Old Photo from the pop-up menu (**Figure 23**). The Script-Fu Old Photo dialog box will open (**Figure 24**).

3. To unfocus the image a bit, select the check button next to Defocus.

4. To add a photo-style border around the image, select the check button next to Border.

5. To change the image's color to old-fashioned sepia tones, select the check button next to Sepia.

6. To add some mottling to the image, select the check button next to Mottle.

7. To create a copy of the original image that will be changed to look like an old photograph (and leave the original image unchanged), select the check button next to Work on Copy.

8. Click OK. The Script-Fu Old Photo dialog box will close and the script-fu will go to work. When it's finished, the image (or a copy of the image) will look like an old photograph (**Figure 25**).

Figure 22. Open the image you want to make look like an old photo.

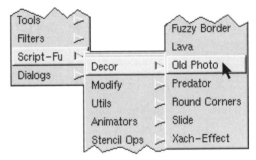

Figure 23. Right-click on the image and choose Script-Fu→Decor→Old Photo from the pop-up menu.

Figure 24. Use the Script-Fu Old Photo dialog box to set the way the "old" photograph will look.

Figure 25. The image is changed into an old-looking photograph.

Figure 26. Open the image to which you want to add a border.

To quickly add a border around an image:

1. Open the image to which you want to add a border (**Figure 26**).

2. Right-click on the image and choose Script-Fu→Modify→Add Border from the pop-up menu (**Figure 27**). The Script-Fu Add Border dialog box will open (**Figure 28**).

3. To set the width of the left and right sides of the border, enter a value in pixels in the Border x size text box.

4. To set the width of the top and bottom sides of the border, enter a value in pixels in the Border y size text box.

5. Click the Border Colour button to open the Script-Fu Color Picker (**Figure 29**). Use the color picker to select the border color.

6. Click OK. The Script-Fu Add Border dialog box will close and the script-fu will go to work. When it is finished a border will appear around the image (**Figure 30**).

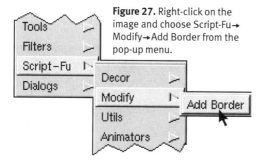

Figure 27. Right-click on the image and choose Script-Fu→Modify→Add Border from the pop-up menu.

Figure 28. Use the Script-Fu Add Border dialog box to set the width and color of the border.

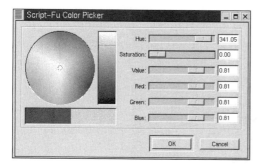

Figure 29. Use the Script-Fu Color Picker to select the border color.

Figure 30. A border appears around the image.

Decor Script-fus

Original image

Add Bevel

Circuit

Coffee Stain

Fuzzy Border

Lava

Old Photo

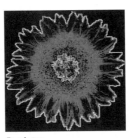

Predator

Round Corners

Slide

Xach-effect

Alchemy Script-fus

Original image

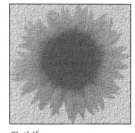

Clothify

Erase every other row

Unsharp Mask

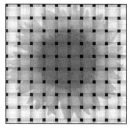

Weave

Animator Script-fus

Color Cycling

Rippling

Spinning Globe

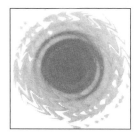

Waves

Modify Script-fu

Add Border

Render Script-fus

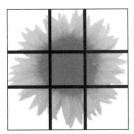

Make grid system

Line Nova

Shadow Script-fus

Drop-Shadow

Perspective

Summary

In this chapter you learned how to:

- View installed plug-ins and script-fus
- Create shapes using Gfig
- Render geometric patterns using IfsCompose

- Add several coffee stains to an image
- Make an image look like an old photograph
- Add a border around an image

CREATING IMAGES FOR THE WEB

17

*T*he GIMP was originally designed as a program to create graphics for the Web. It has expanded from there by leaps and bounds, becoming a full-fledged image manipulation program, but it hasn't lost its Web-based ancestry.

In this chapter you'll convert an image to indexed color mode using the WWW-optimised palette and learn how to reduce the number of colors in an image to make file size smaller. Next, you'll view and edit the color palette created by an indexed image and view the Web color palette. Then you'll create a background and use the Web page theme script-fus to quickly create basic elements, such as buttons and bullets, for a Web page. Finally, you'll find out how to save an image in a Web graphic file format and use the GIMP's special animation filters to create an animated .gif file.

Ruler Units and Image Resolution

The GIMP is set up, ready to create graphics for the Web right from the first time you use it. You may have already noticed that the ruler measurement unit is pixels and the resolution of images is automatically set at 72 ppi (pixels per inch). Both of these settings are exactly what you need for creating Web graphics.

Converting to Indexed Color

One of the first things you need to do when creating graphics for the Web is to convert your image to indexed color. (For details about the indexed model, turn to page 35.) There are several options to consider when doing this. You can convert the image:

◆ To 255 colors to take full advantage of the widest possible color palette (this tends to make file size larger).

◆ To the least possible number of colors, for instance 120 or 50, without sacrificing too much image quality (the fewer colors there are, the smaller the file size).

◆ Using the WWW-optimised palette. This palette contains the 216 colors that display the same in every browser.

To convert an image to indexed color:

1. Open the image you want to convert to indexed color (**Figure 1**).

2. Right-click on the image and choose Image→Indexed from the pop-up menu (**Figure 2**). The Indexed Color Conversion dialog box will appear (**Figure 3**).

3. To convert the image to 255 colors or less, select the Generate optimal palette radio button, then enter the number of colors in the text box.

4. To convert the image to the Web-ready palette, select the radio button next to Use WWW-optimised palette.

Notice that this is an RGB image

Figure 1. Open the image you want to convert to indexed color.

Figure 2. Right-click on the image and choose Image→Indexed from the pop-up menu.

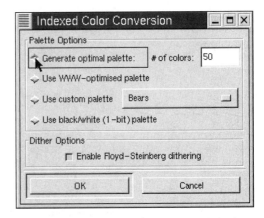

Figure 3. Use the Indexed Color Conversion dialog box to use a palette with a specific number of colors or use the WWW-optimised palette.

Figure 4. You can tell that this image is set in indexed color, because it's noted in the title bar.

5. If you want to dither the image, select the check button next to Enable Floyd-Steinberg dithering.

6. Click OK. The Indexed Color Conversion dialog box will close and the image will be converted to indexed color (**Figure 4**).

✔ Tips

■ If you are trying to use the least number of colors possible and don't like the results of the color conversion, press Ctrl+Z on the keyboard to undo the changes, then try the conversion with a different number of colors.

■ For more details about creating images with the fewest number of colors, take a look at the "Color and Web Images" section on page 40.

To Dither or Not to Dither?

If you select the dithering option when converting an image to indexed color, the GIMP will try to create colors not available in the color palette by mixing adjacent colors. This doesn't create new colors, it just blends existing colors in the color palette. The image in **Figure 5** is dithered, whereas the same image in **Figure 6** is not.

Figure 5. This image is made up of a palette of 10 colors and is dithered.

Figure 6. This image is also made up of a palette of 10 colors, but it is not dithered.

Viewing and Editing a Color Palette

Once you've converted an image to indexed color, thus creating a custom palette, you may want to view the color palette and edit the colors.

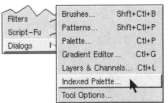

Figure 7. Right-click on the image and choose Dialogs→Indexed Palette from the pop-up menu.

To view and edit the color palette created from an indexed image:

1. Right-click on the image and choose Dialogs→Indexed Palette from the pop-up menu (**Figure 7**). The Indexed Color Palette dialog box will appear, displaying the color palette for that image (**Figure 8**).

2. To edit a color, right-click on the color square. The Color Selection dialog box will open, displaying that color in the old color area (**Figure 9**).

3. Use the color box and the slider bars to adjust the color.

4. When you are done adjusting the color, click OK to close the Color Selection dialog box. The adjusted color will appear in the color square you originally right clicked on (**Figure 10**), and the color in the image will change to reflect the new color (**Figure 11**).

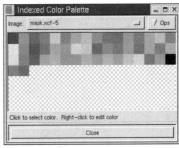

Figure 8. This is the Indexed Color Palette for the image shown in Figure 4.

✔ Tip

■ This is a temporary color palette that will only be available while working on the indexed image. When the image is closed, the palette will be gone. If you want to save the palette to use with other graphics, turn to page 50 for directions.

New color box   Old color box

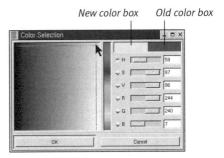

Figure 9. Use the Color Selection dialog box to set a new color (turn to page 42 for details).

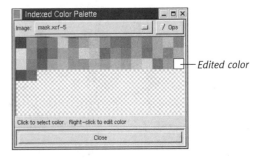

Edited color

Figure 10. The edited color square changes color.

Figure 11. The adjusted color is changed in the image. Notice the light colors around the chin, nose, and eyebrows.

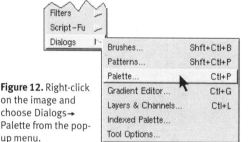

Figure 12. Right-click on the image and choose Dialogs→Palette from the pop-up menu.

The Web Color Palette

If you're designing graphics from scratch, you should use the 216 colors that Web browsers display well. This is often called a *Web-safe palette.*

To view the Web color palette:

1. Right-click on an image window and choose Dialogs→Palette from the pop-up menu (**Figure 12**) or press Ctrl+P on the keyboard. The Color Palette dialog box will appear (**Figure 13**).

2. Use the Color Palette drop-down list to select the Web color palette. The palette will appear in the palette window (**Figure 14**).

✔ Tip

■ To select a foreground or background color using the Web color palette, in the GIMP Toolbox, click in the color selector on either the foreground or background color square to make it active, then click a color square in the Color Palette dialog box.

Color Palette drop-down list

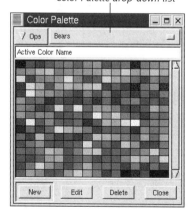

Figure 13. The Color Palette comes loaded with many different color palettes.

Figure 14. The Web color palette contains the 216 colors that Web browsers display well.

Creating Backgrounds

A good background can set the look for an entire Web site. In some cases, a solid color background can be both simple and elegant. In other cases, you may want to create something with more texture or use a pattern. Be careful when creating backgrounds, though, as a texture or pattern that is very busy or brightly colored can make text hard to read.

To create a background:

1. Create a new RGB image with a white fill that is 150 pixels wide and 150 pixels high (**Figure 15**).

2. Use the Bucket Fill Tool to fill the image with a solid color or a pattern (for directions on filling an area with a solid color, turn to page 119; to find out how to fill an area with a pattern, turn to page 121).

3. If you filled the image window with a solid color, you can add texture by applying a filter such as Apply Canvas, Cubism, Noisify, or Randomize (**Figure 16**). (To find out how to apply a filter, turn to page 231.)

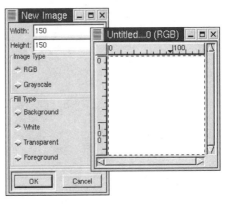

Figure 15. Create a new RGB image with a white fill that's 150 pixels wide and high.

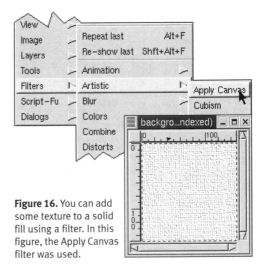

Figure 16. You can add some texture to a solid fill using a filter. In this figure, the Apply Canvas filter was used.

Web Graphics and File Size

When creating graphics for the Web, you should remember that the larger the file, the longer it will take to load in a browser. Suppose you are using a 56k modem. That modem downloads information at 48k per second. This means that a 200k image would take five seconds to load. This may not sound like much, but if you have ten 200k images, your Web page would take at least 50 seconds to load (ugh!). The rule of thumb about Web page load times is that a page should take no longer than ten seconds to load. This means that the maximum *combined* size for all the text, graphics, and other Web elements on a page should be no more than 500k.

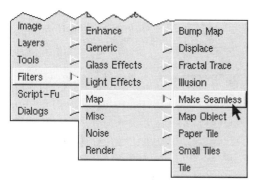

Figure 17. Right-click on the image and choose
Filters→Map→Make Seamless from the pop-up menu.

4. Convert the image to indexed color mode (see page 36). Use as few colors as possible without sacrificing quality to keep the file size down.

5. Right-click on the image window and choose Filters→Map→Make Seamless (**Figure 17**). This will make the background a *seamless tile*, meaning that when it is tiled across the back of a Web page, you won't be able to tell where it is repeated.

6. Save the image as a .gif or .png file (see pages 270–272). Your background is now ready for the Web (**Figure 18**).

Figure 18. The background you created is seamlessly tiled on a Web page.

Help with Web Design

The best source for advice on the Web is the Web itself. There are many sites on the Web that offer advice on Web page design and style. Page design isn't just about pretty pictures—it includes creating user-friendly sites that make it easy for visitors to find the information they need. A few sites that offer interesting advice and tools for Web design are:

Sun Microsystem Inc's Guide to Web Style:
http://www.sun.com/styleguide

Web Designer's Paradise:
http://desktoppublishing.com/webparadise.html

Web design links available at Yahoo:
http://www.yahoo.com/Computers_and_Internet/Internet/World_Wide_Web/Page_Creation/

CREATE A BACKGROUND

Quickly Creating Web Page Elements

Many of the graphics on Web sites are used to emphasize text, or as links to other pages or Web sites. When creating buttons, bullets, arrows, or any other Web page element, it's good to come up with a style and use it throughout the site. This makes for a consistent look and makes it easier for folks browsing your site to find what they want. The GIMP comes with several special script-fus that quickly create Web page elements.

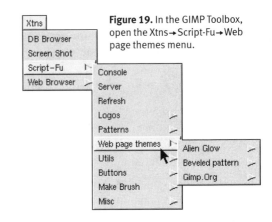

Figure 19. In the GIMP Toolbox, open the Xtns→Script-Fu→Web page themes menu.

To use a script-fu to create Web page elements:

1. In the GIMP Toolbox, open the Xtns→ Script-Fu→Web page themes menu (**Figure 19**).

2. Move the mouse pointer over to one of the styles and from the fly-out menu select the Web page element that you want to create (**Figure 20**). In this example, Xtns→Script-Fu→Web page themes→Gimp.Org→Big Header is selected. A Script-Fu dialog box for the item you selected will open (**Figure 21**).

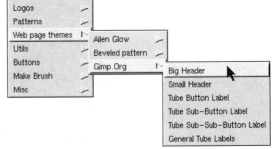

Figure 20. Choose a Web page element from the fly-out menu. In this example, Xtns→Script-Fu→Web page themes→Gimp.Org→Big Header is selected.

3. Use the various text boxes, color buttons, check buttons, and radio buttons to set the different options. (For more information about how script-fu dialog boxes work, turn to page 254.)

Don't Go Overboard

Animations and cute graphics are great for attracting attention, but too many can get distracting and detract from the items you really want to emphasize. Just as one lightly seasons one's food, animations and graphics should be sprinkled sparingly on a Web page.

Figure 21.
Use the Script-Fu dialog box for the Web element you selected to set the various options.

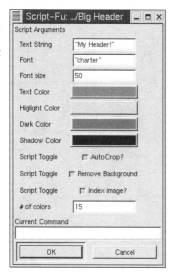

4. Click OK. The Script-Fu dialog box will close and the Web page element will appear in a new image window (**Figure 22**). Try several Web page elements out using a browser (**Figure 23**).

✔ Tip

■ To create text banners for your Web page, try using the Script-fu Logos available in the GIMP Toolbox on the Xtns→Script-Fu→Logos menu. These script-fus are discussed in Chapter 14, *Working with Text*, starting on page 227.

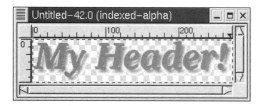

Figure 22. The script-fu quickly creates the Web page element—in this case, a header.

Figure 23. After creating several graphics using script-fus, try them out on a Web page.

Creating Graphics Quickly Using the Web

You can create many custom Web page elements using the great (and easy to use!) tools at:
http://www.cooltext.com

To find other script-fus that create Web graphics, go to the GIMP.org resource page at:
http://www.gimp.org.scripts.html

For some great script-fus and installation details, go to Sven Neuman's Script-fu Megaperls:
http://sven.gimp.org/megaperls/home.html

Which File Format Should I Use for Web Graphics?

Graphics make Web pages visually interesting while helping to bring across the message you are trying to convey. Graphics inserted into Web pages have to be saved in either the .gif, .jpg, or .png file format.

The .jpg (Joint Photographic Experts) file format is ideal for photographs and images with depth and small color changes, such as lighting effects. When saving a graphic as a .jpg, you can set the graphic's quality. The higher the quality, the larger the file size. Keep the quality as low as possible (without sacrificing too much of the image's quality) to minimize file size.

The .gif and .png file formats are typically used for black and white art, line drawings, and indexed color images that contain fewer than 256 colors. The .png file format was created to replace the .gif file format (because of patent disputes) and is actually an improvement upon the old .gif standard. Unfortunately, only the latest browsers are able to read the .png format.

To save a graphic as a .gif file:

1. Convert the image to indexed color. (See page 36 for details on how to do this.) If the image contains transparency, it will be layered. Don't flatten the image. If you do, the transparent areas of the image will be filled with the current background color.

2. Right-click on the image and choose File→Save as from the pop-up menu (**Figure 24**). The Save Image dialog box will appear (**Figure 25**).

3. Use the Directories list box to move to the directory where you want to save the file.

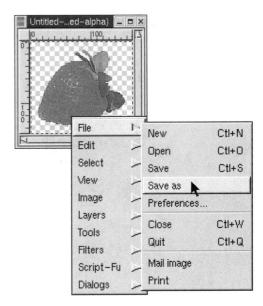

Figure 24. Right-click on the image and choose File→Save as from the pop-up menu.

Figure 25. In the Save Image dialog box, use the Directories list box to move to the directory where you want to store the .gif file.

Figure 26. When you type in the file name, be sure to add the .gif file extension.

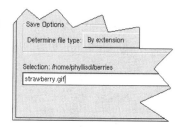

4. Type a name for the file in the Selection text box at the bottom of the Save Image dialog box (**Figure 26**). Be sure to add the .gif file extension after the file name. In this example, strawberry.gif has been entered.

5. Click OK. The Save Image dialog box will close and the Save as GIF dialog box will open (**Figure 27**).

6. If your image is rather large, you may want to select the Interlace check button. This loads the image into a browser gradually, first appearing chunky, then smoothing out.

7. Click OK. The Save as GIF dialog box will close and the image will be saved as a .gif file, ready for the Web. If the image contains transparency, the transparent areas will be preserved (**Figure 28**).

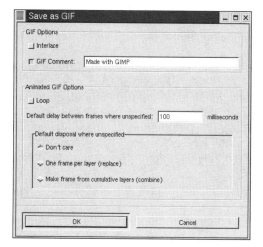

Figure 27. Use the Save as GIF dialog box to set whether the image is interlaced.

✔ Tip

■ The best graphics to save in .gif format are black and white art, line drawings, and images that contain fewer than 256 colors. Photographs should be saved in the .jpg format.

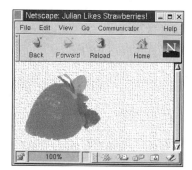

Figure 28. If the image contained transparency before it was saved as a .gif file, the transparent areas are preserved. Notice that the strawberry has a transparent background which lets the background texture of the Web page show through.

Saving a GIF File in JPG File Format

If you want to save a GIF file in the JPG file format, here's what you need to do:

1. Convert the image to RGB color mode (see page 38 for directions).

2. Save the image as a .jpg file (turn to page 273 for directions)

To save a graphic as a .png file:

1. Convert the image to indexed color. (See page 36 for details on how to do this.) If the image contains transparency, it will be layered. Don't flatten the image. If you do, the transparent areas of the image will be filled with the current background color.

2. Right-click on the image and choose File→Save as from the pop-up menu (**Figure 24**).The Save Image dialog box will appear (**Figure 25**).

3. Use the Directories list box to move to the directory where you want to save the file.

4. Type a name for the file in the Selection text box at the bottom of the Save Image dialog box (**Figure 29**). Be sure to add the .png file extension after the file name. In this example, sunflower.png is entered.

5. Click OK. The PNG Options dialog box will open (**Figure 30**).

6. If your image is rather large, you may want to select the Interlace check button. This loads the image into a browser gradually, first appearing chunky, then smoothing out.

7. Use the Compression level slider to set how compressed the file size will be. A setting of 1 is minimal compression. A setting of 9 compresses the file size as much as possible.

8. Click OK. Both the PNG Options dialog box and the Save Image dialog box will close and the image will be saved as a .png file, ready for the Web. If the image contains transparency, the transparent areas will be preserved (**Figure 31**).

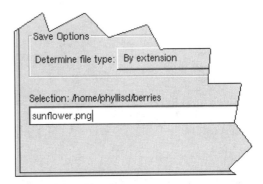

Figure 29. When you type in the file name, be sure to add the .png file extension.

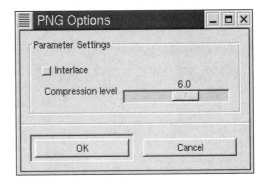

Figure 30. Use the PNG Options dialog box to set the file compression and whether the image is interlaced.

Figure 31. The .png file format preserves the transparent areas of an image.

SAVE A GRAPHIC AS A PNG FILE

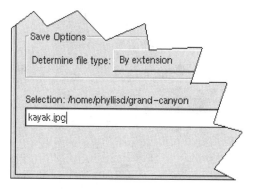

Figure 32. When you type in the file name, be sure to add the .jpg file extension.

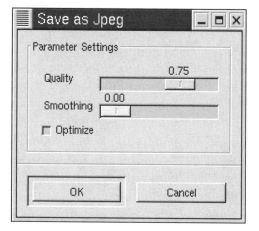

Figure 33. Use the Save as Jpeg dialog box to set the image quality and smoothing. If you want to reduce the image file size a little more, select the Optimize option.

What's the Difference Between GIF and PNG?

To find out more about the PNG file format and how it differs from the GIF file format, go to:

    http://www.cdrom.com/pub/png

To save a graphic as a .jpg file:

1. Right-click on the image and choose File→Save as from the pop-up menu (**Figure 24**).The Save Image dialog box will appear (**Figure 25**).

2. Use the Directories list box to move to the directory where you want to save the file. (Using the Save as command creates a new copy of the file that remains open while the original version is automatically closed. That way, you can use the original version again if the Quality setting you select in step 5 doesn't work out.)

3. Type a name for the file in the Selection text box at the bottom of the Save Image dialog box (**Figure 32**). Be sure to add the .jpg file extension after the file name. In this example, kayak.jpg has been entered.

4. Click OK. The Save as Jpeg dialog box will appear (**Figure 33**).

5. Use the Quality slider to set image file compression. The lower the setting, the higher the compression. You should know, though, that lower Quality settings can sacrifice image quality.

6. Use the Smoothing slider to set whether the edges of the image will be blurred to create a smooth look. A setting of 0 deactivates the option. The higher the setting the blurrier the edge will be (you may not want this look).

(continued)

7. If you want to reduce file size further, select the Optimize check button.

8. Click OK. The Save as Jpeg dialog box and the Save Image dialog box will close and the image will be saved as a .jpg file, ready for the Web (**Figure 34**).

✔ Tip

■ If this is your first time saving an image as a .jpg, try setting Quality to .50 and see how the image comes out. (You can see what the saved image looks like in a browser.) If it looks bad, open the original version of the image that you closed using the Save as command in step 2, and start at step 1 again. Save the image again, nudging up the Quality setting until you find the right setting.

Figure 34. The .jpg file format preserves color depth and quality of photos and complex graphics.

For More Information on Creating Web Pages

Even if you know everything about HTML and coding Web sites, there's more to organizing and designing a great Web site than meets the eye. There are many books available about creating interesting Web sites. A few helpful ones with some provocative ideas include:

♦ *Information Architecture for the World Wide Web* by Louis Rosenfeld and Peter Morville (O'Reilly & Associates)

♦ *The Non-Designer's Web Book: An Easy Guide to Creating, Designing, and Posting Your Own Web Site* by Robin Williams and John Tollett (Peachpit Press)

♦ *Typography: The Best Work from the Web* by Jeff Carlson, Glenn Fleishman, and Toby Malina (Rockport Publishing)

♦ *Web Design in a Nutshell: A Desktop Quick Reference* by Jennifer Niederst (O'Reilly & Associates)

♦ *Web Style Guide: Basic Design Principles for Creating Web Sites* by Patrick J. Lynch and Sarah Horton (Yale University Press)

♦ *Website Graphics Now* by Noel Douglas (Thames & Hudson)

Creating an Animation

If you like to browse the Web, you've probably seen such things as scrolling banners or blinking buttons. Animations enhance a Web site and are really very simple to make.

Animations are created using layers. If you think of it in film terms, each layer makes up one frame and each frame is slightly different than the frame that comes before it. When all the frames are quickly shown in succession, the object in the frames appears to move.

In this section, you'll learn how to create an animated text banner using a gradient. It's fun and easy (even though there are a lot of steps!), and uses a combination of the many techniques you've learned while reading this book.

There are three animation filters you'll use when creating the animation: Animation Playback, Animation Optimize, and Animation UnOptimize.

Animation Playback lets you run an animation you've created without having to use a browser. This lets you see if the animation is choppy or needs fixing. You can work back and forth between the image window and the Animation Playback dialog box, fixing and running the animation until it's just right.

Animation Optimize cuts out any extra space from each layer, making the overall file size much smaller. And, Animation UnOptimize is like the Undo command for Animation Optimize—it returns the image to its original state.

Good Web Site and Page Design

Before you design your Web pages, there are several things you should consider:

Less is more. When you design Web pages, they should present the information you want to convey in an easy-to-comprehend fashion. Users should be able to move through a site without confusion and easily find what they are looking for. In Web page design, as with good architecture, form should follow function. In other words, there should be a relationship between a Web page's appearance and what it is supposed to do.

Plan Web site flow. Web site flow is the way users will move around your site and its pages. Often, this involves navigation through information displayed in a hierarchical fashion. For instance, if part of your site were used to show dessert recipes, there might be a link to the dessert page from your site's main page. (The main page is also called a *home page*.) One way to plan a Web site is to draw a diagram similar to a flow chart showing every connection between the pages. Many folks use low tech materials—a pencil and piece of paper—to do this.

Maintain a consistent look. Use the same design elements across related pages of a Web site. This will give your site a consistent look and feel, and give the site visual cohesion. In order to maintain visual consistency between the pages in a Web site, you should establish standardized fonts, colors, graphic styles, and site navigation tools, such as buttons.

Use graphics and background colors. Since the Web is a very visual medium, it's important to add art to your pages. A picture is worth a thousand words! Be careful, though: dark or busy backgrounds can make text difficult to read.

To create a simple animation:

1. Create a new image with a transparent background. For this example, the new image is 550 pixels wide and 150 pixels high. (See page 25 for directions.)

2. Create some text that fits in the image window. For this example, the word "Animation!" is set in the Charter font at 100 points (**Figure 35**). (Turn to page 208 for details on how to create text.)

3. Anchor the text to a new layer by clicking the New Layer button in the Layers & Channels dialog box. The layer will automatically be named "Text Layer."

4. In the Layers & Channels dialog box, select the Background layer and delete it by clicking the Delete Layer button. Next, you'll need to create the separate layers and rename them as numbered frames.

5. Copy the Text Layer three times using the Duplicate Layer button in the Layers & Channels dialog box. There will now be four layers shown in the layer window (**Figure 36**).

6. Starting at the bottom layer in the Layers & Channels dialog box (this will be the Text Layer), rename the layer **Frame 1** (**Figure 37**). (For directions on how to rename layers, turn to page 95.)

7. Move up to the next layer (probably named Text Layer copy) and rename it **Frame 2**.

8. Move up to the next layer (probably named Text Layer copy copy) and rename it **Frame 3**.

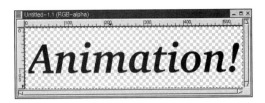

Figure 35. Create some text and center it in the new image window.

Figure 36. Duplicate the text layer three times for a total of four layers.

Figure 37. Rename the bottom Text Layer, Frame 1.

Figure 38.
Use the Blend drop-down list to select Custom (from editor).

9. Move up to the top layer (probably named Text Layer copy copy copy) and rename it **Frame 4**. Next, you'll alter the four frames using a gradient to make them all look slightly different.

10. Double-click on the Blend Tool in the GIMP Toolbox. The Tool Options dialog box will appear (**Figure 38**).

11. Use the Blend drop-down list to select Custom (from editor). This sets the Blend Tool to draw a gradient selected from the Gradient Editor.

12. Use the Gradient drop-down list to select Linear, then click Close to close the Tool Options dialog box.

13. Use the Gradient Editor to select one of the many colorful gradients that ship with the GIMP (**Figure 39**). For this example, Neon_Cyan is selected. (For directions on how to use the Gradient Editor, turn to page 127.)

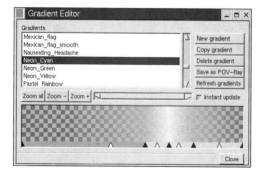

Figure 39. Use the Gradient Editor to select a gradient for your animation.

14. Click the eye icon next to the layers named Frame 2, Frame 3, and Frame 4 to hide them. Only Frame 1 will be visible.

15. Use the Layers & Channels dialog box to select the bottom layer named Frame 1.

16. With the Blend Tool selected, position the mouse pointer at the left end of the text, press the left mouse button, and drag to the right. Create a gradient that stretches about ¼ of the way across the text (**Figure 40**). (For directions on dragging the Blend Tool to create a gradient, turn to page 124.)

17. Use the Layers & Channels dialog box to select the layer named Frame 2. (Leave it hidden for right now. You'll be using the Frame 1 layer as a guide for placing the next gradient.)

Figure 40. The first gradient should stretch about ¼ of the way across the Text Layer.

(continued)

18. Position the mouse pointer at the right side of the gradient you created in step 16, press the left mouse button and drag right to create another gradient that stretches to the middle of the text. (Remember that the Frame 1 layer is visible and the Frame 2 layer is hidden. You'll only be able to see the gradient you just created on the Frame 2 thumbnail in the Layers & Channels dialog box at this point (**Figure 41**).)

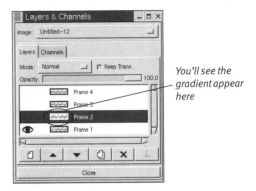

You'll see the gradient appear here

Figure 41. Since the Frame 2 layer is hidden, you won't see the new gradient in the image window. Instead, you'll see the new gradient in the layer's thumbnail.

19. Use the Layers & Channels dialog box to hide the Frame 1 layer, view the Frame 2 layer, and select the layer named Frame 3 (**Figure 42**). (The Frame 3 layer will be hidden for now. You'll be using the Frame 2 layer as a guide for placing the next gradient.)

20. Position the mouse pointer at the right side of the second gradient you created in step 18, press the left mouse button and drag right to create another gradient that stretches to about ¾ of the way across the text. (Remember that the Frame 2 layer is visible and the Frame 3 layer is hidden. You'll only be able to see the gradient on the Frame 3 thumbnail in the Layers & Channels dialog box.)

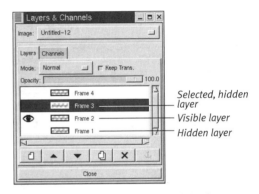

Selected, hidden layer

Visible layer

Hidden layer

Figure 42. Use the Layers & Channels dialog box to hide the layer named Frame 1, view the layer named Frame 2, and select the hidden layer named Frame 3.

21. Use the Layers & Channels dialog box to hide the Frame 2 layer, view the Frame 3 layer, and select the layer named Frame 4 (**Figure 43**). (The Frame 4 layer will be hidden for now. You'll be using the Frame 3 layer as a guide for placing the final gradient.)

22. Position the mouse pointer at the right side of the third gradient you created in step 20, press the left mouse button and drag right to create the final gradient that stretches to the end of the text. (You'll only be able to see the gradient on the Frame 4 thumbnail in the Layers & Channels dialog box.)

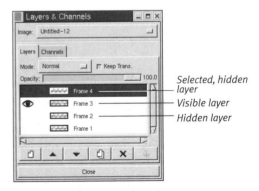

Selected, hidden layer

Visible layer

Hidden layer

Figure 43. Use the Layers & Channels dialog box to hide the layer named Frame 2, view the layer named Frame 3, and select the hidden layer named Frame 4.

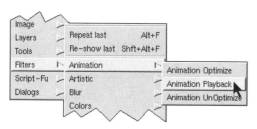

Figure 44. Right-click on the image and choose Filters→Animation→Animation Playback from the pop-up menu.

Figure 45. Use the Animation Playback dialog box to view your animation in action.

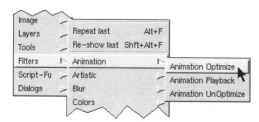

Figure 46. Right-click on the image window and choose Filters→Animation→Animation Optimize from the pop-up menu.

23. To see your animation in action, right-click on the image window and choose Filters→Animation→Animation Playback (**Figure 44**). The Animation Playback dialog box will appear (**Figure 45**).

24. Click Play/Stop. The animation you just created using gradients will play. (Wow! Look at what you just created!) If your animation seems choppy to you or there's something you want to fix, you can work back and forth between the image window and the Animation Playback dialog box to make corrections.

25. When you have finished watching the animation play, click Play/Stop to stop the animation, then click Close to close the Animation Playback dialog box. The next step is to *optimize* the animation, then save it as a .gif file.

26. Right-click on the image window and choose Filters→Animation→Animation Optimize from the pop-up menu (**Figure 46**). A duplicate of the image you've been working on will appear in a new image window.

27. Convert the new optimized image to indexed color. (Turn to page 36 for directions.)

28. Right-click on the optimized image window and choose File→Save as from the pop-up menu (**Figure 24**). The Save Image dialog box will open (**Figure 25**).

29. Use the Directories list box to move to the directory where you want to store the animated .gif file.

30. Enter a name for the animation in the Selection text box. Be sure to add the .gif file extension after the name. In this example, animation.gif is entered.

(continued)

31. Click OK. The Save as GIF dialog box will appear (**Figure 27**).

32. In the Animated GIF Options area, select the Loop check button if you want the animation to play again and again. (If the Loop check button isn't selected, the animation will only play once.)

33. In the Default delay between frames where unspecified text box, enter the amount (in milliseconds) that you want each frame to play. The default, 100 milliseconds, is a pretty good speed.

34. In the Default disposal where unspecified area, select the Make frame from cumulative layers (combine) radio button.

35. Click OK. The Save as GIF and Save Image dialog boxes will close and the optimized image will be saved as a .gif file. If you look at the Layers & Channels dialog box, you'll see that the time delay you specified in step 33 has been added after each layer name (**Figure 47**). (If you want, you can change the time delay, just by renaming the layer and inserting a new number before ms.) Your animation is ready for the Web (**Figure 48**). (Go to http://www.peachpit.com/vqs/gimp to see it in action.)

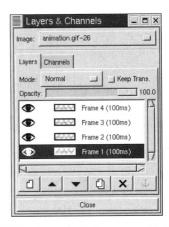

Figure 47. The time delay that you entered in the Animated GIF Options area of the Save as GIF dialog box appear appended to the layer names.

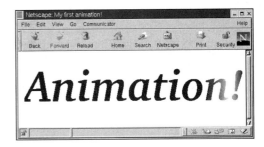

Figure 48. Try out your animation on a Web page!

Summary

In this chapter you learned how to:

- Convert an image to indexed color
- View and edit the palette made by an indexed image
- View the Web color palette
- Create backgrounds
- Create Web page elements using script-fus
- Save a graphic as a .gif or .png
- Save a photo as a .jpg
- Create a simple animation

PRINTING AND OUTPUT

18

*G*raphics are stored by the GIMP as pixels, but when they are printed, graphics are rendered as dots. The quality of the printed page depends upon the resolution of the graphic and the output device. The higher the resolution, the finer and sharper the output will be.

Since the GIMP was originally created as a Web graphics design program, any images created solely using the GIMP will only be saved with a resolution of 72 pixels per inch (ppi). This resolution looks fine for graphics on a computer monitor (because monitor resolution is 72 ppi) (**Figure 1**), but when printed on a page, it will look pretty bad—most definition will be lost and the image will appear very pixelated (**Figure 2**). Thankfully, there are a few tricks you can use to get around this. (The next version of the GIMP promises to have full-resolution printing capabilities—I can't wait!)

Figure 1. While a GIMP graphic looks great on a monitor...

Figure 2. It may not look so good in print.

Creating Images that Print Well (Get Out Your Calculator)

If you are creating an image for printing, the 72 ppi resolution that the GIMP offers just isn't acceptable (**Figures 3a–f**). There's a simple way to get around this right from the start.

Before you even create a new image window, figure out the printed resolution that you will need. Printers, such as inkjets and laserjets, typically print at resolutions ranging from 300 to 720 dots per inch (dpi). Higher quality output devices, such as Verityper and Linotronic imagesetters, create output with resolutions ranging from 1200 to 4000 dpi. So what do you need? If you are creating a flyer for your office, 300 dpi should do very well. But, if you're creating a high-quality art poster, 1200 dpi should be a minimum. (If you're going to do high-end work, contact your printer first to find out what works best for the printer.)

Of course, higher resolutions make for larger file sizes. For instance, **Figure 3b** is set at 150 dpi image and is only 32K, whereas **Figure 3e** is set at 1200 dpi and is a whopping 2MB.

Suppose you want to create a flyer for the local garden club, printed on your color inkjet printer on regular 8.5" by 11" paper. Since the GIMP only creates images at 72 ppi, you'll need to create a large image that will *scale down* to 300 dpi when printed. (When a large image is scaled down while printing, all the pixels are squashed together, making for an image that appears sharper when it prints.)

To create the garden club flyer you'll need to multiply the width and height of the printed image by the resolution (expressed in dpi) that you want to use:

paper width x resolution (dpi) = GIMP image width (ppi)

paper height x resolution (dpi) = GIMP image height (ppi)

Figure 3a. This grayscale image is set at 72 dpi; its file size is 8K.

Figure 3b. This grayscale image is set at 150 dpi; its file size is 32K.

Figure 3c. This grayscale image is set at 300 dpi; its file size is 127K.

CREATING IMAGES THAT PRINT WELL

Figure 3d. This grayscale image is set at 600 dpi; its file size is 505K.

Figure 3e. This grayscale image is set at 1200 dpi; its file size is 2MB.

Figure 3f. This grayscale image is set at 2400 dpi; its file size is 8MB.

So, to create a flyer that is 8.5" by 11" and prints at 300 dpi, you would need to create an image that is 2500 pixels wide by 3300 pixels high because:

8.5" x 300 dpi = 2550 pixels

11" x 300 dpi = 3300 pixels

Even though a 2500 by 3300 pixel image is quite large, the GIMP (thankfully) adjusts the image window size so it is never larger than your computer screen.

I've Created My Image Using These Calculations—Now What?

After figuring out the size of the GIMP image and creating it using the width and height dimensions based on image resolution, you'll want to print it at the correct resolution (of course!). Use the following steps to print your image:

◆ Select your printer using the Printer drop-down list as described in step 2 on page 285.

◆ Select the printer you are going to use following the steps on page 286.

◆ Set page size and paper orientation using the instructions on page 287.

◆ Set printer resolution (if your printer supports this feature) as described on page 288.

◆ Scale the image down to the resolution you calculated following the directions on page 288. Select the PPI radio button and set the Scale slider to the resolution you calculated.

◆ Print your image (see page 285)—if you're creating the printout yourself— or generate a .ps or .eps file for a service bureau or commercial printer (see page 291).

Wait! I've Already Created an Image!

But, what happens if you've already created an image and you want to print it at a higher resolution? You can scale the image up a bit (doubling image size will make the image fuzzy, though), using *cubic interpolation*. The GIMP will compare adjacent pixel colors and fill in the gaps with pixels that are a blend of the adjacent colors.

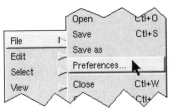

Figure 4. Right-click on the image and choose File→ Preferences from the pop-up menu.

To scale an image up using cubic interpolation:

1. Open the image you want to scale up.

2. Right-click on the image and choose File→Preferences from the pop-up menu (**Figure 4**). The Preferences dialog box will open with the Display tab page in front (**Figure 5**).

3. Select the Cubic interpolation check button, then click OK to close the Preferences dialog box.

4. Right-click on the image and choose Image→Scale from the pop-up menu (**Figure 6**). The Image Scale dialog box will open (**Figure 7**).

5. Make sure the Constrain Ratio check button is selected. This will keep the width and height scaling proportionally the same.

6. Enter the new width and height (in pixels) in the New width and New height text boxes.

7. Click OK. The Image Scale dialog box will close and the image will scale up to its new size (it will take a few seconds depending upon the speed of your computer).

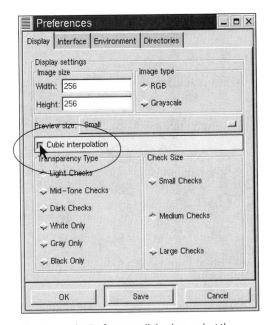

Figure 5. In the Preferences dialog box, select the Cubic interpolation check button, then click OK.

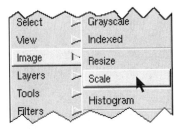

Figure 6. Right-click on the image and choose Image→Scale from the pop-up menu.

Figure 7. Use the Image Scale dialog box to set a new width and height. If the Constrain Ratio check button is selected, the width and height remain proportionally the same.

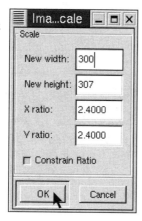

Printing an Image

Once you've created an image, you'll probably want to print it for proofing or as final output. You should know however, that if your image contains more than one layer, only the active layer will be printed. To print an entire image, you'll need to flatten it first (turn to page 106 for directions).

To print an image:

1. Right-click on the image and choose File→Print from the pop-up menu (**Figure 8**). The Print dialog box will open (**Figure 9**).

2. Use the Printer drop-down list to select a printer. Most likely, this is lp, lp0, or lp1.

3. Use the Output Type radio buttons to select whether the image will be printed in black and white or color.

4. Click Print. The Print dialog box will close and the image will print.

Figure 8. Right-click on the image and choose File→Print from the pop-up menu.

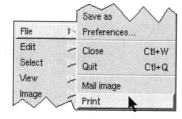

✔ Tips

- Once you set various printer options, they will be set up and ready to go every time you print. You should know, however, that the print options you set aren't permanent. If you exit the GIMP, then restart it, the options in the Print dialog box will return to the default settings.

- To print an image to a file, use the Printer drop-down list in step 2 to select File, then continue setting the various printer options.

- In case you were wondering, when you select your printer in step 2, lp stands for the port that the printer is connected to. If you have more than one printer, they will be sequentially numbered, lp, lp0, lp1, etc.

Image size preview *Paper size and orientation preview* *Select your printer here*

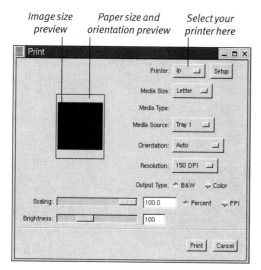

Figure 9. Use the Print dialog box to set printing options.

PRINT AN IMAGE

To select a different printer:

1. Right-click on the image and choose File→Print from the pop-up menu (**Figure 8**). The Print dialog box will open (**Figure 9**).

2. Use the Printer drop-down list to select lp, then click the Setup button to the right of the drop-down list. The Setup dialog box will appear (**Figure 10**).

3. Use the Driver drop-down list to select your printer (**Figure 11**). (At this time, the GIMP only supports PostScript printers, and specific Hewlett-Packard and Epson printers.) If your printer model is not on the drop-down list, but it supports level 1 or 2 PostScript, select one of the PostScript options.

4. If you wish, you can use the Browse button next to the PPD File text box to select the PostScript printer definition file for your printer (this is optional). (This text box is only available if you selected PostScript Level 1 or PostScript Level 2 in the Driver drop-down list.) A PPD file tells the GIMP what features are available on a particular printer.

5. Click OK. The Setup dialog box will close, returning you to the Print dialog box.

6. Choose more printing options or click Print.

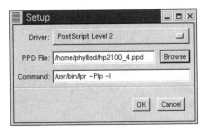

Figure 10. The Setup dialog box is used to select a printer and, if you wish, set a PPD file.

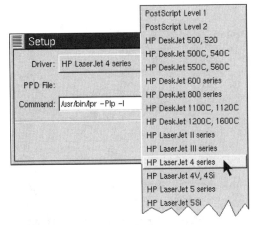

Figure 11. Select your printer from the Driver drop-down list.

Where Can I Find My PostScript Printer's PPD File?

If you want to use a PPD file when printing, you can find it on the floppies or CD-ROM disk that shipped with the printer. Another place to look for current PPD files is at:

http://www.adobe.com/support/downloads/pdrvwin.htm.

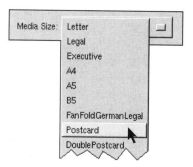

Figure 12. Select a paper size using the Media Size drop-down list.

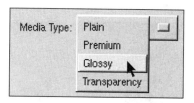

Figure 13. Use the Media Type drop-down list to select a type of special paper.

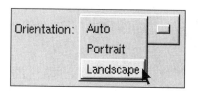

Figure 14. Use the Orientation drop-down list to set paper orientation.

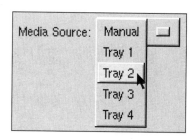

Figure 15. Use the Media Source drop-down list to select the paper tray that the printer will take the paper from.

To set a different page size, paper, or orientation:

1. Right-click on the image and choose File→Print from the pop-up menu (**Figure 8**). The Print dialog box will open (**Figure 9**).

2. Use the Media Size drop-down list to select the size of the paper that the image will be printed on (**Figure 12**).

3. Use the Media Type drop-down list to select the type of paper—Plain, Premium, Glossy, etc.—that the image will be printed on (**Figure 13**). (This drop-down list is only available if you selected a printer that uses special paper.)

4. Use the Orientation drop-down list to set the paper orientation to auto, portrait, or landscape (**Figure 14**). (If you select auto, the GIMP will automatically use the most logical paper orientation.)

5. Choose more printing options or click Print.

To select a different printer tray:

1. Right-click on the image and choose File→Print from the pop-up menu (**Figure 8**). The Print dialog box will open (**Figure 9**).

2. Use the Media Source drop-down list to select which tray the printer will take the paper from (**Figure 15**). (This drop-down list is only available if you selected a printer that has multiple trays.)

3. Choose more printing options or click Print.

To set a printer resolution:

1. Right-click on the image and choose File→Print from the pop-up menu (**Figure 16**). The Print dialog box will open (**Figure 17**).

2. Use the Resolution drop-down list to select a specific printer resolution (**Figure 18**). (This drop-down list is only available if you selected a printer that supports different resolutions.)

3. Choose more printing options or click Print.

To scale down an image to a specific percentage or resolution:

1. Right-click on the image and choose File→Print from the pop-up menu (**Figure 16**). The Print dialog box will open (**Figure 17**).

2. Use the radio buttons to the right of the Scaling slider to set whether the slider will operate in either Percent (of the actual image dimensions) or PPI (**Figure 19**).

3. Use the slider to set the scaling of the image.

4. Choose more printing options or click Print.

✔ Tip

■ The PPI (pixels per inch) option is a more exact way to scale an image. If you used the formula on page 282 to figure out the image width and height based on a specific printed resolution (such as 300 dpi), just select the PPI radio button and use the slider to set that resolution (**Figure 20**). The printed image will scale accordingly.

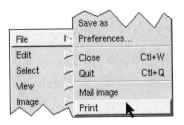

Figure 16. Right-click on the image and choose File→ Print from the pop-up menu.

Image size preview   Paper size and orientation preview

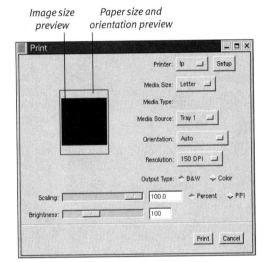

Figure 17. Use the Print dialog box to set printer resolution, and scale and brighten an image.

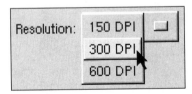

Figure 18. Use the Resolution drop-down list to select a printer resolution. (This is different from scaling an image down in order to create a higher resolution.)

Figure 19. Select either the Percent or PPI radio button, then use the Scaling slider to scale the image down.

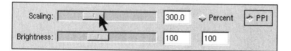

Figure 20. To scale the image down to a specific print out resolution, select the PPI radio button, then use the Scaling slider to set the resolution.

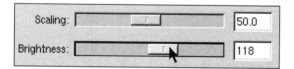

Figure 21. Use the Brightness slider to adjust the brightness of the printed page.

To adjust the brightness of a printed image:

1. Right-click on the image and choose File→Print from the pop-up menu (**Figure 16**). The Print dialog box will open (**Figure 17**).

2. Use the Brightness slider to adjust the brightness of the printed page (**Figure 21**). A number greater than 100 makes an image brighter; a number less than 100 makes an image darker.

3. Choose more printing options or click Print.

ADJUST THE BRIGHTNESS OF A PRINTED IMAGE

The Colors on the Printed Page Don't Match the Colors on My Monitor

This version of the GIMP doesn't include any special *color calibration* tools to set monitor color to match the color on the printed page. Thus, color differences are bound to happen. If you are sending a file out to a printer for high-end printing, you can get around this. Just print a *proof* on a color printer, setting the printed colors to exactly what you want. Then, give both the file and printed proof to the printer, telling her to match the printed proof colors.

How Does Offset Printing Work?

When you prepare a project—a brochure, newsletter, poster, etc.—for commercial printing, you will deal with a print shop and possibly a service bureau.

Traditionally, a service bureau takes your prepared GIMP files and either prints them using a high-resolution printer, giving you *camera-ready* output, or images the files onto film. If you get camera-ready output, the print shop will use a camera to shoot pictures of the output to create film.

With the advent of computers and transportable large storage media such as DAT tapes, and ZIP and JAZ drives, many graphic artists skip the service bureau, cutting out the intermediate step of film or camera-ready output, and go straight to the print shop with disks containing their project files. Most service bureaus and print shops prefer to use PostScript (.ps) or encapsulated PostScript (.eps) files, while others prefer Tagged Image File Format (.tif) files.

The print shop takes any of these media—camera-ready output, film, or computer files—and uses them to make printing plates. The printing plates are usually made of acid etched metal. The plates are then put on large rollers on a printing press by the *pressman*. If your project contains more than one color, the pressman uses *registration marks* to make sure all the plates are exactly aligned. He or she then runs the printing press. As the plates rotate on the rollers, they pick up a very thin coating of ink and an ink impression is transferred to the paper.

After the ink dries, the paper is trimmed and folded using *crop marks* as a guide. The *print job* may then be stapled or bound, depending upon the print job's number of pages. The completed print job is then packed in boxes and shipped to you.

Figure 22.
Right-click on the image and choose File→ Save from the pop-up menu.

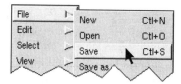

Preparing an Image for a Service Bureau

When preparing files for a service bureau or print shop, you will probably need to generate PostScript (.ps) or Encapsulated PostScript (.eps) files.

To generate a .ps or .eps file:

1. Save your image by right clicking on the image and choosing File→Save from the pop-up menu (**Figure 22**).

2. Right-click on the image and choose File→Save as from the pop-up menu (**Figure 23**). The Save Image dialog box will appear (**Figure 24**). (Using the Save as command creates a new copy of the file that remains open while the original image you saved in step 1 is automatically closed. That way, you still have your original image intact.)

Figure 23.
Right-click on the image and choose File→ Save as from the pop-up menu.

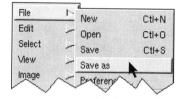

3. Use the Directories list box to move to the directory where you want to store the file.

4. In the Selection text box, enter the name of the file. Make sure you enter the .ps or .eps file extension after the file name (**Figure 25**).

5. Click OK. The Save PostScript dialog box will open (**Figure 26**).

6. In the Unit area, select either the Inch or Millimeter radio button. This sets the unit of measure that you will use in the Width and Height text boxes in the next step.

7. In the Image Size area, use the Width and Height text boxes to set the size of the image (in inches or millimeters). (If the keep aspect ratio check button is selected, the width and height will be sized proportionally.)

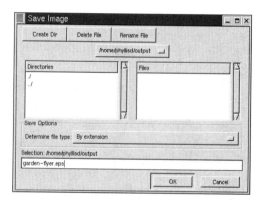

Figure 24. Use the Directories list box to move to the directory where you want to store the file.

Figure 25. Make sure you add the .ps or .eps file extension after the file name.

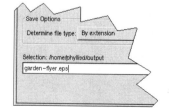

(continued)

GENERATE A PS OR EPS FILE

8. In the Rotation area, select a rotation for the printed image. (Be aware that 90 is the default for this option. This prints a landscape image.)

9. In the Output area, select the Preview check button. This will let the service bureau view the image before it is printed.

10. Click OK. The image will be saved as either a .ps or an .eps file.

✔ Tips

■ By choosing File→Save as in step 2, a new copy of the file remains opened while the original version is automatically closed. This keeps the original version intact (all layers, guides, etc., are preserved).

■ You may have noticed the Encapsulated PostScript check button in the Output area. If you are generating an .eps file, this check button will automatically be selected. If you are generating a .ps file, the check button will not be selected. Leave this check button as is since fully encapsulated PostScript (.eps) is different than plain PostScript (.ps).

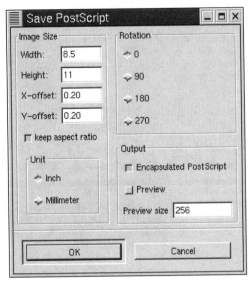

Figure 26. Use the Save PostScript dialog box to set the image's size and rotation.

Call the Service Bureau First

Before creating output for a service bureau, call them first to find out what file type they use and what media you should use to transport the file to them.

Summary

In this chapter you learned how to:

◆ Calculate image size to print at a specific resolution

◆ Scale an image up using cubic interpolation

◆ Print an image

◆ Select a different printer

◆ Select a different page size, paper, or orientation

◆ Select a different printer tray and printer resolution

◆ Adjust the brightness of the printed image

◆ Generate a .ps or .eps file

GLOSSARY

Airbrush Tool

The Airbrush Tool paints soft-edged strokes on an image.

Alpha channel

A special grayscale channel that is used to save selections. These selections are used to protect areas of an image from editing.

Antialias

Antialiasing creates a smooth transition from a filtered (or altered) area to a non-filtered area.

Background color

Set using the color selector in the GIMP Toolbox, the background color is applied when the Eraser Tool is used, a selection on the Background layer is moved, or when an area is erased using the Clear command.

Bezier curve

A curved selection segment created using the Bezier Selection Tool that can be reshaped using its control points and levers.

Bezier Selection Tool

The Bezier Selection Tool is used to select areas with bezier curves.

Bitmap mode

The simplest color mode. It contains no color or shades of gray, only black and white.

Blending modes

A blending mode changes the way a layer's pixels blend with the pixels in the layer directly below it.

Blend Tool

The Blend Tool is used to fill an area or selection with a gradual transition between two or more colors.

Bucket Fill Tool

The Bucket Fill Tool is used to fill areas or selections with solid colors or patterns.

Channel

A component of an image that contains the pixel information for an individual color. An RGB image has three color channels while a grayscale image has one color channel.

Clone Tool

The Clone Tool strokes color onto an image just like the Paintbrush Tool, but instead of painting solid colors, the Clone Tool paints part of a selected image or pattern.

CMYK color model

The Cyan, Magenta, Yellow, Black color model is used in high-quality offset color printing. (Black is the "key color," hence the K initial.) CMYK is a subtractive color model, meaning that as colors are mixed, darker colors are created.

Color mode

A way that color information is specified. For example, an image can be set in RGB mode, then converted to grayscale mode.

Color Picker Tool

The Color Picker Tool selects colors in an image.

Color selector

The bottom area of the GIMP Toolbox that is used to select and switch between the foreground and background colors.

Composite

An image made by combining elements from different images or photographs.

Convolver Tool

The Convolver Tool is used to blur or sharpen areas of an image.

Crop Tool

The Crop Tool cuts away part of an image, leaving only a selected area.

Curves

Curves adjust the tonal range of an image using a plotted curve representation of the image's colors.

Dither

When colors are limited as in an indexed image, dithering simulates colors not available in the color palette by mixing adjacent pixels.

Dots Per Inch (DPI)

The unit of measure that indicates the resolution of a printer or imagesetter.

Desaturate

When an image is desaturated, all color is removed, leaving a grayscale image.

Elliptical Selection Tool

The Elliptical Selection Tool is used to select round areas.

Encapsulated PostScript (EPS)

An image file format that is commonly used to move files from one application to another and also for color printing.

Eraser Tool

The Eraser Tool erases color from an image, leaving the current background color in its place.

Equalize

When an image is equalized, the brightest values in the image are redistributed, making it brighter.

Feathering

Feathering makes the transition from an altered area to an unaltered area smoother.

File extension

The three or four letters that come after the period in a file name. .XCF is the GIMP's native file format.

Filter

Filters are used to apply special effects to an image or selected area.

Flip Tool

The Flip Tool is used to mirror or flip an image vertically or horizontally.

Floating Selection

A selected area that isn't anchored to a layer. A floating selection occurs when a cut or copied portion of an image is pasted or text is created.

Foreground color

Set using the color selector in the GIMP Toolbox, the foreground color is applied when a painting tool is used, text is created, or the Stroke command applied.

Free-hand Selection Tool

The Free-hand Selection Tool works just like a pencil and is used to select areas by clicking and dragging the mouse.

Fuzzy Selection Tool

The Fuzzy Selection Tool creates selections using color. When a pixel is selected, the Fuzzy Selection Tool also selects adjacent pixels that are similar in hue and value.

Grayscale mode

An image set in grayscale mode contains no color, only varying shades of gray. There are 256 shades of gray from black (0) to white (255).

Guides

Guides (also known as guidelines) are horizontal and vertical lines that are positioned on an image to set up exact areas for drawing or selection. A guide looks like a dashed blue line.

HSV color model

The Hue, Saturation, Value color model is used in combination with the RGB color model in the GIMP. Hue represents the color in use, saturation represents the intensity of the color, and value represents the intensity of light on the color.

Image display area

The area in the image window where the graphic is displayed. Also called a canvas.

Image window

The area in the screen where images are created.

Indexed color model

An indexed image contains a specific number of colors from 1 to 256.

Intelligent Scissors Tool

The Intelligent Scissors Tool works like a pencil but has a mind of its own. After a selection has been drawn using the mouse, the Intelligent Scissors Tool goes to work making its best guess as to exactly which edge is being selected. The resulting selection is smoothly shaped, but can sometimes be unpredictable.

Invert

To exchange an image's light values with dark values, creating an image that looks like a film negative.

Layer

Layers are like a clear glass window stacked one on top of the other. Every new GIMP image starts out with one layer, a special layer called the Background layer.

Layer mask

A layer mask controls the way different areas of an image are revealed.

Levels

Levels are used to make exact adjustments to an image's tonal range by setting highlights, midtones, and shadows.

Magnify Tool

The Magnify Tool is used to enlarge and reduce the view of an image. It doesn't change the actual size of the image, only your view of it.

Move Tool

The Move Tool moves selections, layers, and guides.

Opacity

The density of a color in an image that ranges from transparent to opaque. In the GIMP, you can select an opacity for a layer or tool.

Paintbrush Tool

The Paintbrush Tool is used to paint strokes on an image.

Pencil Tool

The Pencil Tool draws hard-edged strokes on an image.

Pixels

A unit of measure that is dependent upon the size of a computer monitor and its resolution setting.

Pixels per Inch (PPI)

The unit of measure that indicates the resolution of a digital image or a monitor.

Plug-in

A little program that lets the user add extra features to the GIMP. Much of the GIMP—except the core features—are plug-ins that have been integrated into the GIMP program.

Point

A unit of measure that indicates the size of text. 72 point text is 1" (2.5 cm) high.

Rectangular Select Tool

The Rectangular Select Tool is used to select rectangular areas. This tool works by clicking and dragging a selection boundary around a specific area of an image.

Resize

Resizing an image changes the size of the image display area, but doesn't change the image size. If the new size of the image display area is smaller than the original size, any part of the image that doesn't fit into the image display area will be cropped.

Resolution

The fineness of detail in a digital image (measured in pixels per inch (ppi)), a monitor (measured in ppi), or a printer (measured in dots per inch (dpi)). The higher the resolution, the more detailed the image. GIMP images are automatically created at 72 ppi.

RGB color model

The Red, Green, Blue color model is used to display a color image on a computer monitor. RGB is an additive color model, meaning that every color can be created using red, green, and blue in varying degrees of brightness.

Sample merged

When this option is turned on, the selected color is a blending of two or more layers.

Saturation

A description of a color's purity that is separate from its hue or brightness. The less gray a color contains, the higher the saturation.

Scale

Scaling an image changes both the size of the image display area and the image itself.

Script-fu

A mini-program that automates special effects containing many steps.

Selection

An area of an image that has been isolated to restrict changes to that area. Unselected areas are protected from change.

Text Tool

The Text Tool is used to create text in an image. When text is created it appears as a floating selection.

Threshold

When the Threshold command is applied to an image, all color or grayscale pixels change to black and white, creating a high contrast image.

Transform Tool

The Transform Tool is used to rotate, scale, resize, shear, or add perspective to images.

Transparency

An area of an image where the pixels contain no color. A transparent area in an image is shown in the GIMP with a light and dark gray checkerboard pattern.

TrueType and Type 1 Fonts

TrueType and Type 1 are technical standards used to create fonts. Both of these font types can be installed and used with the GIMP.

Wilber

The GIMP mascot.

GLOSSARY

INDEX

A

Adobe Photoshop, 1, 33
Airbrush Tool, 6, 41, 107, 116–117, 293
   changing brushes, 110–111
   drawing a freehand line, 116
   drawing a straight line, 117
   setting options, 116
Alien Glow effect, creating, 179–180
Alignment
   of layers, 165–166
   types, 164
Alpha channels, 194–199
   adding, 194–195
   changing stacking order, 196
   defined, 16, 191, 194, 293
   deleting, 197
   duplicating, 195
   how to use, 198–199
   renaming, 196
   reshaping, 198
   saving a selection to, 86
   using to edit unselected areas, 199
Animation graphics for the Web
   creating, 276–280
   defined, 275
Antialiasing
   defined, 62, 293
   turning on, 62–63
Auto-stretch Contrast
   applying to an image, 144
   defined, 144
Auto-stretch HSV
   applying to an image, 145
   defined, 144
Autocrop command, 151

B

Background color, 147, 148, 293
   changing to default, 46
   setting using a color palette, 44

   setting using the Color Picker Tool, 45–46
   setting using the Color Selection dialog box, 42
   switching with foreground color, 41, 46
Background color square, 6, 42
Behind mode, 173
Bezier curve, 293
Bezier Selection Tool, 6, 61, 69–72, 293
   activating, 72
   control points
      defined, 69
      moving, 70
   corners, adding to a selection segment, 72
   curves, adding to a selection segment, 71
   handles, defined, 69
   levers, defined, 69
   setting options, 62–63
   straight segment selection, creating, 69–70
Bitmap mode, 91, 293
   converting an image to, 36
   defined, 35
Blend Tool, 6, 107, 124–128, 277, 293
   gradient
      foreground and background colors, applying
         using, 124
      Gradient Editor, applying using, 127–128
      layer mask, applying to, 205–206
   setting options, 125–126
Blending modes, 33, 126, 169, 170–171, 172, 173,
   221
   defined, 16, 40, 293
   examples, 172–173
   how to test, 170–171
   setting in the Brush Selection dialog box, 111
Blurring an area, 189
Border, quickly adding to image, 257
Brightness, 138
Brush Selection dialog box, 110–111, 169, 225, 251
   adding new brushes to, 112
   blending modes setting, 111
   creating a custom brush, 113–114
   defined, 11

INDEX

INDEX